$9.95

# BLUE DOMINO

## DETECTIVE STEPHEN DEL CORSO
## DETECTIVE BILL ERWIN
## MICHAEL FOONER

BLUE DOMINO is a cop's-eye view of a narcotics case so big and so successful that it resulted in the conviction of 86 major heroin dealers. It is also the story of the "Lady in Pink," a beautiful Puerto Rican drug courier who turned out to be the key to the case. And it is the story of the biggest bribe ever offered a detective in the history of the New York Police Department.

Detectives Steve Del Corso and Bill Erwin had worked narcotics before and knew that the heroin network was almost impossible to breach. It was frustrating work. Then, one day in 1972, Steve and Bill tailed a known dealer to a quiet block in East Harlem, and before their eyes saw millions of dollars worth of heroin changing hands right out in the open, on the sidewalk in front of the local fruit store, barbershop, and tavern. The street was Pleasant Avenue, and its drug traffic was pumping forty to fifty kilos of heroin a week into New York, and from there to other cities in America. The heroin network, the detectives now decided,

was really like a row of dominoes—if they could knock over
Pleasant Avenue, all the major
dealers of the northeast would go
down behind it.

The story of how they did it is a
landmark case in narcotics law
enforcement. This is the case that
could never have been prosecuted
if a detective hadn't received a
videotape camera for Christmas.
Concealed in a window on Pleasant Avenue, that camera eventually recorded thousands of hours
of drug transactions as they took
place. This is the case that would
never have come to trial if Del
Corso and Erwin had not befriend-
ed Dolores Gomez, a tough, street-
smart drug courier who risked her
life by turning state's evidence.
And this is the case that could
have been blown if Del Corso and
Erwin had accepted the biggest
bribe ever offered two New York
City detectives: $250,000 to destroy
the evidence they'd collected—and
kill Dolores Gomez.

*Jacket design & photograph by* STEVE KAPLAN

G. P. PUTNAM'S SONS
*Publishers Since 1838*
200 Madison Avenue
New York, N.Y. 10016

# Blue Domino

—————by—————

Detective Stephen Del Corso
Detective Bill Erwin
Michael Fooner

G.P. Putnam's Sons · New York

To Loretta, to Phyllis, and to wives of peace officers everywhere; to their patience, and to their faith that after each day of keeping the peace we'll be coming home the same as when we went.

Stephen Del Corso
William Hubert Erwin

# BLUE DOMINO

The dramatic story
behind America's most successful
drug bust-- the cops who fought to
keep it honest and the woman who
gave them the key

DETECTIVE STEPHEN DEL CORSO
DETECTIVE BILL ERWIN
MICHAEL FOONER

# PREFACE

More than two hundred people took part in the actual events narrated here—New York City police officers, agents of the Drug Enforcement Administration, government attorneys and U.S. marshals. The story is based upon interviews with people who were there, supplemented by the vast collection of physical evidence gathered and thousands of pages of court testimony.

During the night of April 13, 1973, more than eighty persons, including some of this country's most notorious and high-level narcotics importers and distributors of high-grade heroin were arrested in various states. Former United States Attorney Whitney North Seymour, Jr., termed this top-secret operation "the most historic night in the history of drug law enforcement."

On July 27, 1973, a young Puerto Rican woman, who in this narrative is called Dolores Gomez, disappeared into the government's witness protection program. U.S. marshals guard her and her family, and with a new identity, she pursues her new life. Through Dolores, law enforcement officers found the key that ultimately toppled this drug empire. Detectives Steve Del Corso and Bill Erwin were offered in excess of one quarter of a million dollars to destroy evidence and to help kill Dolores Gomez before she testified. After an investigation, the would-be bribers were rearrested and convicted of all charges, including conspiracy to commit murder.

Insights gained from interviews with Captain Francis McGhee and the members of the Intelligence Division, Captain John Plansker and the members of his unit in the Organized Crime Control Bureau, and with former Assistant United States Attorneys Walter Phillips, Gerald Feffer and John Gross were particurarly helpful.

Several actual events have been consolidated so that the reader can more easily follow the narrative. For the same reason, a few minor incidents have been slightly altered.

# PROLOGUE

Pleasant Avenue comes alive at precisely 6:30 in the morning. The blackness of night has been fading and first light of day opens the scene. At ten minutes before six a pair of heavy workshoes taps out the first morning sounds on the sidewalk of 118th Street. The man in the shoes comes into view and crosses Pleasant Avenue going west. He is about forty-five years old, heavyset, wearing T-shirt and dungarees, bearing a round pasta belly before him, carrying a black metal lunchbox. He is soon out of sight and his footsteps fade out toward First Avenue, to the bus taking him to his job uptown, or to Second Avenue for the bus going downtown. But before the sound of his steps is completely gone, the milk-delivery truck has rolled onto Pleasant Avenue, its engine stuttering quietly as it makes stops at the grocery store, which is still shut, the luncheonette and another grocery store, both shut. The driver has carried boxes to each of them and is rolling away as a tan automobile drives in from 120th Street. It comes to rest between 118th and 117th streets in front of the fruit store. The man who gets out

13

is balding, with his thinning hair combed straight back. His age is close to fifty. Even at this hour, with the street empty, his face is arranged in an open friendly expression, ready to break into a smile at the first human being he encounters. He opens his fruit store and starts setting out vegetables and fruits on sidewalk display trays and boxes. Moments later his partner joins him.

And then it is 6:30.

At precisely 6:30, Daniel Iello appears on the street and takes his position, pad and pencil in hand, in front of the barbershop at 320 Pleasant Avenue, next door to the Pleasant Tavern, corner of 117th Street. Iello is the numbers man. He is fifty or fifty-five years old, a little above average in height, a heavy man with a dark-blue-banded white hat on his head of graying hair. He is never seen without a cigarette between his lips, and he is never without a smile for each of the people who encounter him. The effect is slightly bizarre; he has no upper teeth.

His arrival in front of the barbershop is the upbeat. People are emerging from their houses, moving along with purpose—to work, to shop, to greet each other and move on. Only Iello is stationary as the residents of the neighborhood pass by. One after another they stop, some briefly and some lingering a little to have a bit of conversation with Daniel Iello. They place their number bets, and sometimes money is seen to change hands.

At eight o'clock a new beat is added as a blue car enters Pleasant Avenue from 116th Street and stops in front of the luncheonette. Its proprietor has arrived. He unlocks the luncheonette door but does not stay inside. He goes across the street and engages the owner of the fruit store in conversation. In a few minutes a red-headed woman in her forties, a heavy, hard-looking woman with a large bosom, arrives at the luncheonette to start the day's work going while the proprietor himself moves about the street visiting and chatting.

There is another arrival at eight o'clock. "The Head" comes around the corner from 117th Street and opens the club over

Barone's bar on Pleasant Avenue toward 116th Street. He is a short, stocky, "five-by-five" person who twists his mouth and talks out the side of it.

At ten minutes after eight there is a momentary change in the beat as "The Mona Lisa" leaves her house on 118th Street and steps along the sidewalk, a slender woman of about twenty-two with long black hair, an oval Italian face, and dark eyes. She crosses Pleasant Avenue going west and continues out of sight to whatever job occupies her day, while on 117th Street "The Blond" heaves into view, noisily shepherding her three little children to some destination on the other side of Pleasant Avenue. She will reappear several times during the morning with her three kids in tow, going back and forth from her house.

Shortly after half-past eight, the two sons of the luncheonette proprietor appear and take positions in or near the luncheonette. One is age twenty, the other about thirty-eight, and both work for their dad, taking bets on sporting events. Money is handled, counted, handed to them or handed out by them.

Around nine the young man appears who opens up the Pleasant Tavern, and at about the same moment, the superintendent of the tenement at 320 Pleasant Avenue comes out and opens the barbershop next door to the tavern. The actual proprietor of the barbershop does not appear in person until later.

The housewives are now out in full force, calling at the stores in the neighborhood, carrying groceries, fruits, and vegetables in string bags or paper shopping bags. Children are out on the streets, and dogs are running about. The tavern receives its first customer of the day, Popeye, a short, dumpy man of about fifty-five, gray-haired and unshaven, accompanied by his black-and-white dog. He gets drunk regularly and if he finds someone to talk with, he will always end up urging the other man to throw his heaviest punch, so the drinker can demonstrate how well he can take it.

By ten o'clock the proprietor of the second barbershop on

Pleasant Avenue, at 328, closer to 118th Street, arrives and opens for business. He is a short man with gray hair and glasses who lives nearby, and he begins his day with a visit to Aiello, in front of the first barbershop, to place his number bet.

At about 10:30 "The Polack" appears on the street and wanders about offering to wash people's cars, or doing so without asking. Sometimes he can be dissuaded but often enough he has to be paid a fee to refrain from washing a car.

Between eleven and eleven-thirty, three or four representatives of the gambling syndicate arrive and confer with the luncheonette proprietor and his sons. They discuss trends in the day's betting activity and potential problems of layoffs or collections.

About noon, the proprietor of the first barbershop, next to the tavern, arrives. He has driven his Chevy Caprice station wagon in from Long Beach, steers it into the parking lot, and enters his shop. By this time the proprietor of the second barbershop up the street has taken care of several customers and will continue to give haircuts until closing time. But at the first shop, the boss sits in his own barber chair reading the New York *Times* thoroughly from first page to last. No haircutting will take place here.

The street activity of women shopping, children playing, and people gossiping thins out now as people move indoors for lunch, and the gamblers start to leave at around one o'clock. By 1:30 the gamblers have departed and "Johnny Echoes" arrives.

The detective who has been watching Pleasant Avenue turns away from his videotape monitor for a moment to check the recording deck and see how much tape is left to run on this reel.

Until now he has been switching the camera on and off to catch bits of the street scene on videotape, but for the next nine or ten hours he will leave the camera switched on for long stretches of time. In the carton at his feet are a dozen fresh half-hour reels. Across the room are two more unopened cartons of reels.

16

Johnny Echoes drives up in his cream-colored Pontiac station wagon and parks in whatever space is handy, curbside or double. He is a heavyset man in his late thirties with black curly hair and an invariably pleasant expression. Two or three of the men who work for him and for his associates appear on the block about the same time. People known to Johnny arrive by car and converse. They find him in the tavern, or in the barbershop next door, or they find him on the sidewalk and go with him into the tavern or the barbershop.

Shortly after, "Benjie" arrives. People known to him drive into the avenue, park, and converse with him on the sidewalk, in the tavern, or in the barbershop.

The men who work for Johnny Echoes and Benjie wait around in the tavern or the barbershop. From time to time one of Johnny's men comes out and gets into a car belonging to one of Johnny's visitors. Johnny's man drives the car away, returning in fifteen minutes or half an hour to hand the car over to its owner, who drives away. Sometimes the car is only driven into the parking lot and then its owner drives it out a few minutes later. Benjie's men do the same sort of thing.

"Moe" emerges at about this time. He lives at 323 Pleasant Avenue, across the street from the tavern, and is a principal associate of Johnny Echoes. Moe is thirty-five, stocky, proud of the long brown hair that hangs to his neck. He has light blue eyes. Some people think of him as having "scary blue eyes," and are wary of his moods. He seems hyperactive, frequently grabbing at people near him, the kind of man who is joking one minute and violent the next. He circulates on the block more than the others, who tend to just stand about. People arrive and talk with him, and go with him into the tavern or barbershop.

"Ernie Boy" arrives, having driven in from Port Washington. He is a youngster, barely twenty-four years old, with brown eyes, pallid complexion, and curly black hair. He is a partner of Johnny Echoes, and wears a disagreeable expression most of the time.

Between two and two-fifteen, "Jerry" drives into Pleasant

17

Avenue in his late-model black Oldsmobile 98. He is a heavyset, balding man of nearly fifty, with a large cigar permanently protruding from his mouth. He nods to people or greets them, and there is special attention directed toward him by the men who have arrived during the hour before, a subtle deference. He wears slacks and a short-sleeved shirt which hangs completely open and unbuttoned, revealing the undershirt beneath. Jerry enters the barbershop next to the tavern and removes his shirt, which the *Times*-reading proprietor takes from him and hangs on a nail in the wall. He stands in the doorway of the barbershop and the owner of the tavern comes to speak with him. All afternoon and evening, the regulars who have arrived earlier approach him, speak, and then turn away. Even in his sleeveless undershirt he has an air of command.

By now the street has been enlivened by the reappearance of the women of the neighborhood, out shopping or gossiping, and the kids on roller skates, skipping rope, running about, licking ice creams, climbing on the parking-lot fence, banging sticks on trash-can lids.

Shortly after four o'clock, "John the Carpenter" comes home from work. He is the living image of the carpenter in Tenniel's illustrations of *Alice in Wonderland*. He is six feet and slender, but his hunched-down posture makes him seem short and stubby. He is thirty-five, with blondish-brown hair and brown eyes, and is invariably dressed in a torn T-shirt, gray workpants, and workshoes with untied shoelaces. People enjoy calling him "Stupid" or "Boob," but the teasing is always affectionate. He is believed to be a good workman. He is also believed to have built "traps" all through the neighborhood, secret stashes for heroin. John lives on 118th Street just off Pleasant Avenue, and until dinnertime he slowly traverses the avenue, making everyone who greets him feel good about being smarter than he is.

Between four and five in the afternoon "The Fat Man" arrives in his large black Cadillac. His chauffeur parks double and walks around to open the door for him. A three hundred-pound mound of flesh emerges from the automobile, and there is a noticeable shift in the car's body alignment as the right side rises by inches.

The deference previously offered to Jerry now tilts very abruptly toward the Fat Man, Gigi. He speaks to Jerry and the contrast between the two of them is striking. Jerry is unsmiling and businesslike, his brow furrowed as if he were driving a bargain. But Gigi acts out the jolly-fat-man role, laughing gruffly and coarsely, joking and teasing like a good-natured uncle.

The Fat Man does not come around every day, and when he does not, Jerry continues to be the focus of respect.

Some days, "Funzie" comes in the afternoon and stays awhile. Some days, "Johnny Hooks" comes. Like Jerry, they stand about and receive visitors to the avenue.

In midafternoon the parking lot, only half full till now, begins to fill up. As the early evening comes on, so many cars are moving in and out that the congestion spills out over the sidewalk into the roadway. People go back and forth opening and closing trunks. By evening, most of the women have left the street to prepare supper, kids are being called in, and at seven "Danny" makes his appearance. He is the evening numbers bets collector.

A pair of sidewalk telephone booths stand on the corner in front of the tavern. During the afternoon and into the evening the phones ring with incoming calls. Whoever is passing or nearby answers the phone, then goes to find the person called, on the avenue, in the tavern, or in the barbershop. During the mornings, the gamblers make outgoing calls over these phones, but in the afternoons and evenings the phones are mainly in use for incoming calls, mostly to Johnny Echoes, "Ernie Boy," Moe, Benjie, and a few others.

Between eight and nine o'clock, men and women bring chairs out on the sidewalk and sit and chat with each other. Elderly residents of the avenue are always treated with marked respect by Johnny Echoes, Benjie, and the other regulars, who

19

always ask after the older person's health or enjoyment of life or the welfare of a child or grandchild.

The tavern has been doing a steady business since afternoon. By ten, some patrons have had their share of booze and begin the exodus homeward.

Sometime between nine and midnight, Jerry and Johnny Echoes and Benjie and Moe and Ernie Boy and other regulars put shirts on, sometimes jackets, get into their own cars, and ride off, alone or in pairs or in groups. The children have gone home, the residents of the buildings on the street have taken their chairs indoors. most of the tavern drinkers have gone away.

It is past one o'clock A.M. and the streets are quiet. Blue-eyed Moe, who has been out of the neighborhood for several hours, returns to his apartment at 323 Pleasant Avenue and comes back down leading his dog. They walk along the curb and cross to the parking lot, the dog making stops to relieve himself at three locations. They return to 323 and go in. It is approaching two A.M. Pleasant Avenue is empty, silent and dark except for six streetlamps. Streamers from the last church parade flutter in the light breeze, reflecting a little light from the streetlamps.

It has been an average day on Pleasant Avenue. Between twenty and thirty pounds of French heroin have been sold to dealers and brokers for ultimate distribution in Manhattan, Westchester, Connecticut, northern New Jersey, Long Island, Queens, and Brooklyn; on special days additional pounds are sold for distribution in Detroit, Pittsburgh, Philadelphia, Boston, and places in between. Transactions on the average days add up to two and a half to four tons of heroin a year.

# 1

The telephone is ringing with a soft "burrrr" sound because the bell is muted, but it gets through to Steve on the second "burrrr" and his right hand is reaching for it on the third, while his eyes automatically focus on the watch around his left wrist, registering 3:49. The lighted flashlight has fallen into his lap along with the book he had been reading, *A Lovely Corpse*, yellow letters on a red background. The television monitor hooked up to the video camera shows a deserted street, with only an overflowed garbage can signaling that the area is inhabited; the television set, on which he had been watching *The Bride of Frankenstein*, is blank now and glows a flickering bluish white.

He switches the television set off as he holds the telephone to his ear and focuses his attention, saying nothing, waiting for the caller to make the first identifying sound.

"Gas company."

It's Bill's voice. Steve's tension eases. "Hi!" He yawns.

"How ya doin'?"

"Got a swell party going here. C'mon over."

"Be right up. Could you use a fresh case of champagne?"

"Where are you?"

"Nyack."

"What's playing there?"

"I was visiting a friend."

"Sorry, I'm not home."

"You think I got no other friends?"

"Haw! Name one."

"Anthony Evans."

"Who's he?"

"Lives at eight Broad Terrace Drive."

"Hey, in Nyack? That's just down a couple streets from me."

"I know. I passed your house after I put him to bed. I picked him up leaving Pleasant Avenue and tailed him. This is where he took me. I'm phoning you from the booth outside a service station called George's. You know it?"

"It's where Loretta buys gas. You must really be in Nyack."

"Like I said. You know Evans?"

"Not by name. I might by sight, might have seen him around town, or at church or someplace. What's with him?"

"Drives a tan Lincoln, with tag Queen-Jack-one-oh-nine-eight. Registered to a Lenore Evans. I got an NCIC on husband Anthony—shows a couple of homicides, some gambling violations. In the morning we can check him out on junk. Think he knows you?"

"Don't know. If he's got kids they probably go to school with mine."

"Well, next time you drive to work and notice a tan Lincoln is following you, say hello to your friendly neighbor."

"Sure, and seeing we both work on Pleasant Avenue, we could make a car pool."

"And you could borrow his lawnmower."

"Thanks. What time did you start tailing him from here?"

"About midnight. He came out on 120th Street and turned north on the Harlem River Drive."

After hanging up, Steve checks back on the log and finds an

observation listed at 12:08 for a Lincoln, tag QJ1098, leaving the area. As he runs his finger back up the log, his thoughts go to his own home, where Loretta and the three children are sleeping peacefully. Then he finds the listing he wants—the Lincoln entered the scene at 10:43. Putting the log aside, he locates the reel of videotape covering that time period. He puts the reel on the playback machine and thinks of what he will say to Loretta; he will ask if she knows Mrs. Evans, to talk to. He'll have to alert her not to discuss his work with that particular neighbor. And he'll have to do it, somehow, without making Loretta anxious.

He runs the reel until the spot where the Lincoln comes into view, and thinks of Kathy going to school in the morning. What do you say to a child, seven years old going on eight, about a classmate whose father is a mobster?

Watching the screen, Steve sees a white male step out of the Lincoln, about five-nine, 160 pounds, full head of hair, dressed in slacks and patterned sport shirt; he could be any one of twenty residents in Nyack.

On screen, the driver of the Lincoln approaches a man and the two of them go into the tavern. The second man is a major drug dealer, nicknamed "The Animal." They are off screen for a stretch, and Steve thinks of Loretta again.

On screen, "Georgie," a courier working for the dealers, comes out of the tavern, gets into the Lincoln, and drives it into the lot on Pleasant Avenue, parking out of the camera's angle of vision. Georgie comes back on the screen and goes into the tavern; he comes out again and goes into the parking lot; he comes back once more and into the tavern.

The reel of tape rolls along, and Steve tries to visualize Broad Terrace Drive and house number eight. It doesn't come to mind, though he must have passed by at some time. The driver of the Lincoln comes out of the tavern, and Steve tries to remember seeing him in the village. He goes into the parking lot, and moments later the Lincoln comes out, turns right, and drives out of the picture.

Steve figures that between half a kilo and two kilos of heroin are resting in the locked trunk of that Lincoln. It would be an easy arrest. But would that remove the mobster from their neighborhood? Not likely. He'd be out of custody the next day, out looking for the cause of his arrest.

Steve gets back into the chair next to the video camera. Its monitor still shows an empty, silent street. He puts his mind to the question of what to tell Loretta; what to tell Kathy. He is thinking hard. Suddenly there is a knock, knock-knock-knock on the door to the apartment.

He opens his eyes and sees bright daylight in the six-inch strip of their window opening. His body feels stiff from hours in one position. His watch shows eight o'clock.

He goes to the door, draws his gun, and says softly, "Yes?"

From outside a quiet voice says, "Steve."

He holsters his gun and opens the two locks. Ralph Tomas comes in carrying two containers of coffee and a paper bag with one roll, plain, for Steve, and two Danish pastries for himself.

Ralph is Puerto Rican, a slender man wearing wire-rim eyeglasses, a yellow windbreaker, and blue jeans. Both men are silent until he is inside and Steve has locked up behind him.

As they divide the breakfast, Ralph asks, "How'd it go?"

"About the same."

"How's the family?"

"Fine. How's yours?"

"Fine. You on tonight?"

They work in twelve-hour shifts, eight to eight, two days or nights on, two off.

Steve says yes, he's on tonight.

Ralph says, "You know those Italian ices you brought in last night? Very good."

"Sure, I'll try to remember."


Steve, watching the monitor, is voice-recording the action as the videotape deck whirs softly: "2132 hours, September 8,

24

1972 ... male Hispanic about five-six, one-sixty-five pounds, short black curly hair, mustache, leather jacket, gray slacks, with unknown female, light-skinned Hispanic, exiting Pontiac, license nine-five-four-seven-Yankee-Peter. They leave it double-parked in front of the barbershop. They are speaking with Moe. Moe walks away to speak with Johnny Echoes; the Hispanic male and female enter Pleasant Tavern. ..."

The telephone rings. Steve picks up but says nothing, waiting for the caller to identify himself.

"Who's the broad?"

"Hi, Bill."

"Yeah. Who is she?"

"She? You mean the swell-looking woman with terrific dark eyes, nice olive complexion, long dark hair, in a lacework dress looks like she was poured into it?"

"Right," Bill says.

"I don't know."

Moment of silence. Steve, his eyes on the video monitor, holds the phone to his ear with his left hand while his right hand pans the camera along the entire length of Pleasant Avenue. He's looking for Bill's car, but he does not see it.

He figures it must be out of camera range, probably at the north end of the avenue. "You parked at 120th Street?"

"No. I'm in the office."

Steve lets out a small laugh. "That's funny. I had the girl on camera up here, and when you asked about her I thought you were watching her, too, from up the street. Whatcha doin' at the office?"

"Screening videotapes. Checking logs."

"How come?"

"Fitzgerald switched me out of the surveillance car to work on tapes and ID the subjects."

"Suppose we meet after I finish here."

"OK. What about the broad?"

"What are you looking at?"

"She's on this reel of tape, shot"—Bill paused a moment, probably to look at the markings—"on September 5, seventy-two, at 1918 hours. Whoever taped it doesn't say who she is, just 'unknown female.' "

"I guess nobody's made the ident. His name is Melicio, Pedro, you'll find a file on him. He's a regular the last three weeks—buys from Moe Lentini and Johnny Echoes. She comes with him, his girlfriend, just a broad."

Bill reacts with put-on astonishment. "Just a broad? With a shape like that?"

"Hey, man, don't get horny. We're not screen-testing for the movies."

"So how come you knew so quick who I was talking about?"

"I get horny."

Steve shifts the camera's field of vision so that the monitor picks up action at various spots. Moe Lentini goes into the tavern. Johnny Echoes has walked off camera. The Hispanic couple has come out of the tavern, the girl walking to the passenger side of the Pontiac. She opens the door and sticks her head in, her behind protruding, while her companion does the same on the driver side. The scene is more interesting on the passenger side.

Steve, still holding the phone to his ear, has twisted the mouthpiece aside and voice-records: "2155 hours, September 8, 1972 ... The Hispanic male and his female companion lean into the Pontiac; they come out and shut the doors; he carries something in his hand. They go back into the tavern."

Steve speaks into the telephone again: "He's probably making a deal with someone in there. Pretty soon Georgie will come out of the tavern and go into the barbershop to get a package."

Bill asks, "Didn't anybody try to get an ident on her?"

Steve asks, "Why? She's with him."

"Don't we know her from someplace?"

"Do we?" And suddenly Steve is racing his mind over female faces as though he were flipping through a drawer full of mug shots.

"Wait a minute," he says. "There *is* something about her ..."

26

Steve's imaginary mug shots dissolve into one picture—a laughing, slender woman with shining black hair, young and beautiful. The laughter fades and her eyes are frightened. He smells a strange fragrance, his hands feel silky arms and soft shoulders, and he tastes a tingling sensation somewhere in his throat.

"Hey, are you still there?" Bill's voice sounds far away, then louder. "Hello?"

"I know her," Steve says.

"Give."

"She . . . Wait!"

On the video screen, Georgie comes out of the tavern and enters the barbershop.

Steve is voice-recording again: ". . . and he exits the barbershop, he goes to the Pontiac . . . he leans in . . . and he is going into the tavern again." After a short silence while camera holds on tavern: "Puerto Rican male exits tavern with female companion. They enter their Pontiac and . . ."

Steve has focused the camera on the woman until: ". . . they are driving away, out on left of the picture tube."

He is animated as he speaks again into the telephone: "Bill? You still there? Will you be on until eight? Wait for me. When I finish this shift, I'll shoot right down to the office and meet you. OK?"

"Sure."

"I think I got something."

# 2

Steve drove the department's royal-blue gypsy cab downtown on the FDR Drive and parked in a small lot on 29th Street just east of Second Avenue. He walked the rest of the way to 432 Park Avenue South, a privately owned office building whose tenants were mainly importers, sporting-goods firms, used-furniture dealers, and the like. The lobby directory showed a listing for "C.I.B., Inc." in Room 300—that was the secret location of the Police Department's Intelligence Division. The top-secret Drug Intelligence Group to which Steve and Bill belonged had two rooms in the office, crowded with desks, filing cabinets, and three videotape playback machines.

Steve greeted Bill and couple of other guys who were there at the moment. He ran the tape Bill had been looking at back to where Melicio and the woman came into the scene, and watched it twice.

Bill watched with him. Steve had a funny look on his face when he switched off the machine.

They pulled chairs over to a desk in a corner and Bill waited for Steve to start talking. By way of goosing him to it, Bill said, "Not a bad-looking broad. You got hots for her?"

"Don't be a jerk."

"No?"

"No. But all of a sudden I remembered her."

"Who is she?"

"Dolores Gomez. She used to live on Pleasant Avenue, across the street from where our apartment is now."

"What's with her?"

"When I was a rookie my first assignment was Harlem. You know how you get to know neighborhood characters? There was a guy up there named Gabby Condotti. She used to go with him."

"So?"

"Gabby was a big, handsome son of a bitch, in his fifties. He used to dress swell and spend big. He had a wife and kids, natch, but she was his girlfriend. He got rich and moved out."

"He make it in junk?"

"Big. He was close to Zanfardino and Inglese. He used to come to Pleasant Avenue regularly to do business, and she would be with him. I'd see them once in a while, driving in big expensive cars."

"He still around?"

"No. The feds dropped him. He drew fifteen to twenty. Atlanta, last I heard," Steve said.

"Where'd they drop him? Not on Pleasant Avenue."

"Of course not. Nobody gets in trouble on Pleasant Avenue. Even in those days, Pleasant Avenue was always safe for big junk dealers."

"So?"

Steve leaned back in his chair. "I've been thinking. She could be the one."

"One what?"

"The key to that chain of evidence McCrae's been talking about, to make a case."

30

"You mean," Bill said, "we drop her, and flip her, and get her to bring in the undercover agents. Sounds good."

His voice made it clear he was entirely skeptical.

"She used to go with an Italian dealer who took a fall," Bill continued. "Now she goes with a spic dealer. That doesn't add up to so much."

Steve said, "I remember her. She's no ordinary broad."

"What's special? She's got big tits and you get horny. You remember her now—how come you didn't recognize her before? You said she's been coming on the avenue for the last three weeks."

"Because I'm watching the dealer, not the woman with him. The dealer's the one we want. A broad's just there, and one of them is like another. But after you mentioned her on the phone, I took a good look at this one. Why did *you* notice her?"

Bill said, "Something about her."

"Something about her." Steve mimicked Bill's voice. "You know her, too!"

"I do?" Bill puckered his face in a frown, then suddenly lit up. "Hey! Yes! The Blue Lounge." He closed his eyes, pushing his memory. "When was it?"

"The day the Meat Market blew," Steve said.

"Oh, yeah—the day we were trying to figure out who was the wise guys' friend in the department," Bill said. "You told me then there was something special about her. Why didn't we follow up?"

"Because we were worried our whole operation was about to collapse. Anyway, we really had nothing to go on then."

"That was eight months ago. Have we got so much more to go on now?"

"I think so."

"Your 'think so' won't take this case anywhere. The lieutenant won't even listen."

Steve leaned back, lowered his voice, and spoke slowly: "We've been screwing around with this case for more than a year, and all we got to show for it is what? One bust—and that was eight months ago. Since then, we lost the Meat Market; we lost the Havemeyer Club; we lost the Stage Delicatessen. We've been on Pleasant Avenue since the beginning of June, and here in September we've got nothing to show for it except a few miles of videotape."

Steve smiled. "If McCrae won't listen to us about the Gomez broad, what else has he got?"

"OK, let's tell him. We drop her, we flip her, we get her to bring in our undercovers," Bill said.

"It might just work."

"Or someone might just get killed."

# 3

The Drug Intelligence Group had been formed in September 1971, almost a year before Steve and Bill began surveillance work on Pleasant Avenue. It consisted of sixteen picked men and a lieutenant.

They were outside the department's regular Narcotics Division, functioning separately, working out of the Intelligence Division's secret offices. They had been instructed to avoid discussing their assignment with anyone outside their unit they even avoided mentioning the unit's name, Drug Intelligence Group. There were only three individuals in their chain of command up to the commissioner—Inspector John Kramer, the CO of the Intelligence Division's Organized Crime Section; Chief of Intelligence Al Terborg; and First Deputy Commissioner Arthur McNeil.

The men were not told why all the hocus-pocus of secrecy, but naturally, they guessed. Many of the men selected were from units outside of narcotics activity, to minimize possible exposure to corruption.

Inspector Kramer was pleased by the "ethnic balance" he had put into the group—five Italians, four Hispanics, four Irish, one Greek, and three blacks, under a Scots-Irish commanding officer.

Kramer had combed the department for them, and then had carefully explained to each one that this assignment would be very chancy, so if the candidate had any doubts, he could and should reject the assignment. Kramer said they were going to try something new—"innovative," he called it, in the language fad of the day—in a department that was notoriously hostile to innovation.

He said the new unit would have support from the top but might get lots of flack from the ranks. A man who couldn't take it shouldn't come in. But for the men who did join, it would be something new and exciting, with lots of opportunity for initiative and original ideas, and if they succeeded, there'd be no telling how their careers might be affected.

He spoke glowingly of the lieutenant he had picked to be commanding officer, and said they could have twenty-four hours to think it over. Most of them accepted there and then.

The exceptions were Barton and Macon, two black detectives. Maybe Kramer had been overanxious in talking with them, or overly conscious of their being black. Maybe he felt he had put so much effort into screening black candidates—he wanted to be absolutely sure he was getting the best—that he felt it would be intolerable if they refused.

Somehow they got the impression they were not being asked but ordered. They accepted after the twenty-four-hour grace period, but began work with a residue of skepticism. During the first days they instinctively tested the other men to see if any harbored shreds of racism.

Bill and Steve, taking a break one afternoon, ran into Barton in the corridor and invited him along for coffee. They had formed the impression that Barton was a good cop. They called him "Archy." His name was Arnold Barton, but somewhere he'd been dubbed "Archy Brown" and he liked it.

They took their coffee breaks at the Belmore Cafeteria, down the block from their office. The Belmore was famous as the hangout of New York City taxicab drivers. Two or three detectives dressed in windbreakers and slacks could talk in complete privacy at a corner table, their conversation thoroughly covered by the normal sounds of a busy eating joint.

As the three of them sat over their coffee cups, Archy felt an impulse to test how far their friendly feelings went, how much trust he could expect from them. He was cautious, not because they were white and he was black, but because they were longtime tight partners.

He asked how they felt about the new unit. It had been in existence now for nearly two months and seemed to be unproductive, going nowhere.

"Do you sometimes think," he said, looking up at the ceiling, "that maybe, in the end, it's going to come up the same old shit?"

That was the cops' way of referring to the sweetest racket ever, Police Department code-language for a long-established system of dealing with the city's drug problems. About eight hundred lucky cops might get in on it at any one time, according to the Knapp Commission, which had been investigating corruption in the Police Department.

Under department rules, cops assigned to narcotics squads had to make four felony arrests a month. In practice, the Knapp Commission was saying, a detective or plainclothes patrolman would develop some informers, go out on the street, make four arrests, and then he could goof off for the rest of the month. Mostly they made easy arrests of pushers and junkies, but it didn't matter who was arrested as long as the cop's record showed he was making his four collars eleven months of the year. With experience, a narcotics cop could knock off his whole month's quota in several days or a week. In some cases three would team up so that two of them would make twelve arrests during the month and credit four to the third cop, who wouldn't have to work at all.

The system was very important. With a force of about eight hundred cops assigned to narcotics, the department ran up impressive arrest statistics to show the public they were doing a great job on the drug problem.

Some of the men simply took it easy for the rest of the month, once their four arrests had been made, but others used the time advantageously, to study for promotion, take college-credit courses, or rip off pushers and small-time dealers.

Judging by what the Knapp Commission was showing on television in the winter of 1971, ripping off pushers and small dealers was a popular choice among narcotics cops. Basically, this involved arresting pushers and small dealers, then letting them go after taking their cash or their stock of drugs, or both. The cop could then sell the confiscated narcotics to some other pusher. There was an extra dividend for a cop who followed this routine. Once a pusher had bought from a cop, he was always vulnerable to pressure. The cop could threaten him into becoming an informer against other pushers. This way, the cop could maintain a supply of prospects for future collars and ripoffs.

Archy Brown Barton said, "When I was interviewed for this assignment, they told me the four-busts-a-month shit would be out."

Steve said, "We had the same interview."

"And everybody in our unit was going to work together, they said, share information, go after heavy dealers and their connections. No more trying to make individual credit, no more of that statistical bullshit."

"It's what the man said."

Steve was getting a little irritated with Archy, but Bill stood by him. Steve had grown up in an exclusively white neighborhood, but Bill had come from a mixed community and could understand what was deep down under Archy's anxiety. Making a big success of his career on the force was of the greatest importance to him. It was his ticket to self-esteem, and to recognition for his family in their community. He was giving his trust to the group in this new, experimental project which their maverick boss was trying to shove down the throat of the hidebound Police Department. Archy had already brought in some good information to share with the unit, and under the four-a-month system he would have scored credits on his own service record. But their group was isolated. If the project didn't pan out, if the unit didn't make good, where would he be when promotions were handed out?

"One thing bothers me," Archy said. "The lieutenant is always harping on how we have to keep what we are doing absolutely confidential. You think maybe he thinks they have a friend on the inside?"

"They" was a code word for the big narcotics dealers their unit was supposed to go after. "Friend" was code for someone in the department who was placed where he could get information and earn big money by tipping off the dealers when the heat was coming their way.

"We don't know yet."

Steve didn't need to say what was in everybody's mind—that if they had a friend on the inside this time it was almost certainly because the bosses wanted it that way.

That was what the Knapp Commission investigation was all about.

In November 1971, as Barton, Del Corso, and Erwin sat in the Belmore Cafeteria, the Knapp Commission was on television telling the world that some cops were on the take, and that they were making it easy for the bad guys to operate. Everybody had known that before. But the Knapp Commission was also saying the bosses in the Police Department were letting it happen that way.

Bill said, "All we know is the lieutenant. His career is on the line. We think he's solid."

"And it's Kramer's idea," Steve said, "so he must be clean."

Archy said, "I thought it was Terborg's idea—he's chief of

37

intelligence, and this is supposed to be a strictly intelligence operation."

"So he'll keep it clean," Bill said.

"Then all we got to worry about," said Archy, "is the first dep and the commissioner."

That brought a little laugh. Commissioner Murphy was making news headlines with his reorganization of the department, which, he kept saying, was intended to root out corruption. Everyone knew the rumors, that half the men on the force hated him.

"I guess you could say," Archy went on, "that since only the first dep, the chief of intelligence, Inspector Kramer, the commissioner, and us in the group are supposed to know about Operation Discover, we got nothing to worry about."

"What the hell is Operation Discover?" Bill asked.

"Didn't you know? We got a high-class thing here, and when you are high-class you have a code name. According to a memo that Lieutenant McCrae wrote, Operation Discover is supposed to be a demonstration to the public"—here he began to intone like a preacher—"that our department can function innovatively and without corruption against organized crime, and it will therefore be a strong response to the Knapp Commission."

Steve said, "Is *that* what we're supposed to be doing? I thought we were going to investigate the big heroin dealers."

"It's not so simple," Archy said. "The idea is, we identify the top dealers and when they are arrested, it shuts off the supply of heroin to the middlemen, and that will dry up the connections, who will then be unable to deliver it to the runners and street pushers."

"Yeah? Who said all that?" Bill asked.

"McCrae."

"When?"

"In that memo."

"What memo? Where'd you see it?"

"Over Richie Regan's shoulder as he was typing it. It was addressed to the first dep."

"What a crock of shit all that is."

"Why?"

"He's gonna stop heroin distribution in New York? With three sergeants, four detectives, and nine patrolmen?"

Archy was laughing. "Why not, when the four detectives are Bobby and me, and you and Steve?"

# 4

As Stephen Del Corso saw himself, it was his destiny to become a cop. His family originated in Naples, where, according to a local legend, the best crooks and best cops are born. His Uncle Ralph had been a cop, and as a kid Steve used to love to listen to Uncle Ralph tell stories, mostly tales of the Mafia. By the time Steve began to grow up, those same tales were the subject of televised United States Senate committee hearings and big-budget movies. By then Uncle Ralph was a sort of minor celebrity, retired and traveling the lecture circuit, getting paid for telling those same stories to college boys and girls, and debating college professors on "Does the Mafia Really Exist?"

By then Steve was starting to make his own way, as a newly appointed cop in Harlem.

"That's when I grew up," he once told Bill, after they had become partners and were getting to know each other. "It was like I was seeing the real world for the first time."

"Didn't you have gangs where you lived?"

"Sure. Tough street gangs. I used to play with them all the time, stickball and basketball in Crotona Park, stuff like that. But I didn't really know what they were doing when they weren't playing ball."

"So now you know."

"In the Bronx we had neighbors who were in the rackets, but we never thought of them as bad people. They were our friends. When my pop was out of work, hell, there was always someone around to offer him jobs."

"What kind of jobs?"

"Like driving. That would have paid very well. It wasn't till after I became a cop that I found out what kind of driving he was offered."

"Joe Valachi started as a wheel man. You could have been 'Son of Joe.' "

"My father's name was Stephen. I guess things were different for me because I was interested in athletics. I got my kicks being a good athlete. But they were real friendly people, they never held it against me."

Steve married Loretta before he became a cop. They met one Saturday afternoon at the Fordham Road Roller Skating Rink. She had blue eyes and brown hair, and was as Irish as she could be, with a mother born in Dublin and a father in County Cork, he having served as a lieutenant in the IRA before emigrating to the Bronx.

Still, when Loretta, the youngest of five children, brought Steve home it wasn't all that much of a novelty. One of her sisters was married to an Italian and her older brother, Joseph, was already a veteran cop when Steve told her about his boyhood dream of joining the force. At the time, the idea seemed fine to her. Joe and his family had a pretty good life. There was no way she could have known about the disquiet that would come into her life later on.

Steve had to wait until there were openings for new applicants and meanwhile he took a job in the construction industry, building small homes in Westchester. Their first

42

child, Kathy, was six months old when the police lists opened up and they moved out to Long Island. After training, Steve was assigned to Harlem, then Brooklyn, then Harlem again. Loretta adjusted to the little changes these shifts brought, but their life wasn't really affected too much until he was assigned to narcotics undercover, with crazy hours. Then he was promoted to detective, they moved to Rockland County, and her life became very trying.

She was expected to make all the wrenching adjustments, and she did. She automatically blanked out any thought of the consequences of her husband's job. He went to work every day like other family men in their neighborhood, but from that moment on she had no idea where he was, what he was doing, when he was coming home, or even if he was.

There was no power in the world that could make her pay attention to the blanked-out piece of her mind. Her day-by-day concerns were those of the other wives on her block in Nyack, a small suburban town north of New York. There were the kids and their schooling, the shopping and the PTA, running the house, and her classes in ceramics, where she couldn't help competing fiercely with eleven other women for approval from the bearded youth who taught the class.

She was an even-tempered woman, serious, thoughtful, concerned about the kind of world her children had been born into, there now being three of them since little Stephen and Mary had come along. Before marriage and children, she had worked in the bustling midtown world, in the executive office of a major textile company, but her worldliness was tempered by her strong attachment to church and religion.

Her smile was always ready and warm, that of an attractive woman who was determined not to transfer her anxieties to her children. There was that time when Kathy, age seven, came home from school and asked, "Mommy, what does it mean, there's a contract on Daddy?"

Loretta remained perfectly calm, she believes.

"Where'd you hear such a thing?"

"A boy at school said it. In the schoolyard."

"He probably watches too much television," Loretta said. "Would you like to help Mommy bake a chocolate cake?"

Steve quietly checked; it *was* a kid who watched a lot of television. Probably he had just been showing off for Kathy, who was pretty and bright, someone an eight-and-a-half-year-old boy would want to impress.

By September 1971 there was a year out of their marriage that Steve had not shared with Loretta. He had shared it intensely with Bill Erwin, his partner in Narcotics Intelligence, and now there was to be even more involvement between them because their new unit was so damn secret. It was not as if they were close friends or brothers, but more as if they'd become two halves of one person. Whatever it was that had brought them together, chemistry, chance, or fate, when it happened it was as if it just had to be. They didn't in any sense look alike, but, curiously, people seemed to remember them as if they did. Actually, Bill was taller, muscular, and handsome, if you liked the brooding looks of the black Irish. Steve was a little shorter, husky, with a round face. Bill was often serious, and Steve was full of laughs.

When Steve and Bill were growing up, their families lived on opposite sides of the city, Bill's in south Brooklyn, Steve's in central Bronx. Steve took academic subjects in high school and played on the football team. Bill took a mechanical-trades course and worked after school in a gas station. Steve was popular and gregarious; he graduated, and kept a large circle of friends. Bill dropped out in his third year, was always a loner, and took a job as an auto mechanic, ultimately working his way up to service manager at a Chevrolet agency. Then their separate worlds converged. Both entered the Police Academy the same day, got their guns and badges the same day, and graduated at the same ceremony. They were rookies in different parts of the city, but, curiously, six years later, both were promoted to detective the same day. By that time, each

44

one's chain of assignments and transfers had brought him into the Narcotics Division—on the same day.

How much closer could two men get? Phyllis Erwin was the wrong person to ask. Her family and Bill's had lived on the same block in south Brooklyn. When they married, he was twenty, she was eighteen. "We'd been going steady for eighteen years," Bill says, his dark face breaking into one of his engaging smiles.

Phyllis was good at her studies, good at the piano, an honors student at St. Joseph's High School, and obviously smart enough for college. She married Bill instead, and then she was ambitious for both of them. She let him know she was pleased and proud when he moved up to agency service manager, but she was suggesting to him from time to time that he ought to go into the cops, that there might be more of a future in it for him, and for them. Her sister, Rita, was married to a postal employee. It had advantages, the civil service.

There were six years of marriage behind them, two kids at table and a third on the way when he came home one day and said he was going to do it. She smiled, her thoughts on the security of a job with the city, just what a guy from a poverty-haunted childhood needed most.

Then she started filling in a missing corner of her own life. She registered at a local community college and found she still had the touch for scholarship. Bill was proud of the way she was able to wrestle the house chores, the kids and their schooling, along with her own studies.

Only gradually did it seep into her awareness that she was sharing Bill, that she had been moved in on, that his partner, Steve Del Corso, lived a whole part of Bill's life from which she was excluded.

By then they had been married for fourteen years and had

45

moved up to Hartsdale, in upstate New York. Bill's hours meant nothing; he left the house early and came back late. But she demanded no explanation. Since he had become a detective there had always been an unspoken understanding between them that she would not ask about his work or about the cryptic telephone conversations she sometimes overheard when he was home.

Her own college work absorbed a lot of her attention. Often she would study until he got home, seated at the dining-room table with her books and papers. Around midnight she would hear the car turn into the driveway, and be vaguely aware that his arrival was accompanied by an easing of her tension.

On one of these nights she heard the sound of the car unexpectedly early. It was only 11:09. She continued reading and taking notes, half her attention on the sound of the car door slamming. Bill came up the steps, scraped his feet outside the door, turned the key in the lock, and came through the entrance hall. He said, "Hi, honey," and she turned her face up sideways for his kiss, her eyes staying on her book as she read to the end of the paragraph. She wrote a few more lines in her notebook and then looked up and smiled. "You're early."

"West Side Highway gave me a break," Bill said. "I did it in fifty-two minutes. How's it going?"

He nodded toward the scatter of books and papers.

"All right. I have to do a paper for my sociology course. Dinner is on the stove. Just let me finish something here and I'll get it for you."

"No, finish what you're doing. I'll get it."

He sat down at the opposite end of the table and ate while she studied, watching her read and take notes. She stopped after a bit, closed her books, shuffled the papers and notebooks, and slipped everything neatly into a plaid plastic zippered pouch. She sat back as he was finishing.

"How is it?"

"Very good. Delicious." Bill leaned back, looking at her. He

46

was aware of the dinner and the good feeling flowing through his body, the day's tensions draining out.

Phyllis said, "We had a little excitement around here."

"Oh?"

"A murder."

"Oh?"

"They found a burned-up car with a body in it. In the woods out past the Eggerton place. It must have been put there during the night, with a bomb set to go off in the morning. The fire company went out but couldn't do anything. The state troopers said the man was dead before the fire. He was in the trunk."

"Who was it?"

"They don't know. He was hacked up as well as burned. Gangster-style killing, just like in the city. It'll probably be in the morning paper. You can imagine the excitement in a place like this."

"The kids know about it?"

"Of course. It was on the radio, and all over their school."

"Radio didn't say who it might be?"

"The body was pretty well scorched. And stabbed. Lots of times." She swallowed. "And the head was cut off. It's still missing. A state trooper said on the radio the murder was done somewhere else and the body just dumped out here."

Bill looked at her in silence. He was amazed at how calmly she had said it all, as if untouched by the horror. He knew she was deeply distressed but had herself under control. That's my Phyllis, he thought. The family must not be upset by this horrible intrusion from the filthy, terrifying world they had escaped, the world that was a one-hour drive away from their home. He'd bet there were hysterical women in half the houses of their village that day, but not Phyllis.

He watched her closely as she poured coffee for the two of them. Only her hands showed any signs of her real reaction. He went to her and kissed her, properly this time, with his arms around her, feeling her soft, slender body beneath her

47

blouse and skirt. She clung tightly to him. "Let's go to bed," he said.

But even in bed, Phyllis was restless. She wasn't turning on. Then he realized he wasn't turned on either. The headless burned man was intruding on their thoughts, vague and shadowy.

He stretched out in bed looking at her. She was lying quietly, eyes open, looking at the ceiling. He wondered why today's event had moved her to such an effort of control. He reached over and touched her with his fingertips, her ear, her cheek, her neck and shoulder. She moved her hand toward him, and he held it.

"How did you hear about it?" he asked.

"Mrs. Martin phoned to tell me. She had me on the phone for over an hour."

Mrs. Martin was a policeman's widow who lived several streets away in their village. She had been doing her best to become close friends with Phyllis.

"What did she find to talk about for all that time?"

"She heard about the murder on the radio. I didn't have our radio on, so she told me about it. Somehow, she kept on talking and couldn't seem to stop. She talked about her husband, Joe, and the time he was killed. It happened in Brooklyn. In what was supposed to be a quiet section. It must have been terrible for her."

Bill listened and wondered.

"She said, before that she used to worry a lot, while he was away at work. Sometimes she'd be terrified when she didn't hear from him, and the only time she really had peace of mind was when he was home off duty. She asked how I stand it when you are away on the job."

"Do you stand it OK?"

"I stand it OK." Phyllis turned and embraced him fiercely.

"Mrs. Martin said they brought the dead man out here for a reason," she said after a moment. "As a warning to somebody."

48

"No," Bill shouted. "No! That doesn't make sense. That guy has nothing to do with me. They just picked this area because it's an hour or so from New York. That body could just as easily have ended up in New Jersey. What the hell does that Mrs. Martin know?"

Suddenly Phyllis' body was in his arms, convulsed with sobs and trembling. He held her tight against him. With his big hands he stroked her hair, her neck, her shoulders, the fine curves of her back and legs. He had told her the truth about the body, but he wondered if she believed him.

She felt small and fragile against him, but her body held rigid. He started to speak, but her mouth bore down on his, hard, lips open as if she would drink him in. Her body remained closed and unyielding for one more moment; then she shook herself and went limp.

In another moment it was over. She turned to him and smiled at the anxious look on his face.

"You all right?" he asked.

"Sure, darling, I guess it's been more of a day than usual. Let's forget it."

# 5

Bill was sitting with Steve, Archy Brown, and Archy's partner, Bobby Macon, over coffee at the Belmore a few nights later. Bobby asked, "How could they tell who it was if the head was missing and the fingers were scorched?"

"From the bridgework," Bill said. "At the autopsy they found teeth in the throat, and ran down a dental record which showed the same bridgework."

Bobby persisted. "How'd they know where to look?"

"He was one of Sperling's guys. Sperling must have wanted it known. The information came in over the transom. He was putting out a warning, I guess."

"Was he flipped?" Archy asked.

"Not that I know of. My guess is he was skimming, and Big Herby don't like that no way. I'm sitting on Herby."

Bill was assigned to surveillance in the area of the Stage Delicatessen on 7th Avenue just north of Times Square, where a major drug dealer named Herbert Sperling was believed to be conducting business. Bill was paired with Richie Spinelli.

Steve was paired with Ralph Tomas and assigned to surveillance at the El Sombrero, a nightclub in Queens. Steve and Bill had agreed to split up temporarily in order to train men in their unit who'd had little experience in narcotics investigation. Steve was also trying to learn a little Spanish at the same time.

The El Sombrero was located between the center of the city and the airports, in the heart of New York's South American "colony" where thousands of Colombians and other Latin Americans lived. It was known to shelter the mainstream of cocaine smugglers from South America, who had lately been carrying sideloads of heroin.

Lieutenant McCrae had chosen four locations reputed to be principal drug distribution centers and had organized team surveillance of those spots. Archie and Bobby were working to get a handle on the Black-Hispanic dealers, but couldn't tell yet if the Lilac Lounge would be productive. Charlie Cabalo and Jake McNamara were sitting on Chinatown locations. The Stage Delicatessen where Bill and Spinelli worked had long been suspected of being a meeting place for the Jewish-Italian drug dealers' network.

All the men alternated field surveillance sessions with work in the office, coordinating information they gathered with material in the Department's intelligence files.

Their object was to identify the top dealers and get them arrested, thereby shutting off the middlemen's heroin supplies, and drying up the connections, who would then be unable to make deliveries to the runners and street pushers.

Their job was strictly intelligence, which was to be handed over to operating police units to make arrests and seizures.

All of them were finding the work tedious, and they were becoming restive. Archy said, "The word's going around what we're into is strictly a snow job."

Bill said, "Guys see us sitting on places that have been under surveillance before and they hear we're searching old records—hell, our unit's been going two and a half months with nothing happening."

Steve said, "Maybe we should get some new locations, something we can call our own."

"Maybe I got something," Bobby said.

"You could take penicillin for it."

"Or Tums."

"Or Preparation H."

"I got a contact at the Westchester County sheriff's office."

"That's swell," said Steve. He got up to leave.

"This contact is a friend of a friend of my sister, a detective up there. I asked him, the detective, do they get much junk up there."

Bill said, "They probably do, but what's it to us?"

"He said yes, and that there's people bringing it over the county line from the Bronx."

"Have they made any of them?"

"Negative."

"Well, I got to get home," Steve said.

"But he jotted down some license numbers of their cars," Archy said.

Steve sat down. "Might be worth checking out," he said.

"We already did, me and Bobby. The cars are registered to females, residents in the Bronx. Three cars. Guys drive up to Westchester with girls and make rounds of the bars and roadhouses."

"Any records on them? The registered car owners?"

"We called BCI. Negative."

Bill said, "How about putting a tail on those dudes?"

Bobby Macon said, "All the way up in north Bronx? For a couple of nickel-bag pushers?" No one in the entire unit had up to that time worked anywhere in the Bronx.

Bobby said, "It's not just a couple, it's three guys. There's girls go with them, so that's six. So here's these three guys who track around certain bars, they got cars and they got girlfriends, and after they've been, there's lots of junk for sale all over Westchester. My friend Charlie has never had enough to collar them—up there. They've got no one to make undercover buys, nor the money for it. But here's my question—if some-body's dealing all over Westchester from a base in the Bronx, would that look like what the lieutenant calls a network?"

Bill asked, "What's it like where they come from?"

"The cars are registered to these three women who live in different housing projects, middle-income projects."

Steve said, "How about we get a wire in?"

Bill said, "We don't have enough for a court order."

Archy said, "Maybe not with what we have, but if we can add what the Westchester sheriff has—Charlie will get it for us—it could make an application heavy enough for some judge."

Part of McCrae's system was to have the entire unit meet about once a week, to exchange information and suggest ideas.

The four detectives put forward their idea for investigating a Bronx-Westchester connection for possible leads into a network operation, and for wiretaps on a Miss Cleo Dingle, a Miss Laverne McBride, and a Miss Mary Hogin, the owners of the three cars. Dingle and McBride had Pontiacs, but the car registered to Miss Hogin was a new white Mark III Lincoln Continental.

Lieutenant McCrae took his time accepting the idea. In those days, each wiretap had to be served by six men, in pairs, doing twelve-hour shifts—two days on, two days off. Three wires going at the same time would tie up their entire unit, and the only basis for it was a lead from a black detective outside the city. McCrae wasn't saying he was against it, but he was thinking of what they'd be saying around the depart-ment: with all of New York to work in, with tons of junk flowing through the city, here's this hotshot unit of McCrae's sitting out in the boondocks checking up on half a dozen black pushers working bars across the city line.

He looked around at the other men, and saw that some of them were persuaded it was a good idea. He suspected that several of them liked it because they lived in Queens or nearby Rockland County and traveling to the wiretap locations would be convenient, save them travel time. But, like McCrae, they did want a chance to move on something that would show tangible results: and this just might. McCrae said OK. By November 14 the court orders had come through and the telephone company had installed the taps. On the night of the fourteenth they divided into teams and moved into the three listening posts in the Bronx.

Bill Erwin's suspect was Laverne McBride, 715 Noble Avenue, in a public-housing project called the Butterfield Estates. His listening post was four blocks away in another public-housing project. Archy's suspect was Cleo Dingle, who lived on Convent Avenue near Terrace, and Steve's suspect was Mary Hogin, who lived in Co-op City.

Detective Richie Salvesen, temporarily assigned to the group, was taking the first shift with Bill Erwin. The building superintendent, a fat West Indian who was probably an illegal immigrant, was very eager to oblige them with working space when they identified themselves as cops working on a murder case in New Jersey. He showed them a small basement room, just vacated by a previous tenant, asking if it would be OK.

The two detectives stared; the West Indian stood aside, his face impassive. Opposite the open door, the entire wall was covered with pictures clipped from pornographic magazines. After a moment, the detectives looked at each other and shrugged. The room was a good size, and opened on a passageway leading to a door in the backyard where they could park. They said, "Yeah, OK," and ignored the West Indian's sudden grin.

They moved in with three tape recorders, two tables, three lamps, a typewriter, two straight chairs, one folding deck chair, a carton of writing materials and a small TV. The confidential unit of the phone company installed two telephones, one a direct line to their unit's office, the other to the outside world.

Arriving for their first day, Bill brought a can of roach spray and liberally clouded the room, giving particular attention to the equipment so the insects would not eat the insulation and short it out. Laverne McBride's telephone revealed she had a very lively life-style. For detectives Erwin and Salvesen, her

55

conversations were like episodes of a soap opera. First her girlfriends would call in, reporting that Laverne's man had been seen with other chicks. After a few of these reports, Laverne got furious and decided to kill her boyfriend. He must have found out, because he didn't call for a while. During that time, Laverne discussed with her girlfriends how she could kill him without making too much of a mess in the apartment, and what information a lawyer would need to get her off. Finally there was the conversation with the boyfriend in which he denied everything. At first she rejected his denials in some pretty strong language, then finally relented. They agreed to get together later that night.

Every time Laverne made or received a call, her telephone activated the wiretap equipment, automatically recorded the phone number if she dialed, started two tape recorders, and turned on the audio for the cops to hear both sides of the conversation. When each pair of reels was finished, the cops had to seal one reel in case it was later needed for evidence. The second copy was used for playing back on the third machine and for making reports.

On the day after Laverne McBride's reconciliation with her boyfriend, the telephone was quiet for a long time. Erwin and Salvesen speculated how long the quiet would last. Just before midnight they had their answer; the tape system was suddenly activated, and Laverne came on, calling a gypsy cab to take her boyfriend to a hospital with a gunshot wound.

Salvesen thought they ought to call the cops, and Erwin thought not, unless it was a homicide, which didn't seem to be the case, since the man was evidently going to the hospital on his own power. But before they could do anything either way, Laverne's phone activated the machines again. She was calling a girlfriend for advice on how best to remove bloodstains from her white wall-to-wall carpet.

These personal calls broke the monotony of what soon became a dull routine surveillance. Evidently their suspects had their activity neatly organized, with due precautions against eavesdropping. Phone contacts were usually:

"Meet me?"

"Yes."

"Same place?"

"Yes."

Or, "No, the other one."

Amounts were referred to as "How many?"; "What he asked for"; or "Same as last time."

In comparison, Steve Del Corso had a ball at his plant about a mile from Bill's. He set up his surveillance in the lower level of a shopping mall in Co-op City, an enormous housing development in the north Bronx. The room he used was a storeroom back of quarters occupied by a church cult of some sort. It was dry and warm and airy and clean. But Steve and a partner, Tony Norman, had their own cross to bear. Del Corso's tap was on the phone listed in the name of Mary Hogin, who had a child, Rita. At age twelve, Rita was a nonstop telephone talker. Together, Del Corso and Norman were treated to an encyclopedic overview of the interests, opinions, and deep concerns of American preadolescents. Rita had a seemingly unlimited number of friends, with each of whom, every day, she had something to discuss. On the five weekdays, the detectives came to dread 3:15 P.M. That was when Rita got home from school and the Hogins' telephone went into action. There was no escape.

Nor could the cops ignore Rita's calls, because she also took and passed messages for the adults. At first the cops thought that, being a kid, she might let something slip that would give them a clue, but evidently she was well-trained and savvy. Her message-handling was nicely cryptic, and left the eavesdroppers frustrated.

Richie Spinelli and Danny Fiorentini, two others of their unit, were sitting on the wire to Cleo Dingle's telephone. Inexperienced in narcotics investigation, they let Bill know immediately when they heard a man converse with Cleo about having three shirts and about someone's boy delivering "half a shirt." That bit of talk occurred a week after they had set up the equipment. Two days later Cleo received a call to "get

57

ready," the caller would come by to tell her where.

Something was happening that night. Lieutenant McCrae said they'd put a tail on her, and they'd need several more men to tail other people she met if they separated.

Moving rapidly now, he worked the phones all morning and through lunchtime, getting his boss, Inspector Kramer, to approve a quick call to the New York joint task force's Captain Hugot. What McCrae wanted, and got, was ten detectives from the task force to assist on mobile surveillances.

Archy Brown Barton and Bobby Macon were watching Cleo's house when Herby Wright, a detective from the task force, appeared on the scene. They told him that two black females had entered the building and might be calling on Cleo Dingle. As they were talking, the same two females came out with a third, whom Archy recognized as Cleo. The three women separated as soon as they were on the sidewalk, each one looking for a separate taxicab. Archy and Bobby got into their car to follow Cleo, and Herby Wright got into his car to follow the taller of the other two. The third they simply had to let loose, hoping she'd join the others later. Herby noticed that the one he was following was very beautiful, but didn't think anyone could say he followed her rather than the other one for that reason.

In the end, it didn't matter. All three women went to the same address by different routes, 294 Convent Avenue, still in the Bronx. The three detectives waited awhile, but when nothing further happened, Archy went in and listened at doors on the first two floors. Then Bobby went in and listened at doors on the second two floors. Then Herby went in to listen at doors on the top two floors. On the fifth floor he heard unmistakably female voices, several of them, and the women were clearly doing something other than socializing.

Archy called McCrae, who got going again, rushing a search warrant out of the Bronx County Court House and additional task-force detectives to the scene. With fourteen men deployed, they raided the fifth-floor apartment and found a drug mill in full operation.

Six girls were working at cutting heroin with adulterants and bagging tiny amounts in little cellophane envelopes. The girls, all young and pretty, had stripped down to bras and panties. Their hair was covered by cloths tied in elaborate turbans. A short black male sat in an armchair in the adjoining bedroom, watching. The windows were covered and taped, and the room was hot.

They were all hustled down to the courthouse, and police teams came in to confiscate the drugs and equipment and to gather technical evidence.

The raid at Convent Avenue in the Bronx sharpened expectations in McCrae's unit. The six detectives sat patiently on their wires, sure something new would turn up. It did.

Steve and Tony began to notice a somewhat different pattern in the phone calls Mary Hogin was receiving. A male voice frequently answered the phone; the male was evidently in residence.

Steve requested a surveillance of the man and once more McCrae went back to the task force for assistance. Detective Herby Wright was put in as a tail, and a picture of life in the Hogin apartment rapidly emerged. The man was called "Willy," and he regularly drove the white Mark III Lincoln Continental that was registered in Mary Hogin's name. Tailing him wasn't difficult, Herby reported. The man who drove the Lincoln was a cool-looking black, a sharp dresser with porkchop sideburns, long mustaches, and an air of self-importance—in fact, Herby reported, it was sort of funny to see, since Willy was hardly more than five feet tall.

Herby checked regularly with Steve and filled him in on the little family he had come to know so well, although he had never seen them. The gentleman who answered to the name "Willy" on the phone was actually William J. C. Abraham, Herby reported, and he was proprietor of the Gold Lounge at 124th Street and Seventh Avenue, a well-known watering place for black Harlem's hotshots. The Gold Lounge was frequently mentioned in Police Department records and was suspected of being a hangout for gambling racketeers and narcotics dealers.

Steve remembered the Gold Lounge. It was just around the corner from the Two-Eight Precinct station house, where he had first served as a patrolman.

Steve phoned Bill, and Bill talked to his friend Frank Jackson, a joint-task-force detective. Jackson's response to Abraham's name was immediate. He had a long-standing interest in "JC," as Jackson called him.

According to information assembled by Jackson and his partner, Jim Nauwens, JC was more than just a drop. He handled heavy weight and was a big dealer.

Steve and Bill were elated, sure that JC would make things pop soon. But JC and Mary were too shrewd, their conversations too guarded. Finally Steve got something specific off Mary's line: The whole family—Mary, JC, and Rita—were going to Hawaii for Christmas vacation.

The day Mary booked the tickets with American Airlines, Steve was ready to pack it in. The wiretap was turning out to be a big letdown, and soon there would be no action on it at all. He decided to ask McCrae for an outside assignment. With Willy and the family going on vacation, there'd be no point in continuing the telephone surveillance until they returned. McCrae agreed.

On December 14 Steve came in for his last turn. He looked at the log showing calls overheard by the detective he'd relieved. One entry showed that Mary was meeting Willy at the Gold Lounge, so they'd probably be out for the evening and it would be a very quiet night.

Steve snapped on the TV, unwrapped a sandwich he'd brought from home, and opened his thermos of coffee. He adjusted the beach chair and was soon involved in—what else, he thought—*Hawaii Five-0.*

The wiretap mechanism switched on, activated by a phone call to Mary Hogin's number. He heard Mary's voice ask, "Did she call?"

Rita's voice came on. "No."

"OK, call you back."

60

Just after the second commercial break, the mechanism activated again. It was Mary Hogin. "Did she call?"

"Not yet."

"Call you back, honey."

"Whatcha doin'?"

"I'm with Daddy. How about you?"

"Watching television. You coming home?"

"Soon, honey; call you back."

There were further calls at intervals of twenty and thirty minutes.

"Did she call?"

"No."

Rita was patient about these interruptions, and her voice sounded bored.

Steve, however, began to feel a small charge of nervous energy. It was becoming obvious that the "she" in question was not just a friend of Mary's. He leaned forward when the next call came in. It was a different voice. Female.

"She" gave no name, did not question who was answering or where anyone was. What she said was obviously a prearranged message.

"Everything is OK. Tell Willy and Mary. I'm in room two-oh-three at—"

"Wait a minute." Rita's voice cut in over hers. "Let me get a pencil."

There was silence for an interval. The caller's phone clicked off.

Rita came back on.

"Hello. Hello? Hello? . . . Hello?"

She hung up.

Steve grabbed his own phone and dialed the group office. No answer. He looked at his wristwatch. It was getting on to midnight.

He phoned Bill at home. Phyllis answered. He left word for Bill to call him back as soon as possible.

He called the lieutenant at home.

61

"Sorry if I'm disturbing you, but I thought you'd like to know at once."

"No sweat, Steve, whatcha got?"

"I think there's going to be a meet tonight. Right away. Wait, hang on! There's a call coming in. . . ."

The equipment activated. The same unknown woman's voice said to Rita, "What'd you hang up for?"

Rita said, "I didn't hang up, I went to get a pencil, and you hung up. Didn't you hear me say 'wait till I get a pencil?' "

The unknown woman was either annoyed or jumpy. "Oh, for Chrissake," she mumbled.

Rita said, "OK, what's the number?"

Steve's tension was way up.

"He knows the number. Just tell him it's OK, and I'm in room two-oh-three."

End of conversation. Steve got back on the phone with the lieutenant.

"Sounds like a meet, all right. Room two-oh-three sounds like a motel."

"Any idea where?"

"There are several in this area. Can't be many where a black woman checked in by herself tonight. We should be able to check all the motels until we find her."

"OK, let's do it."

"We'll need manpower."

"Call Regan and tell him I said to round up as many of our guys as he can reach and have them report to you. I'll call the joint task force and ask them to authorize manpower to help locate the motel."

Steve hung up and opened the Bronx yellow pages to the "Motels" classification.

He spread out a street map of the Bronx and began ticking off motels with addresses in the north Bronx and southern Westchester County.

"Holy shit!"

The check marks were thick on the page. He had never realized how many motels there were in the Bronx.

Bill called in.

"Where are you?"

"On my way home. I called Phyllis and she gave me your message."

"Well, better get your ass down here. Willy's got something going tonight, and you wouldn't want to miss it, would you?"

During the next hour detectives started checking in. Steve briefed them as they arrived, and gave them lists of motels to check out. By dawn they'd covered every motel in a radius of about five miles, including nearby Westchester and Connecticut.

No motel in the area reported a black woman checking in alone that night.

By sunup Steve called off the search, and let the task-force detectives go home. About eight o'clock the wiretap machines activated. Rita answered and she arranged to meet her chum Shirley so they could go to school together. In the background he could hear Mary telling Rita to hurry up and finish her breakfast.

At 8:30 Steve phoned Frank Jackson and told him what had happened. Frank listened, then quietly asked, "What made you think the meet had to be in the Bronx?"

Steve was silent. Then: "Oi!" he said.

He now pictured the map of the entire city, with Queens just across the East River, and closer to Co-op City than half the Bronx locations he'd been searching.

Frank said, "It's natural your people think only west of the river. But the junk dealers think of Queens, too. The airports are there."

"Of course," Steve said. "The Gold Lounge is on 124th Street. He shoots across the Triborough Bridge, makes a meet between there and the airport, and circles back home."

Steve's voice was glum. He sat down wearily, blaming himself for the wasted chance.

To his astonishment, Frank's voice came to his ear full of heartiness.

"Yup! That's exactly it!"

"Huh?"

"You said it!"

"What?"

"Like you said—*he circles back home.*"

"Jeez, we just called it off and sent everybody home."

"Get going, Steve. Call your boss. He better get his ass up to the Bronx County Courthouse soon as it opens, for a search warrant, and tell him to buzz my boss for all the task-force guys he can spare."

Steve called McCrae at his office, just as McCrae was arriving. As he explained why he needed a search warrant on the Co-op City apartment, his outside phone rang. "Hold it," he said to McCrae.

It was Herby Wright. "Something's up. JC just left the apartment, drove to a corner phone booth three blocks away, and made a call. I'm going to follow him."

Steve got back on the other phone and repeated this to McCrae, as the outside phone rang again. "Hold it," he said.

It was Bill's relief man on the Laverne McBride wiretap. He said, "Hey, maybe something's going on. She just got a call from a male, saying, 'Get ready.'"

Steve went back to McCrae, who said, "OK, let's get on this—on the warrants, and on a turnout of manpower."

Herby Wright called in. He had followed JC to a small apartment house on Olmstead Avenue in the east Bronx. A few minutes later Mary Hogin went in. Shortly after that a man went in, carrying what looked like a folded airline shoulder bag.

McCrae now applied for a search warrant for this new address and sent ten more men over to join Herby. Ralph Tomas called in. He and his partner were assigned to tail Laverne McBride, and they had followed her to an apartment house at 1186 Seventh Avenue in Manhattan. McCrae called the task force for more men and sent ten of them to that address. Another warrant was requested.

By noon more than fifty men were deployed around four locations, with four search warrants issued.

A man came out of the Olmstead Avenue place. Wright recognized him as the man who had gone in with the folded airline bag. He was now carrying it unfolded and full. Two detectives followed him for three blocks and arrested him. There were two one-kilo packages of white powder in his bag.

Mary Hogin came out of the Olmstead Avenue building a quarter of an hour later, carrying a shopping bag. Two detectives followed her for three blocks and arrested her. She had a kilo package of white powder in her bag.

Herby Wright was now the only detective outside Olmstead Avenue. The others were all deployed to surround the building from the rear and from rooftops. Fifteen minutes later a man came out of the building with a paper-wrapped parcel under his arm. Herby Wright recognized him as Melvin Coombs, one of JC's couriers, but he couldn't follow him and leave the front of the building uncovered.

As he headed for a phone to request more detectives, Wright saw JC himself emerge, carrying an oversize attaché case. He was heading for his white Lincoln Continental. Wright decided he'd have to let Melvin go and move on JC.

As JC got into his car, Jackson and Nauwens drove up. Wright waved frantically to them as he started running up to JC, hollering, "Police! Freeze!" Jackson and Nauwens jumped from their car and ran too, yelling the same thing.

JC zipped into action. He slammed his door and started the car, aiming straight for the three cops coming toward him. They fell back just in time to avoid being hit, and JC was gone.

The cops got back into their two cars and started after him. Wright reported in on his car radio and called for reinforcements, while both cars scoured the streets, drawing a pattern of parallel streets and turns.

JC was evidently a demon driver. They caught sight of him in the distance a couple of times, but he eluded them at high speed in the narrow streets of the east Bronx. He was fearless about going the wrong way, fast, on one-way streets.

Another car joined the chase, then another. Jackson knew

JC was worried when he saw the dealer throw first one white package out of his car, then another as he disappeared from sight around a corner. Moments later, from his car, Wright caught sight of more white packages being thrown out.

JC spun into Castle Hill Avenue, getting close to the Cross Bronx Expressway and the Bruckner Boulevard Interchange. The cops now began to worry that if he got on the highway system their chances of catching him would fade fast.

JC picked up more speed and swung into Harmony Avenue—only to discover it was a temporary dead end, blocked by a construction project. He slammed on his brakes and swerved into a fence, crushing his right fender. As the detectives pulled up to surround him, he stopped, then immediately went into reverse and started to bulldoze back the way he came. They were out of their cars now, shooting at his Lincoln. But JC kept plowing on in the Lincoln, striking Nauwens and knocking him to the ground.

The Lincoln was still moving, and the cops still firing, when the front-left door opened and JC slithered out. He started to run in a crouching position, heading into a parking lot, running between parked cars, with several men after him in different lanes. Herby Wright came around, got close enough, and made a flying tackle. Jackson and another detective caught up. Jackson got a grip on his collar, and JC stopped struggling the instant he saw the gun pointed in his face.

"Let's not be hasty, gentlemen," he said.

# 6

At the Bronx County Courthouse, the district attorney held a joint press conference with the Westchester D.A. to announce the arrests and the big haul of heroin, thirteen kilos. The two D.A.s appeared in a group photograph..

At Lafayette Avenue and Taylor Street, Detective Bill Erwin packed up his small truckload of wiretap equipment and said farewell to the cockroaches in residence.

In his basement hideaway at Co-op City, Detective Steve Del Corso packed up his wiretap gear, sent it on its way in a department truck, and stopped at a coffee shop for a Danish and milk. To everyone, it seemed like a very good day.

Later that day, at headquarters of the joint task force, Frank Jackson was on the phone talking to Bill and Steve, by now back in their office on Park Avenue South. "Stupid bastards," Frank said. "Fifty thousand dollars bail for a guy like JC? How dumb can they get? He'll be off and running before they finish counting it."

After they'd hung up, Sergeant Fitzgerald came in from the

courthouse. "There's a rumor that JC's going to take it on the lam," he said.

Archy Brown Barton called in on the lieutenant's line. McCrae wasn't in, so he asked to speak to Bill. "The word is out on the street—JC disappeared. Tell McCrae when you see him." McCrae came in. He'd already heard, and he got on the phone to the Detective Bureau to try for the latest information.

A half hour later he came out of his office putting on his overcoat. "They caught him in Queens. I'm going over to the One-Fourteen. One of their detectives picked him up."

As he walked out of the room he paused at the door and said to Sergeant Fitzgerald, "The detective who picked him up said he thought there was a green Chevy tailing him. See if you can find out who that was."

Bill phoned Frank Jackson. "You were right about JC running, but they got him."

Jackson knew about it. He knew something else—two federal agents were on their way over to the One-Fourteen. He laughed.

Bill asked, "What's up?"

"Stick around a little longer, then call me back."

After a while McCrae came back. He had a peculiar look on his face. There were half a dozen of his men in the office, looking at him expectantly, and finally he opened up.

"The feds came in and took JC."

After a pause for dramatic effect he explained: "They got a federal indictment and have taken over the case. Sonsabitches. Cutting in after we did the work."

Steve said, "That's good news, isn't it?"

McCrae stared at him as if he were a traitor, and the rest of the men were silent, expecting McCrae's anger to explode.

Steve continued, "The D.A. has lost out to the feds, not us. We got the evidence on JC's mob, so the feds can't make a case without us. And the feds are out to drop Sisca, which is why they're hot after JC. So what we got as evidence is more important than the Bronx D.A. could make it."

McCrae was silent for one more moment, and his face took on an entirely different expression. He turned to Fitzgerald and said, "Sergeant, get Martinson on the phone, at the U.S. attorney's office."

While Fitzgerald did that, Bill got on the phone to Frank Jackson and signaled to Steve to pick up on an extension, as Jackson was saying, "... so while the Bronx D.A. was getting his press coverage, the feds rushed through an indictment."

Bill said, "He really hasn't got a beef, since the guy was jumping bond."

"He wouldn't have got away. The feds have been on his tail constantly. The fifty-thousand-dollar bond practically guaranteed his making a run, and that set it up for the feds to take over."

Steve said, "That must have been the feds tailing him in the green Chevy when the One-Fourteen detective picked him up in Queens."

"No, the feds use Fords. What's this about a green Chevy?"

Steve told him. Jackson became thoughtful and ended the conversation abruptly.

Next day, McCrae came to the office in the afternoon, bursting with good feeling. He'd been down to the U.S. attorney's office while they were interviewing JC, working on him to turn informer.

"And they turned him, all right. Worked on him for a couple hours. The guy's really terrific! He must be one of the biggest black dealers in the country. He deals with Sisca! And—get this—he's into them for a hundred and twenty-eight thousand dollars."

Sergeant Fitzgerald said, "You mean they give credit? to a black? A hundred thou—?"

McCrae's audience was really impressed. Steve asked whether JC had really turned or was just wavering.

"Well, it's not final, but it looks good. They talked to him about how serious the charges were and how he'd go away for life, and all that sort of crap, but what really turned him was

talking about how tough it would be on his family, his wife—
the woman he lives with—and mostly the kid. It's his kid, you
know, this Rita."

Steve explained for the benefit of the other men. "We taped
the kid till it came out of our ears."

McCrae said, "We talked to him a lot about what would
happen if the child were deprived of her father while she was
growing up and both parents in prison."

"A lovable child," Steve said, shuddering. "But it was worth
it, if on account of her he gives us a couple of big Italian
dealers."

Bill and Steve got the rest of the story that evening. They
met Jackson and Nauwens at Caruso's Bar & Grill across from
the Federal Courthouse. Frank and Jim were glum.

"That fucking green Chevy," Frank said.

"One of their guys was tailing JC," Jim said.

"Martinson's people had him all set to be a cooperating
witness—that was where your boss left—they were taking a
coffee break, and suddenly, there's Gino Gallina standing in
the doorway."

"Gallina?" Bill asked. "The Mafia mouthpiece? How'd he
get into the act?"

"The green Chevy. So they knew the feds had taken JC and
would turn him. Gallina is Sisca's lawyer and didn't waste
time. It was way after six o'clock and he walked in unan-
nounced. He just walked in the courthouse and knew which
office.

"He stands there and says, 'I understand you have my client
here.' God, it was funny. The federal attorneys sat with their
mouths hanging open. And poor JC was in a state of shock.
They were like kids caught with hands in the cookie jar.

"Gallina looks JC straight in the eye and says, 'For the
record, gentlemen, my client is not cooperating.' Then he
hands around his business cards and says that at the earliest
opportunity he would like to confer with his client. He gives
JC that big, phony smile of his and says not to worry, his

family will be taken care of by his friends, and they'll take care of his child—and out he goes.

"Man, it was pitiful. That was one scared black man the attorneys had on their hands. They couldn't do a thing with him, just book him and ship him off to the slammer."

"Couldn't we promise protection?" Steve asked. "We thought the feds had that witness-protection system going."

"Gallina moved in too fast. And of course he was shrewd, talking about the kid. When he mentioned her, JC turned to jelly."

Jim added, "You know, they wacked JC's brother, Solly, couple of months ago. At first that was good for our side, since he would have liked to get even, but after Gallina came with the message, it just made him that much more scared."

Bill said, "Anything more on the green Chevy?"

"Must have been one of their guys," Jim said.

"Or could it have been one of ours?" Steve said out loud when they were in their own car on the way home.


Lieutenant McCrae was in excellent spirits when he held the next meeting of the unit. His group had successfully set up the knockoff of the JC network, with major dealers among the eighteen arrests, with seizure of heavy weight in heroin, and confiscation of one Lincoln Continental (somewhat damaged), four Cadillacs in excellent condition, $70,000 in cash, and five guns.

In a way, it was a Christmas present to the department. It gave the commissioner something positive to report to the mayor at a time when the Knapp Commission was on TV putting the police in a terrible light as various top-rank officers and former officers attempted to explain why the department had so much corruption and why it had taken so long to find it out. The JC case also gave the mayor something to say when his political critics got their licks in, especially when Congressman Charles Rangel threatened to lead a march of angry black mothers on City Hall to protest the open drug pushing that was allowed to take place on the streets of Harlem.

McCrae didn't actually say any of these things at the meeting with his men. He didn't need to. But he thought it would help their morale to see their job in perspective. Just seven months before, he reminded them, in June, the President had declared a "War on Drugs." His announcement had come on the heels of two major drug busts—first the breakup of a drug ring operated by the French Secret Service, followed by the arrest of Auguste Ricord and the breakup of a big South American heroin network. The U.S. Secretary of State himself had announced that bust, calling Ricord the "Kingpin" of heroin traffic in the Western Hemisphere.

So, said McCrae, their unit was putting their department into the big leagues, with a case and quality arrests as good as any made by the feds' Customs Bureau and Bureau of Narcotics and Dangerous Drugs. He made no reference to their own Department's 800-man Narcotics Division and its policy of arresting thousands of junkies and pushers. He didn't need to. The men knew that was his point. He was telling them again that statistics didn't mean anything; the real thing was to kill drug traffic at the roots, to chop off the main stems.

"I hear the lieutenant is catching lots of flack," Steve told Bill a couple of days later over coffee at the Belmore.

Bill said, "What's the beef? He's been talking like they'd be giving him a medal."

"They want to skin him alive."

"Who does?"

"The Narcotics Division, that's who. They been yacking it up with the chief of detectives and the first dep. The crap is flying thick."

"So what's the beef? That our case puts their chickenshit arrests in a bad light?"

"We exceeded our authority. We were only supposed to do intelligence. When we had something, we should have passed the information to them, for them to handle."

"So they could louse it up?"

"And you want to hear the biggest crock? Some joker has been saying the commissioner will be attacked by the liberals in the administration because it was blacks that got arrested. There's a rumor the C.O. of Intelligence was on the carpet for half an hour."

"Wonder how McCrae's making out?"

Back in the office, McCrae came breezing in. After a short spell behind his closed door, he came out. Fast information, he knew, would dispel rumors.

"There have been some questions at headquarters," he began.

"Our procedures were questioned," he continued.

"Oh, shit—here's what it's all about. The Narcotics Division was bitching because we tied in with the task force when we needed extra manpower. You probably noticed in the *Daily News* how the task force got credit. Narcotics said that this kind of operation was too sensitive to take outside the Narcotics and Intelligence divisions and there's no need to go outside—they have lots of experienced personnel to lend us anytime we want it.

"So our C.O., and the chief of Narcotics Division, made an agreement. They will assign manpower to us whenever we develop a case. Squads from the Special Intelligence Unit of Narcotics will be assigned to work with us.

"The C.O. wants you men to know the department appreciates the heavy hours you've been putting in, and the strain on your families. From now on, with a squad or two from the SIU on our next go-around, we won't have to kill ourselves."

He beamed.

Bill said, "We got trouble."

# 7

He didn't say it very loud; it was more like he was talking to himself. A couple of the men sitting close by started to turn toward him, but McCrae's next remark reclaimed everyone's attention. He was announcing they could all have Christmas off—the entire week including the weekends before and after. Smiles lit up faces all around the room, and McCrae basked in the glow of good feeling.

At the Del Corso home in Nyack, Christmas of 1971 was the happiest time Loretta could remember. It was like the old days, with Steve at home and thinking of the family instead of his job. In fact, it was better than the old days, since Mary, the baby, was getting her first chance to know Daddy. They went skating and visiting, and ate in restaurants, and even took a trip into New York to see a movie at Radio City and the Christmas tree in Rockefeller Center. It was all just as she dreamed family life should be. On January 2, 1972, the life she dreaded started again.

At the Erwin home in Hartsdale, Phyllis watched and

wondered as Bill instantly became absorbed in the lives of Valerie and Andrew and little Eric. There were a hundred things he'd spoken of doing around the house when he had some time off, but almost everything he did for these ten days involved her and the kids. She wondered at how he seemed to be able to turn off thinking of his job. He took them hunting, hiking, even camping out overnight in tents. He taught little Eric to ice-skate. Phyllis wondered if the period when she had half lost Bill was over, so complete was their family life. Then, on January 2, she saw the imperatives of the police job take over again. As Bill walked out the door to his car, his mental gears were meshing for the pursuit of narcotics dealers. She wondered briefly, once more, what made a man tick that way, and a woman endure it.

Driving home around midnight two weeks after they'd returned from Christmas vacation, Steve asked, "Did you see McCrae yet, about the trouble you were talking about?"

"Been trying to all last week, but he's too fucking busy. He's been out of the office most of the time."

"What's it about?" Steve asked.

"That SIU deal, for Chrissake."

"They're supposed to supply us with extra manpower. What's wrong with that?" Steve asked.

"We shouldn't tie in with them. They are not to be trusted. You know that."

"Sure, they've got some bad guys, but not the whole unit."

"A lot more than you think."

"Wouldn't the lieutenant know about it? He was in the Narco Division before he came here."

"He was in a field unit. Corruption there ain't nothin' compared to the SIU. And something else he doesn't know— the SIU is under heavy investigation by the feds. When it comes out, there's gonna be a helluva stink."

"How come you know so much about it?"

"Because of what they did to Ruby Braddock. You remember Ruby."

"Braddock? Sure, he was with us in the Narco Division. He was transferred to SIU. What'd they do to him?"

"Ruby was a good friend, and a good cop. I worked a couple of cases with him. When he transferred, he also made detective."

"Well, what about him?"

"After he was there a short while, he phoned and asked me to meet him. I said, sure, and after that he called me quite a few times—he said he just had to talk to someone."

Steve said, "Don't tell me it was the first time he met cops on the take?"

"That wasn't it. He was assigned to a team, a sergeant and four detectives, and from the first time we talked he said there was something funny about them.

"Ruby said half the guys in SIU had an angle for each thing they did, something kinky or slightly illegal. One time he said they were doing illegal wiretaps, another time he found they were taking money and drugs off pushers and selling the drugs they ripped off."

Steve asked, "Was Ruby thinking of doing something—or did he?"

"He hesitated because other people knew about it and did nothing, including his own sergeant. And Ruby was new to SIU. Another thing was that some guys seemed to have deals going with people in the D.A.'s office, with judges, criminal lawyers, cops in the other squads.

"All I could do was listen and tell him to keep his nose clean. Then, one morning four of them were on a surveillance—Ruby, two other detectives and their sergeant. It ends up with the arrest of a dealer. The sergeant takes the dealer aside and comes back with a fistful of bills.

"Right there he divides it and hands a share to each of them.

"Ruby walks away. He says he wants no part of that and

he's gonna go ahead with the arrest. But the sergeant gets in front of him, takes the prisoner around the corner, and comes back without him.

"Then the three of them start pushing Ruby to take his share, and Ruby refuses, and finally the sergeant says he'll get Ruby's shield if Ruby holds out.

"Ruby was in a sweat. He was mighty proud of that shield. If he reported them, the sergeant would report him as the guy who let the prisoner go, and it would be his word against theirs. He figured he'd lose the shield and get kicked out, too.

"That's lousy," Steve said. "I guess your point is that the SIU is so dirty they won't let a clean guy stay that way—assuming, of course, that Ruby was telling it like it really was."

"He was. After they were all arrested, one of the other guys confessed and told how Ruby refused to go along, and Ruby was exonerated.

"The sergeant and two other detectives had split money before, and so had others in SIU. And you know that shit only comes down if the higher ranks are in on it."

"You were right," Steve conceded. "Guess you better see McCrae, before we get involved."

"I hear he's been in the Bronx the last few days," Bill said, "up in the Four-three Precinct."

"That's because of something I put him onto."

"Can't be too important. He took that lightweight Bernie Turner with him."

"Wanna bet? It's our next target."

"What is?"

"Back in December while I was sitting on JC's phone, I caught a meet between him and a couple of white guys, Italians. McCrae's been saying that for our next case we lay off black junk dealers and try for whites, right?"

Bill nodded.

"There was this phone call," Steve continued, "from an unknown male. JC himself answers, and the voice says, 'Meet us, you know where.'

78

"I call Herby Wright where he is watching JC's apartment building. Herby trails JC in his own car, and puts in a radio call for backup. Two task-force detectives pick him up in another car and they all follow JC to the Jacobi Hospital parking lot, where he meets two white men. Then Herby follows JC, but he only goes back home. The other detectives follow the two white men, and they drive to the intersection of Westchester and Wilkinson avenues.

"The detectives see them go into a small building at 3203 Westchester Avenue, with a sign on it, 'Wilkinson Avenue Meat Market.' "

Steve said he read all this in the surveillance reports when he was preparing documents for the prosecution in the JC case.

"I told McCrae somebody ought to take a look at that place, that club on Wilkinson and Westchester avenues. I know the neighborhood. I was brought up near there, and my first two kids were born at the hospital practically around the corner. It's a hundred percent Italian neighborhood.

"The building with the meat-market sign is a private social club, one of those storefront clubs they have in old-time Italian neighborhoods.

"JC's two white contacts had to be Italians, and they could have been his connection. I told the lieutenant it's a fair possibility that junk dealing goes on there. We know JC got his supplies from Funzie Sisca, and you can't get much bigger than him."

Bill said, "You must have got a rise out of him if he's been going up there himself."

"Rise? Man, he came back jumping, like he had a flea up his ass. He saw people up there that he remembered from when he worked in Harlem Narcotics and in Midtown Detectives. He drove around the neighborhood and passed the club several times. Each time, he saw someone he remembered, someone who deals in heavy weight.

"I couldn't tell him much about the neighborhood. It's a quiet, respectable community. Hardly any street crime. If there was junk dealing, I knew nothing about it when I was growing up. There were the usual rumors that Gonsalvo's Funeral Chapel was burying Mafia corpses in double-bottom coffins, and that Rinaldi's Bakery and Catering Hall had a Mafia tie-in. Other than that, it's middle-class respectable."

Bill laughed. "How respectable can you get, if Funzie's involved? Sisca and Company, hoodlums and killers."

Steve said, "The lieutenant laughed, too, when he came back. He said somebody around there had a weird sense of humor, calling the club the 'Wilkinson Avenue Meat Market.'"

The following night, McCrae told the unit about what looked like a new case for them. As he put it, "There's good news and bad news."

The "good news" was that in McCrae's opinion they had located a very important target. According to FBI records, many of the club regulars were members of the Tramunti branch of the Gaetano Lucchese organized crime family in the New York "Cosa Nostra," as the FBI used to call it. Several had been arrested at one time or another on theft, assault, extortion, and homicide charges, including the violent death of the principal witness in a check-fraud case. But neither the FBI nor the Four-three Precinct had information indicating heavy drug dealing there.

The "bad news" was that McCrae and his special unit had been invited to stay the hell out of the territory. The Four-three Precinct detectives said they "knew all about" the club, had their own way of dealing with it, and didn't need a bunch of new guys coming in to do who knows what on their own. Also, the Bronx D.A. had sent word through his principal assistant that he resented the implied criticism that violations of law were openly practiced there without interference, that both the Police Department and his own office "knew all about" the club and were handling it, and that if any headquarters unit had acquired new intelligence, they would do better to coordinate with the D.A. and not start working it

80

themselves. And another thing, someone had talked about applying to put a wire into the club. The D.A.'s man said that if McCrae knew what he was talking about, he'd have known that all the telephones at the club had been yanked out after the gambling raid several years back.

Bill came in later, after McCrae had finished telling the men about these developments. He asked Steve what the lieutenant had said, and what the men thought he would do.

Steve laughed. "You can't help liking the guy. He says, 'Well, sounds like exactly our kind of target—what we're in business for.' He's either pure bullshit, or he's really got guts."

Mike Larusso, a hearty six-foot two-hundred-pound veteran cop who chain-smoked cigars and was full of laughs, called over to them, "Gonna take more than guts. The C.O. in the Four-three Precinct is Deputy Inspector Pat Milazzo."

Sergeant Harry Fitzgerald, a tall skinny, easygoing black, said, "You mean Pasquale Milazzo takes care of his own? Come on. Those guys had their chance. They've been sitting up there with that club all along and doing nothing."

"Maybe they'll fight McCrae on it," Steve said, "but he can fight back. He's got support from the bosses down at headquarters."

"That was last month," said Larusso. "Now that he's a success, they'll be gunning for him. He could get his head handed to him."

# 8

Steve, Bill, and Archy Brown Barton were sitting at a corner table in the Belmore Cafeteria three nights later with their nightcap cups of coffee.

"The lieutenant is happy as a kid with a new toy," Archy said. "What gives?"

"He's *got* a new toy," Bill said. "It's Bernie Turner's fancy movie camera that he got for Christmas. He brought it in to show around the office, and McCrae got interested."

"What's fancy?" asked Archy.

"It shows movies through a television," Steve explained. "There's a gadget you attach."

"You mean a videotape," Archy said.

Bill said, "Bernie's a camera nut, and his wife got it for him. McCrae and Bernie have been going out in the field with it."

"What for?" asked Archy.

"Beats me," said Bill.

"They want to make movies up in the Bronx, at that social club on Wilkinson Avenue," Steve said.

"He's nuts," Bill said. "If it's really an organized-crime

83

hangout, he'll never get close to it. They have watchers in those neighborhoods."

McCrae's first visit to Wilkinson Avenue had been noticed. On his second visit he went in a different car, which Bernie drove while he sat in the back. They were observed within minutes, after which nobody entered or left the club.

He waited a couple of days and then took Bernie and his video camera in a station wagon driven by Richie Spinelli. Turner sat in the back seat with the camera, both of them concealed inside a carton from a washing machine. Flaps had been cut in the sides of the carton, which Bernie could raise when he wanted to use the camera.

They parked across the intersection from the club, and McCrae and Spinelli got out and went away.

From inside the carton, Bernie photographed the scene for about three hours. He had a telephoto lens on the camera and got shots that were fairly clear, including closeups of people going in and out of the club and having sidewalk conversations.

Steve said, when he heard about it, "He's nuts, nuts about show business."

Bill said, "That Bernie Turner could become the Gabe Pressman of narcotics intelligence."

"Or he could take over *Candid Camera*."

"It's better than working as a cop," Bill said.

"This isn't being in show business," said Steve. "This is only Bernie taking home movies in the Bronx."

Two days later, McCrae called a meeting. Sitting on his desk was a television set with a gadget attached. Explaining that it was a video playback machine, Bernie Turner ran through the tapes he had made in front of the club. The men made jokes at first as they watched, but gradually they became absorbed in the people they saw walking, talking, going in and out of the club, the drugstore, the candy store.

Then McCrae asked Bernie to run through it again. After a few seconds he said, "Hold it!" and Bernie turned a knob, causing the tape to stop running. A scene was frozen on the screen.

"This guy here," McCrae said, "looks familiar. I think we arrested him once when I was a sergeant in Manhattan North."

Steve said, "That looks like Edward Castellazzo. I once had him under surveillance in Queens. He's a courier for his brother Benjamin, who handles deals for Sisca's group. They were JC's suppliers and they're listed as major violators in Intelligence files. Edward makes lots of phone calls from a telephone booth in Jackson Heights, near the nightclub we have under surveillance, El Sombrero."

McCrae said, "OK. Whenever you men see someone on the tube who looks familiar, holler, and Bernie will stop the machine for a good look."

Motion resumed. Edward Castellazzo was seen going into the club. Seconds later two men were seen coming out, and Archy Brown said, "Hold it. That one on the left looks like Frank Stasi. I seen him regularly in Harlem, on Second Avenue. I hear he delivers heroin for someone, and that he buys cocaine."

McCrae said, "He's been in and out of the club several times each day we've been up there. Anybody recognize the other guy? No? OK, Bernie, roll it."

On the screen a sporty-looking man entered from the right. He was stocky, with dark curly hair. A shorter man came out through the door of the club. He too was well-dressed, about the same age as the first man, but with a slighter build.

Bill said, "Hey, hold it, that's 'Johnny Echoes' Campopiano on the right! He's a regular at the East Side nightspots. I've had him on surveillance several times and followed him to Bachelors III on Lexington Avenue. Can't miss him—he looks like Dean Martin, doesn't he?"

McCrae said, "The other looks familiar."

Bill said, "Sure. It's Johnny Capra. 'Johnny Hooks' they call him. I see him couple times a week on Seventh Avenue talking to suspects we have under surveillance. Capra's listed in the files as a big, big dealer. He lives in Pelham Manor, Westchester, and he owns restaurants in New Jersey."

The second runthrough of the tape progressed slowly. One after another, persons appearing on the screen were identified: "Ernie Boy" Abbamonte, who lived out on Long Island; "Moe" Lentini, who lived in East Harlem; Ralph Tutino, also from East Harlem; Alphonse "Funzie" Sisca, from upstate New York; Jerry Zanfardino, from Long Island; Joe Gernie from Brooklyn. All were known to be involved in drug rackets in various sections of the city, but it had not been previously suspected that they all dealt with each other.

The question uppermost in everyone's mind did not need to be asked: what were they all doing in a remote corner of the Bronx?

One impressive-looking person on the tape was familiar to no one in their group. He was a jolly fat giant of a man, about forty, and although he must have weighed more than three hundred pounds he appeared to be what they called a "sharp" dresser. When he appeared on the tube he seemed extremely good-natured, laughing and joking with his companions.

The next day Steve located a mug shot of him in the files of the Bureau of Criminal Identification, then checked him out in intelligence files, and with detectives at the task force. He was Louis "Gigi" Inglese, also known as "Fat Louis" or "Fat Gigi." His police record showed arrests for assault, robbery, drug dealing, and homicide in the Bronx, with a six-month jail sentence as his total prison record.

Task-force detectives told Steve they heard he had shot one person dead and had beaten another to death with a baseball bat.

No one felt the need to speculate why the club had been undisturbed for so long.

Steve put together a folder of information showing that Inglese operated the club. He also operated a bar, the Blue Lounge, two blocks away. He lived nearby, on Dwight Avenue, in a quiet neighborhood of undistinguished but expensive houses, all worth upwards of $200,000. Inglese lived there quietly with his wife, son, and two daughters. Unlike most of his neighbors, however, he went to work every day in a large black Cadillac driven by a chauffeur named Donato Cristiano, also known as "Big Mouth Finnegan," who had never been known to smile at anyone.

Evidently Inglese was an important link connecting this conglomeration of heroin dealers from all over the city and beyond. Richie Regan got the job of putting together a folder of known information on each club member or patron, while the rest of the unit hit the streets or the phones gathering more intelligence.

McCrae disappeared for nearly a week, then returned and called a meeting. The television was set up again, and Bernie Turner ran the tape. It was different this time. Instead of just looking like a home movie, it now looked like a regular TV show. McCrae himself was in it, sitting at a desk like Walter Cronkite and explaining what the tape was all about. He displayed charts and closeup mug shots of people shown in the street scenes.

He was saying that this obscure social club in a remote corner of the northeast Bronx was the base for a large heroin-distribution network. The tape, he said, showed big-time drug dealers walking about without a care in the world, without fear of interference, driving up in big, expensive cars.

"Bulk drug dealing here," he intoned solemnly, "is controlled by members of several organized-crime families who meet at the club daily to arrange their nefarious schemes."

He named them and summarized their crime careers. They supplied a large part of all the heroin moving daily through the streets of New York and other cities of the eastern seaboard. The JC Abraham operation had been part of this network, he said.

He ended by saying he planned to launch Operation Discover against this syndicate as soon as additional manpower was assigned to him.

The men watching were too astonished to wisecrack. Mc-

Crae spoke from the tube with an air of confidence and authority that was larger than life. When the tape was over, they applauded.

He grinned, then put on a solemn expression and said, "I am happy to announce ... we are now legal.

"We had some complaints before about working in this territory. But after I played this videotape for the chief, he took it and played it for the chief of intelligence, and for the first deputy commissioner, and for the commissioner."

McCrae looked very happy. The commissioner himself had said they should go ahead with Operation Discover. McCrae said he was applying for a wire into the candy store where the club members did their telephoning, and for a bug into the club itself.

The men were all to drop what they had been doing and switch full time to Operation Discover. The backup was already on its way: a squad of ten detectives from the SIU of the Narcotics Division was coming over tomorrow to work with them.

As McCrae went back into his office, Bill hurried over to speak to him. From across the room Steve saw that the conversation was brief. McCrae listened, shrugged his shoulders, and disappeared into the office, closing the door behind him. Steve went over and asked Bill what had been said.

"I tried to talk to him again, about not getting involved with guys from the SIU. He's not even taking time to check them out individually."

"What'd he say?"

"He said he knew some of them were on the take but they'd have no opportunity for that with us. They would not be making arrests, so they couldn't expect to be offered bribes. I said they could screw us other ways. He said he had a meeting to get ready for and we'd talk about it another time."

# 9

Lieutenant McCrae was in heaven. His idea for Operation Discover had grabbed the top brass. In a massive institution like the New York Police Department, lieutenants could simply not expect to come in with new ideas and have them accepted right off the bat.

He knew that, as much as anything, it was the novelty of his Walter Cronkite presentation that had caught their fancy. He had packaged this idea just right, making it look like something that would be highly salable to the mayor, who was himself a handsome displaced actor and who ran his administration like a lavish showbiz enterprise. To the top police brass, still smarting from the revelations of the Knapp Commission, Operation Discover looked like something likely to improve their image in the public eye.

McCrae ran the videotape as part of the briefing of the SIU squad. Then he outlined his plan, taking time to remind them that investigations of organized crime are often frustrated because of the system of neighborhood "watchers."

While police and Federal agents had developed over the

years some rather sophisticated methods of surveillance, including electronic devices, organized crime had an effective countersystem, primitive perhaps, but effective. In each neighborhood, said McCrae, they have these watchers—men, sometimes women, even children, who are constantly on the lookout for strangers, hostile, suspicious, or just unfamiliar. Watchers might be loungers, on or off the street, or they might be sidewalk peddlers, or work in stores on the street, or at a local service station, but their main responsibility was to signal the presence of police, detectives, inspectors, investigators, enemies or suspicious unknowns. When they signaled, those who needed to do so took evasive action or dropped out of sight.

McCrae's scheme for evading the countersurveillance that protected Inglese's club was to place investigators in observation posts at a distance from the Meat Market. From that distance they would observe people leaving the club or arriving, and would radio information to detectives in cars parked four or five blocks away.

In principle, the drug dealers who arrived would have no reason to be on guard, and the watchers would not have anything to report, so when the dealers left, the detectives in pursuit cars could tail them without detection.

The object was to observe dealers actually passing heroin to customers in bulk. The evidence thus assembled by the unit could lead to arrests and prosecutions.

Once the SIU squad had been briefed, the sergeants divided the SIU men and McCrae's unit into teams and sent them out to set up observation posts and man the surveillance cars. One team dressed as subway workers went into a signal shack on the subway's elevated trestle. One team parked in an electric-company repair truck. Another team, dressed in bus-company-supervisor uniforms, took turns with a notebook, monitoring the city buses. Steve and Bill, dressed in slacks and windbreakers, got a surveyor's tripod, a measuring stick and tape, and slowly traversed the roadbeds of the area.

Each team carried concealed radio equipment for signaling the pursuit cars.

McCrae had seen a delivery of bottled water going into the club. He arranged with the distributor to install a miniature bug on one of the crates, to pick up conversations inside the club after the next delivery.

The first day, everything went well. The cops seemed to blend into the neighborhood.

On the second day of Operation Discover, Bill and Steve went into the office to make out reports before taking their shift at the club. Jake McNamara said that Larusso had called in to say there was "something funny" about the neighborhood.

Bill grabbed Steve's arm and said, "C'mon, we'll do the reports later."

They drove up to the surveillance area and saw immediately what the "something funny" was. All the other commercial streets in the Bronx were bustling with afternoon traffic, people and vehicles. The intersection of Wilkinson and Westchester avenues was dead. Normal street sounds seemed muted, broken at intervals by the thundering overhead passage of an IRT train riding the high trestle suspended above Westchester Avenue.

"We better call in," said Steve, and drove to a sidewalk telephone booth.

Richie Regan answered. "The Meat Market blew, we think," Bill told him tensely. "Tell McCrae."

Minutes later they stopped at another phone booth and Bill got Richie back on the phone. "What's happening?"

"The shit has hit the fan. It's wild down here."

"We're coming in."

As Steve made the turns that would head them back to the office, they passed the Blue Lounge, the bar operated by Gigi Inglese, who also ran the Meat Market Club. They would have gone right by, but slowed down when they saw a man and a woman at the door, evidently trying to get in. The door seemed locked and the place deserted.

Steve pulled over to the curb and both of them darted out, coming at the man and woman from opposite directions as the couple returned to their car. They flashed their detective shields and said, "Police."

Bill asked to see a driver's license and car registration. The man, a dark-skinned Puerto Rican,, promptly became nervous. Saying nothing, he got a wallet out of his pants pocket and fished around till he found his license, then reached into the car's glove compartment and came up with the registration.

The woman meanwhile stared from one officer to the other. Then, with an edge to her voice, she said, "What's the problem, officer?"

She had light olive skin, black eyes, and long black hair which framed her head and shoulders smartly, and Bill noticed that under the leopard fur coat her figure promised to be very good.

Steve did not answer at once, ignoring her question while he studied the license and registration. Bill was looking into the interior of the automobile through its windows.

"I asked what's the problem, officer." She spoke sharply and slightly louder this time.

"Just checking," Steve said.

Addressing Bill, she asked, "You got any probable cause to go poking around in there?"

Steve said, "We were wondering what you were doing around here."

The man spoke up now. "Just stopping for a drink. Anything wrong with that?" The driver's license said his name was Pedro Melicio.

Steve said, "We were just wondering why someone would stop off for a drink at a bar that's closed, Mr. Melicio."

She spoke again, with the edge still in her voice but more relaxed now, confident that nothing was going to happen. "Obviously, officer, we didn't know it was closed."

Bill said, "There've been quite a few holdups and robberies of bars in this area. We were just checking."

"Nobody robs this place." She almost sneered as she said it.

"How do you know?" Bill asked quickly. "You come here often?"

92

Her face broke into a smile. "Can we go now, officer? Can we go along now?"

Steve handed the license and registration back and said, "Sorry to trouble you both. Just doing our job."

The two detectives went back to their car as the couple got into theirs and drove off.

Bill said, "Do we tail them?"

"She's wise. Be a waste of time. We better get back to the office."

As Steve headed for the expressway Bill asked, "Did you notice her pocketbook? Bet a buck she had a gun in it."

"From the way she was hefting it, yes. That means one of them was carrying a bundle. Obviously they were there looking to buy junk."

Steve added, "The car was registered to her name, Dolores Gomez, with a Bronx address. I know her from someplace. I used to live in the Bronx. But, no. It was when I worked in Harlem."

"You remember her for her looks or her temper?"

"I didn't have cause to find out about her temper back then." Steve turned thoughtful. "Now I recall. She used to go around with a junk dealer then. Italian, major violator. Maybe we should have tailed them."

But he made no move to change course. Next time Bill looked at him there was a peculiar look on his face, and then a half-smile. "What's funny?" Bill asked.

"I'll tell you something I never told anybody before. Back when I was a rookie in Harlem, there was a shoot-out, and a young spic junkie caught it. He was dead when I got to the scene, and the cops had things pretty much under control on the block. Suddenly a girl shows up and has hysterics, and starts to collapse. The dead guy was her brother.

"She comes close to where I was while she's screaming, so when she starts to collapse, I reach out to grab her before she hits the sidewalk. It was this Dolores Gomez.

"At that time she was living on Pleasant Avenue and a bystander told me her address. I put her in a police car and

93

drove her home. She was shook up, weak, so I helped her up to her apartment, practically carried her."

Bill asked the obvious. "Anything happen?"

Steve smiled and half-closed his eyes for a moment. "If you think she's good-looking now, you should have seen her then. She was in her teens, not so big in the tits and hips, but enough. The feel of her when I had to hold her up—slender, silky-smooth, perfume like I never smelled before. And the dress she had on—short, no sleeves, felt like she had nothing on. . . ."

Bill took a long look at his partner. "Nothing happened, right?"

"Right."

Back at the office on Park Avenue South, the men of the Drug Intelligence Group had been assembling, and about a dozen were milling around until someone resolved the uncertainty of what it all meant. Drawing Mike Larusso aside, Bill and Steve asked him what had happened.

The two-hundred-pound six-footer took the perennial cigar from his mouth, sighed noisily, and said, "It was pitiful. . . . So pitiful," he continued, "it was funny." He shook his head. "There's four of us in the office, checking the intelligence reports, phoning, that sort of thing. Richie takes a radio call and goes into the lieutenant's private office, but we don't pay attention, and then he comes out. A couple minutes later, the lieutenant's door suddenly opens and he walks two steps into the room. . . .

"The look on his face is . . . Well, he's flushed and kind of glassy-eyed, and all stiff, and he stands there like a statue, and then he says, quiet-like, 'The Meat Market blew.'

"We all stop and stare at him. And then he starts to swear. He curses like you never heard. He stares over our heads and he curses like he expects it will make the building fall down. He raises his fist as if to smash the nearest desk, and then he suddenly controls himself.

"He puts his hand down slowly and he says, 'I should have known.' That's all he said, 'I should have known.'

"Then he goes back in his office and closes the door."

Bill asked after a pause, "And that's it?"

Larusso said, "He sent out word he wanted everybody to come in for a meeting at five-thirty, just our own group, not the SIU guys, not to even let them know about it. He said there's to be absolute security on this meeting."

Steve asked, "What's funny? You said before it was funny."

"McCrae swearing," Larusso said. "I didn't know that guys who graduated from Fordham knew those words."

Bill said, "He was in the Marines. You didn't know, and he didn't say, but I checked him out."

Mike Larusso laughed. "Well, he comes by his swearing honestly." But there was no mirth in his laughter. "What blew it?" he asked with urgency.

"We don't know," Steve said. "They have watchers all over, and they could have made a couple of our guys."

Larusso's best friend, Dan Fiorentini, came over. "What blew it?" he asked.

Richie Spinelli came over, "Maybe the bus inspectors were trying to work too close," he said.

"I was on that with one of the SIU guys," Fiorentini said, "but I thought it could've been the guys up on the subway trestle in the signal shack."

Ralph Tomas came over and said, "They were SIU guys, using binoculars, and they could have been spotted, easy."

Spinelli said, "What about that surveillance truck? Who brought that in?"

Steve said, "Bernie Turner was in it, shooting more videotapes, and an SIU guy was shooting photographs through the one-way windows."

Bill finally said it. "Yeah, they could have made one of us.

95

Or it could have been a leak." His voice became tense. "A goddamn leak."

The others said nothing for the moment, then he added: "Son of a bitch McCrae. I tried to tell him, and now he comes out and says he should've known. What the hell's that mean?"

Mike Larusso said, "If there's a leak, we are fucked but good. This operation is supposed to have total security. If there's a leak, it means they got somebody on the inside."

Richie Regan had joined the circle. He was administrative officer for the unit, clerk and record keeper, a quiet Irishman whom McCrae had come to rely on because of his methodical abilities, and because he himself was Scots-Irish.

He told them now that what McCrae had said was, "I should have known in the first ten minutes."

The morning of the SIU briefing, Bernie Turner had been only a few minutes into the tape when there was a sort of disturbance in the back of the room, muffled exclamations, and some whispering, and then one of the SIU men had gone over to talk with the SIU lieutenant, Clem Shandel.

When the tape was finished, Shandel simply commented that it was a helluva good job, and that the Meat Market should be a very interesting assignment for all of them.

After the meeting, when the men had dispersed to their posts, McCrae had asked Richie Regan what the disturbance had been all about.

"A detective named Paul Butler."

"What's with him?"

"I don't know," Richie had said. "Sounded to me like he was telling his lieutenant, 'That's our case, that's our case.' He seemed upset."

McCrae had said, "Very peculiar. Crazy. Does he think he owns this case?"

"I don't know. Maybe we should check him out."

"We don't need to. He may have worked on someone in that club, but obviously he accomplished nothing. He's got no beef about our coming into it."

"He could cause trouble. Or some of the others could, if they feel we gypped them out of an important case."

"I'll speak to Lieutenant Shandel and let him take care of it," McCrae had said.

Now Bill and Steve were even more convinced that there had been a leak. They all waited for the lieutenant to arrive and tell them what came next.

McCrae appeared at 5:30, carrying a heavy paper bag from which he pulled a gallon jug of red wine. The men broke out their coffee mugs and passed the jug around.

Lieutenant Robert McCrae knew the crucial importance of morale. He'd commanded troops in the Marines and knew that when the enemy kicks the shit out of your unit, you regroup and start aggressive action right away. You also level with the men about mistakes and weaknesses as well as strong points.

OK, said McCrae, something had gone wrong and he was digging around to find out what. OK, he'd talked with the top brass, and their unit still had the complete confidence of Inspector Kramer and the first deputy commissioner.

OK, this exercise at the Meat Market Club blew, but the system, the idea back of Operation Discover, was still good. They had had more experience now; they'd find another target as good or better, and they'd give it another try.

He did not mention the possibility of a leak, but he said anyone who wanted to talk with him one-on-one should feel free to do so, and he looked at Bill when he said it.

The meeting had started with the men anxious and alienated. McCrae let them talk their resentments out and had them arguing about what to do next. The twilight outside their windows had turned to night, the streetlights had come on, and across the street were the lighted windows of the Ashland Hotel, a local fleabag, where couples were going at it in full view. The men of the unit shared a jug of wine and ended up feeling that they were together, against the world of bad guys.

* * *

A week later, Bill, Steve, Archy Brown, and Bobby Macon were at a corner table in the Belmore Cafeteria, sharing a cup of coffee before the long, late trek home.

"Was it them?" Archy asked. "The SIU guys?"

"I don't know," Bill said.

"What's the lieutenant say? You talked with him."

"He don't know either."

"Is he going to try to find the leak?" Bobby Macon asked. "Wouldn't that make sense before we work with them again?"

Bill said, "We won't be working with them again."

Archy said, "Well, at least that's something, if the lieutenant dumped them."

Steve said, "He didn't. They dumped him."

The other three turned quickly toward Steve. He said, "They like his idea. They figure they can use it themselves, without McCrae, and get the full credit."

Bobby Macon wanted to know, "How'd you find that out? What did the lieutenant tell you?"

"He didn't tell me—we told him," Bill said. "Steve and me."

Archy said, "What's this all about?"

"You know my friend Frank Jackson on the task force?" Bill asked. "I talked to him right after the Meat Market blew, and he told me he thought he knew of a case we'd like to take over.

"They were running heavy surveillance on a dealer named John Ramos. He led them to Johnny Hooks Capra, who operates a big setup—bigger than Inglese's—in a private club on Havemeyer Avenue, near the Cross Bronx Expressway. They dropped Ramos and tried to turn him to give up Capra. They've postponed his trial for months, expecting he'd crack. Jackson suggested that the club at Havemeyer Avenue would make a good target for McCrae's system, and we could take over the case."

Archy said, "What do you mean, take over—why don't they do it themselves?"

"Jackson says they can't. There's something funny going on with the feds, out of Washington."

Bobby said, "What's funny?"

"Beats me," Bill said. "All I can tell you is, it's got to do with something called ODALE. Some Nixon guys in Washington are reorganizing all the narcotics enforcement in the country. Originally, the feds put money and people into our task force, but now, on account of this reorganization, they want to take it back. They transferred some of the task-force units to this ODALE organization, which has opened an office in New York and is running their New York operations."

"What's ODALE?" Bobby asked.

"And what's it got to do with Ramos, and busting Capra?" Archy asked. "I read about ODALE—it stands for Office of Drug Abuse Law Enforcement. Heavy stuff."

Bill said, "Somebody told Frank those guys are out to make a big showing. They have to prove they can do things better than the local cops. In other words, they need lots of cases, fast, and where can they get them? By picking them up from the locals. So they've ordered all pending task-force cases brought to trial right away—and that would have to include Ramos."

Bobby said, "They have to try him sometime, so why not?"

"Frank says if they take him to trial now, good-bye Capra and the Capra organization—nobody will be able to touch them. And Frank says they'll even lose Ramos—the case against him is pretty weak."

"Why don't they tell that to ODALE?"

"ODALE, they say, is not interested. The president's men want cases right away, to build up their statistics, they say."

Archy was enthusiastic. "So why *don't* we take over the Capra case? We don't have to take any crap from the president's men."

"Right. Steve and I made up a report for McCrae, and McCrae said it sounded good to him. He said we should get on it right away. On our way to work we detoured past the club to get a look at it.

"It's fantastic. That club is a three-story frame building, about eighty by a hundred feet, standing detached on its own

99

lot, near the approaches and exits at the interchange of the Cross Bronx Expressway and Bruckner Boulevard. No through streets have access to it. No one could possibly approach it without being seen by neighborhood watchers. No one could come in except on business connected with the club. It's a perfect safe house for drug dealing."

Archy and Bobby were already tasting the excitement of the new investigation. Bill said McCrae had started mapping the location of his surveillance cars and even helicopters, if he could get them. He had applications drawn up for authority to place wiretaps and bugs. Then all preparations stopped.

The applications came back disapproved. Authorized wiretaps and bugs were already outstanding in those premises. McCrae inquired, and learned that the SIU squad, headed by Lieutenant Clem Shandel, had acquired the authority.

Bill and Steve went back and toured the whole area. They found it was ringed with detectives at observation posts and surveillance cars standing by on roads leading into and away from the clubhouse.

They figured that a couple of the SIU men who had been in on the Meat Market must have tailed a dealer, perhaps Capra himself, from that club to this one, and had reserved the information for themselves.

"Makes you wonder," Archy said, "when the SIU gets something as big as this for themselves."

"Makes you wonder," Bobby said, "did someone blow at the Meat Market, or leak it."

Steve said, "Makes you wonder, did they do both."

Bill said, "The thing we do know is that Richie Regan had the answer, that time McCrae said to him, 'I'll speak to Lieutenant Shandel and let him take care of it.' Shandel took care of it."

# 10

Bill Erwin entered the huge apartment house at 837 Seventh Avenue and rode the elevator to the fifth floor. He had on a shoulder-length wig of dark brown hair with blond streaks, large green-tinted eyeglasses, and a Fu Manchu mustache. His flower-patterned shirt was unbuttoned halfway down his chest, exposing a large-link chain with a big medallion. His faded blue jeans had twenty-four-inch bell bottoms that swung as he walked, and he carried a black guitar case by a strap over his shoulder.

On the fifth floor, he walked quickly to suite 5H and pushed the button, setting off two chimes. A card read "Golden & Starr, Artists' Representatives, Hollywood, London, New York." A buzzer sounded and he went in.

Beyond a small vestibule, its walls covered with framed theater posters featuring rock 'n' roll stars, was a larger room with more of the same, and with chairs along three sides.

Through a doorway on the right he could see a short stout man with receding hair, heavy black-framed eyeglasses, a telephone in one hand, a smoldering cigar in the other, and he said, "Hello, Mr. Starr."

Starr, without breaking his phone conversation, looked up, smiled, waved. Bill waved back and pointed to the doorway on the left.

"Still on the coast," Starr said. "Go on in. Don't disturb his papers."

Bill said thanks, went in, and shut the door of the office quietly. Opening the guitar case, he took out a 35-mm. camera, a telephoto-lens cylinder, and a tripod, which he set up for later. He opened the window to the chill March air and looked around to make sure that his host's papers would not blow.

Standing well back from the window, he aimed the camera toward the street below and focused, first on one spot, then another. Without looking for them, he saw Tony Norman and Jake McNamara in their surveillance posts.

This would be his fifth day making surveillance photos. The shots he'd gotten the first two days had led McCrae to decide this was the target with most promise. The squad needed a promising target urgently; McCrae needed it too, Bill was aware, needed it desperately. First Inglese's Meat Market had blown; then he'd missed out on Capra and the Havemeyer Club; and before that, the JC case had ended without giving him a shot at the Funzie Sisca setup.

Telephoto photography was new to Bill, and he enjoyed it. Camera pressed to cheek, he moved the viewfinder to bring in the Gold Rail Bar, the Ballantine Barbershop, the Stage Cigar Store, and the Stage Delicatessen almost directly across the street. At intervals he clicked off pictures. Two previous days' shots were at the police lab being processed.

One of the men Bill had under surveillance was Herbert Sperling, listed in police intelligence records as a major dealer in heroin, but his only convictions were for assault, theft and gun violations. Bill saw him now in his viewfinder, moving in and out of the two restaurants, the cigar store and barbershop, meeting and talking with people who came to him, now inside this place, now in that, now outdoors on the sidewalk.

At intervals Bill would shoulder his guitar case and go down to the street. Assuming an expression of vagueness—as if he were a spaced-out or unemployed rock musician—he walked around near Sperling, trying to get close enough to observe and listen. But Sperling's conversations never took very long. He was never seen writing notes or records or handling money or parcels. He seemed to have a perfect system for eluding surveillance.

That night Bill received a packet of eight-by-ten blowups from the police photo lab. Two pictures produced the little "zing" of adrenaline a detective feels when something drops into place. He remembered making those shots.

A black Cadillac had stopped in front of the barbershop, and the driver had talked with Sperling at the curb. Bill got pictures of the two in conversation and of the car's license plate as it drove away after the meeting.

The registered owner of the car was Maria Lombardy. Now that Bill had the blowup of the meeting, he recognized the driver: Donato Cristiano, chauffeur and general go-for to Louis "Gigi" Inglese. Maria Lombardy was Inglese's daughter.

Inglese had not been seen at either the Meat Market Club or the Blue Lounge, his accustomed haunts.

One photo showed Sperling leaning on the sidewalk mailbox as he talked with Cristiano, and flipping through other pictures, Bill saw he did that time and again.

McCrae found out the Manhattan South Narcotics Unit had put a bug inside the mailbox, a small microphone attached at a small hole near the top. He assigned Richie Spinelli to work with Bill, to make sure their photo surveillance was thorough, and perhaps tie in with conversations tape recorded at the mailbox.

Cristiano again appeared on Seventh Avenue and met

Sperling. Leaving Spinelli to handle the camera, Bill dashed down to his car, pulled a parking ticket off his windshield, and drove into Seventh Avenue in time to see Cristiano drive away. As they went east on 54th Street, Bill removed his wig, shades, and mustache. He buttoned up his shirt and slipped on a black bowtie.

Cristiano led him north up First Avenue, and east again on 116th Street. He turned left for a block and a half, stopped, and double-parked. Bill cruised slowly past and saw him go into a barbershop. Bill himself kept going to 120th Street, turned, circled the block to where Cristiano had parked the Caddy, and drove slowly past it. He was about to stop, but noticed there were three men on a bench staring at him from one side of the street. Another in a leather cap and long coat watched him from the other side.

He kept going. He retraced his route back to the Golden & Starr agency office and left a message for Steve, who was out in the field.

Bernie Turner came in with a carrying case of filming equipment and greeted Richie and Bill, very jolly and spirited.

"What's up?" Bill wanted to know.

"We're going to film motion pictures here."

"Who says so?"

"It's OK with the lieutenant," Bernie said. "He wants it."

"Sorry, Bernie, there's just no room here, and he didn't say anything to me about it. Try someplace else."

Bernie's expression darkened. "McCrae OK'd it. And it's no use calling him now, he's not in. I won't be in your way. I've looked around, and I can get a better angle from the bathroom."

Bill said, with exaggerated patience, "This is a man's private office. He has visitors on business. They have to use the bathroom."

They were interrupted by the telephone. It was Steve calling back. He explained, "I couldn't call back before, I was tailing someone. I'm in a phone booth now in a gas station on 116th Street and St. Nicholas Avenue."

Bill said, "It's OK."

"Guess where I just came from?" He paused dramatically for a moment. "Barone's Bar, in East Harlem."

"It's why I called you to—"

"I remembered Barone's Bar from when I was a rookie working Harlem—"

"The reason I called you—"

Steve was charged up and kept talking fast. "This is a funny one. I get a call from Richie Regan. Seems a couple of detectives are working a truck-hijacking case in Astoria, and they're sitting on a wired corner phone booth. Some guy they are not interested in keeps using the phone, and they are not listening to him, until they suddenly realize he's making junk deals—pickups and drops of heroin.

"So they take down the license number—he drives a red Mustang—and send the information in to Intelligence. Richie monitors stuff that comes in there, you know, so he picks it up and passes it onto Charlie Cabalo and me because we're working Queens.

"Turns out the guy driving the Mustang is Tony Salina, who moves junk for Funzie Sisca. We tail him, and he leads us over the Triborough Bridge and, *boom,* there he is turning off at 116th Street. He double-parks in front of Barone's Bar, which is between 116th and 117th, and there is Eddy Castellazzo on the sidewalk. Salina opens the trunk, they both look in, slam it closed, and both go into the bar.

"I would have stayed, but right away people are watching me, so I take off."

Bill said, "I been trying to tell you. I just been tailing Inglese's Caddy to East Harlem."

"When?"

"Today. Must have been a couple hours before you were there. I tailed Inglese's chauffeur to a barbershop there."

"Maybe the big junk dealers are coming back out of the woodwork."

"Maybe they been out all the time. We didn't know where to look."

"I'm going in to write a report. How about you?"

"I'll meet you."

In the office on Park Avenue South, Archy and Bobby Macon were talking with Mike Larusso when Steve came in and said, "How you doin'?"

Archy said, "We were up in your neighborhood today."

Steve looked his question and Archy continued, "Over in East Harlem. Didn't you say you come from East 109th Street?"

"Not me. My mother's family used to live there, though, on First Avenue and East 109th. What's on up there?"

"Me and Bobby were tailing a major violator on the west side of Harlem, and he took us to East Harlem. Actually, we were a little further up the line, on 117th Street."

When Bill came in, Steve called over to him, "Listen to this."

Archy said, "We were on surveillance of a Hispanic named Lopez. He leads us to a place called Diane's Bar on Second Avenue and East 105th, and when he comes out, Joe Gernie is with him."

"Joe Gernie is from way out in Brooklyn, out on Kings Highway, for God's sake," Steve said. "What's he doing in East Harlem."

"We had the same thought," said Archy. "So we let Lopez disappear and stayed with Gernie. He starts driving up Second Avenue; then, next we know, he turns east, all the way over, and he drives into a parking lot between 117th and 118th streets."

The others waited while Archy made a dramatic pause.

"So," he said, "maybe you wanted to know where Beansie Delacava is since he disappeared from the Meat Market Club in the Bronx? Right there in East Harlem. Gernie parked in the lot, and Delacava is waiting for him on the sidewalk. Gernie hands him an envelope and they go into a corner bar together."

"Tell them, Arch, tell them who else we see in the neighborhood," said Bobby Macon.

Steve and Bill looked at each other, then told Archy and Bobby about their own trips to East Harlem that day. Maybe their work on the Meat Market Club dealers in the Bronx wouldn't be wasted after all. As McCrae had shown in his videotape report, the idea was to identify the dealers' channels of bulk narcotics distribution. They seemed to be on to something worth following up. They were talking excitedly when a phone call came in for Bill from Richie Spinelli.

Bill listened for a moment, cursed, and listened some more with his expression deadpan. "Let him do it," he said, and hung up.

"Seventh Avenue blew," he said.

Steve asked, "Does the lieutenant know?"

"Not yet. And all I'm going to say is, I want to work partners with you again."

They looked at each other in silence. Bobby came right out and asked the question. "How come Bernie's always nearby when something blows?"

Bill said, "I don't think it's him."

"I don't think he's the leak," Steve said. "He's just a meathead with a fucking movie machine. He's gone nutty over solving crimes with a movie camera."

Archy, still suspicious, asked Bill what had happened.

"I told him, 'Not the bathroom,' so where's he shoot from? The bathroom window. First thing you know, one of Starr's clients is knocking on the door to use it. Bernie's got this clever cover story: he's an NBC-TV cameraman doing a documentary. The client turns out to be a TV actor, so pretty soon he and Bernie are yakking it up. Then the guy looks through the window and says, 'Hey, you can see my bookie from here. When I go down I'll walk up to him on the sidewalk and you take his picture.' Next thing you know, a couple of guys from the barbershop are on the sidewalk looking up, then they go into the bar and the cigar store and the delicatessen, and next after that, no more Sperling, and no more any of the guys we've been watching.

"And you want to know something else? Bernie hasn't even noticed. He's still up there filming."

# 11

Steve, at his desk writing a report, felt someone come up behind him and heard a sudden throaty growl. Turning and looking up he was startled by an enormous human eye floating above his face.

It was Bill Erwin, holding a large magnifying glass in front of his face.

Steve politely acknowledged the joke with a half-smile and was turning back to his writing when a packet of photographs landed with a slap in front of him. It took seconds for the pictures to grab Steve's full attention.

"Spinelli took these pictures from the theatrical agent's office while I was out on the street," Bill explained. "We just got them back from the lab."

Steve was flipping through nearly three dozen fairly clear photographs of Seventh Avenue near the Stage Delicatessen. Herbert Sperling was in most of them. In one shot Sperling was talking with Zanfardino. In another he was with Eddy Castellazzo. In two others he was talking with Johnny Hooks

Capra, and there was one of him in earnest conversation with John Campopiano. In three pictures Sperling was evidently very angry and disgusted, while Moe Lentini stood there laughing in his crazy way. They took the pictures to the lieutenant.

McCrae's adrenaline began to run as soon as he saw them. He had already heard Bill's report of seeing Inglese's chauffeur in action, Steve's that he'd seen Castellazzo and his courier in action, and Archy's that he'd seen Delacava's partner in action. He agreed with his detectives that their friends from the Meat Market were no longer underground. They were on the move again, and the unit was on their track.

The break came at a good time. It was now March of the new year and they'd had nothing tangible to work on. Lieutenant Shandel's SIU squad were already two months into their investigation of Capra's club on Havemeyer Avenue.

McCrae called the whole unit in for a meeting. The group's top priority, he told them, was to find out where the big dealers were operating from. He was hyped up and he infected them with his excitement. He told the sergeants to reshuffle the teams and forget the Bronx. Based on the information he'd gotten from Erwin and Del Corso, Barton and Macon, and Spinelli, the likeliest spots were East Harlem, Queens, and Seventh Avenue mid-Manhattan. Their orders were to keep moving, and tail anyone they'd previously seen at the Meat Market Club.

Steve and Bill ended up working in Queens, centering on Roosevelt Avenue and the El Sombrero bar. The April weather was beautiful and people were striding along the street without overcoats. On a Tuesday evening about six, Bill nudged Steve as they sat in Steve's Mercury outside El Sombrero. A tall, elderly man, partly bald and slightly hunchbacked, had parked on the street near the club entrance.

"Frank Stasi," Steve said as they watched him enter the club. "The Meat Market."

After about an hour, Stasi came out, got into his car, and

started toward Manhattan. They had no difficulty tailing him. Completely unsuspecting, he led them to the Brooklyn-Queens Expressway, into Grand Central Parkway, and over the Triborough Bridge. He turned south onto the East River Drive, then turned into East 116th Street and took the first right turn after that.

He double-parked and got out. Steve drove on past.

Out of the side of his mouth, Bill asked, "What street are we on?"

"Pleasant Avenue."

It was a balmy early-spring evening. Children roller-skated and licked ice-cream cones. Several men sat on a bench in front of the parking lot, others stood on the sidewalk between parked cars.

Steve and Bill rode by in their car, staring straight ahead, flicking their eyes rapidly to take in as much of the scene as possible in the minute or two it took to roll down Pleasant Avenue. From 116th Street they rode to 119th Street, and Steve made a left turn going west.

Two blocks farther along, he stopped the car. They turned to each other and grinned. Steve said, "Do you believe it?"

Bill said, "I don't know about you, but I ain't been drinking. I saw them."

"It was Inglese, wasn't it?" Steve asked.

"And Zanfardino."

"Yes, it was. And Lentini."

"And Capra."

"Did you see Delacava coming out of the tavern?"

"Did you see Eddy Castellazzo's brother then?"

"Where?"

"In the telephone booth. He was leaning out talking to a little old lady while he had the receiver to his ear."

"Did you see where Stasi went?"

"He said something to Delacava as he passed, then he spoke to a man who looked like Campopiano, and they went into the barbershop."

They sat for a few minutes, thinking of their next move.

"Do we go back for another look?" Steve asked.

"It's taking a chance on being noticed. We don't want to blow this one."

"Jesus, no. How about tomorrow?"

"Let's try it."

Bill checked the Sanitation Department and learned they had a route scheduled for Pleasant Avenue the following afternoon. He and Steve borrowed uniforms and joined the crew of the garbage truck. While picking up and emptying garbage cans on Pleasant Avenue, they observed Lentini and Zanfardino, and this time Leo Guarino, another major dealer. Campopiano came out of the tavern, and Delacava stood in the doorway of the barbershop. Stasi was talking to a young girl near the candy store. Inglese's Cadillac came up Pleasant Avenue as the garbage truck reached the end of that street and turned into 116th Street.

At the office, they knocked on Lieutenant McCrae's door and went in, closing it behind them, shaking the doorknob to make sure it was shut.

"We found it."

"What?"

"Where the Meat Market Club gang hangs out. Pleasant Avenue, in East Harlem."

"What's it like?"

"A regular Italian neighborhood. Kind of rundown. But it's where they all meet to do business."

"I mean, what's it like where they do their dealing? A club, a bar, or what?"

"We can't tell yet; the dealers seem to be in and out of a number of locations all along the street."

"Well, man alive, you got to get specific if we want to put a wire in or a bug. We can't ask a judge to authorize wiring up the whole neighborhood or bugging every house on the street."

"We'll find out. Meanwhile, there's one main thing. They got watchers there like you wouldn't believe. All our guys gotta stay out of the neighborhood. If anybody has a surveillance and the subject leads into Pleasant Avenue, he has to break off, not go in."

McCrae squinted at them. "If we start without a wire or a bug, and the men break off surveillance when subjects lead them in, how will we work on this? I better take a look myself."

He noticed the two detectives had funny expressions on their faces. There was silence for a moment.

Steve said, "I hope you won't take this the wrong way, Lieutenant."

Bill said, "Steve's Italian, and I'm dark enough to pass for one. Steve's mother's family is from that neighborhood. If they start watching, we leave, and that's it. Nobody thinks twice about it."

McCrae said, "You mean if they see me with my Irish face they instantly know the cops have an investigation going? And everything blows? Oh, come now."

Steve squirmed and said, "Well, that's what we think."

Bill said, "And don't send Bernie with his movie camera, either."

The lieutenant became sarcastic. "You taking charge here? I'll notify our commanding officers."

Bill said, "That's another thing. We better say nothing about it to them yet."

Steve glanced at Bill, wanting to say "Lay off" or "Don't push him too far."

Bill was looking McCrae square in the eye. He said, "We got a leak somewhere. We still don't know where, or how to plug it."

McCrae sat back in his chair, too astonished to be angry.

"You're talking about the C.O., Inspector Kramer? And Chief Terborg? And First Dep Commissioner McNeil? You think we should suspect one of them as a leak?"

Bill said, "No, but each of them has a staff, an office full of guys we don't know. And Shandel's squad knows what we're doing and how we work. And in our unit, maybe everybody's a straight arrow, but some are still a little green at narcotics investigation, so they could screw up."

Steve said, "Bill's only saying we gotta be real sharp so this target won't blow."

"I'm saying we're an intelligence unit, but they got their intelligence too. They've got a lot to protect, and they don't mind killing to protect it. They can afford to buy information at anyone's price. And they only need one friend on the inside."

He smiled then and said, "It's just a suggestion, Lieutenant."

"Some suggestion. Keep a plan secret from the commanding officer; keep my own men in the dark about what we are doing. You're out of your skull."

Steve said, "Figure it this way. We can use the system of observation posts and pursuit cars. The men bring in information which you coordinate, so everything is under your control until you see there's a solid case, then you decide who's to be told, and how much."

McCrae said, "Suppose I decide this is the target, how do we get in?"

Bill said, "We'll find a way. Soon as you tell us you want to make it the target, we'll look for a way in."

"I'll think it over."

Steve and Bill left McCrae's office, went down the elevator, and headed for the Belmore.

Steve said, "Nobody's gotten in before."

Bill shrugged. "You listen to the Knapp Commission, you have to wonder—was anybody really trying?"

# 12

"You know Louis Olivares?" McCrae asked.

"Louis Afro? I worked on the case," Bill said. "He caught a big six at Sing Sing. The task force ran the investigation, I worked on him too. What's up?"

"He's sent word he wants to talk."

"So?"

"So I was thinking, maybe he could become our informer, to put us into Pleasant Avenue."

Bill and Steve looked at each other, and Steve half-smiled. McCrae had really meant it when he'd said he would think about it. Bill said, "What's he want?"

"To make a deal for reduction of sentence, or maybe to get out. What do you think?"

"Olivares? Sounds Hispanic," Steve said.

"He was dealing to Hispanics," Bill said, "but his connections were in East Harlem and on Pleasant Avenue."

"Could he do it?" McCrae asked. They caught the note of eagerness in his voice.

"Possible. Let me ask around a little. Who's handling his request?"

"The task force, but we can be in it when they make the deal," McCrae said. "Bill worked on the case."

Then he added, "We're going to need an informer."

Bill said, "You have to know Louis, his good and bad sides. He was a flashy son of a bitch, a show-off; wore long flowing coats; full of swagger; big spender. When I was doing surveillance, I'd see him with kilo people in the afternoon at Tina's East, and at night I'd see him huddling with guys I could swear were undercover cops.

"It was all very cute. He was working as an informer and using that as a cover to buy for himself—nickel bags and ounces for the feds, half-kilos and kilos for himself."

"What could he do for us?" Steve asked.

"He used to deal on Pleasant Avenue. If he turns and works for us, he can name half the dealers there and who they work with. And maybe we could put him in there making buys."

McCrae said, "Well, I better touch base on this with our C.O. Don't worry, I won't say 'Pleasant Avenue' to him—I'll just talk in general about East Harlem. That way there'll be no harm even if he mentions it to the chief or to the first dep."

"You have to tell him?" asked Steve dubiously.

McCrae was irritated. "Listen, putting together an investigation on Pleasant Avenue is going to take lots of explaining, especially when we request additional manpower, as we'll have to. It's going to take lots of diplomacy not to step on toes."

The detectives backed off as he made his meaning perfectly clear: "Pleasant Avenue is in the Two-five, and the Two-five is in Manhattan North. I don't want to start any arguments with the bosses there—Donegan especially, he's heavy at headquarters. He could screw us on the street, real easy."

Their silence seemed to increase his irritation. "Shit! Everybody knows the story on organized crime in East Harlem *and* Pleasant Avenue. Everybody knows it's untouched—the gambling, loan-sharking, fencing, *and* narcotics. I don't want us to look like we're trying to embarrass Donegan."

In another moment he cooled off. "Don't worry. I know how to talk to Kramer, and we'll keep his support at headquarters."

McCrae approached the inspector at their next bimonthly conference. Of all 282 major violators listed in Narcotics Intelligence files, he told Inspector Kramer, more than a third were either based in East Harlem or frequently conducted business there.

"The next statistic," McCrae warned, "may blow your mind. For that area, there is no record of arrests. Not last year. Not the year before, nor the year before that. No arrests at all."

"But hold on, Bob," Kramer said. "You can't go by arrest statistics in the Two-five. Remember, that area has been changing. Sure, East Harlem always was a home for organized crime, but haven't most of the major violators gotten rich and moved away? I thought you were on the right track looking in Queens, and the Bronx, places in outlying sections."

He leaned back in his armchair and swung around to face the window. He was a thoughtful man, and an avid collector of oral police history. He knew hundreds of stories of East Harlem from the 1920's through the 1940's: the "105th Street Mob," the "107th Street Gang," the clashes between the Italian gangs of East Harlem and the Irish and German gangs from Yorkville, the making of alliances between the youth gangs of East Harlem and those of the Lower East Side when they met in and around Times Square at moving-picture shows, dance halls, and pool parlors. Kramer could describe the East Harlem scene vividly, for hours, even though most of the events took place a decade or so before his time.

Hoping to avoid a trip down memory lane, McCrae declared his agreement very emphatically. "That neighborhood certainly has changed. Must have been terrific in the old days." Then, quickly, as if it were an afterthought, he added, "That's why all this is so puzzling ... really puzzling."

Before Kramer could speak, he continued, "I mean, they get rich and move away from the place where they know we can find them easily. They spread out to secluded distant places, Long Island, Westchester, Jersey, Florida—where it takes so much work to keep track of them that we usually don't. So then why the hell do they keep coming back to the old neighborhood? Because that's what my men seem to be finding: they continue to come back. Surveillances, time and again, lead into East Harlem. Other places, too, but regularly East Harlem. Makes you wonder what all the changes mean, doesn't it?"

He hoped Kramer would not notice he was not specific in discussing his plan. He hoped to avoid mentioning Pleasant Avenue. He went on to say he thought his unit could target a network of major drug dealers in East Harlem and eventually make arrests that would produce prosecutable court cases.

But the inspector was still mulling over McCrae's rhetorical question about what all the changes in East Harlem might mean. When he finally spoke, his answer was sociologically interesting, but not very helpful to the lieutenant.

"Those people have a very strong sense of family identity," he told McCrae, "as well as a strong sense of identity with the home. They gain wealth and move to luxury locations, but their parents do not easily abandon their roots, and the sons keep close ties with the parents."

McCrae nodded along with him. "They come back to the old neighborhood to be with Mom and Dad."

Inspector Kramer nodded, too. "But don't they take Mom and Dad with them to the suburbs?"

"Or send them to live in Florida?" McCrae asked.

"Jewish doctors do that," Kramer replied, but he looked at McCrae sharply, as if suspecting him of levity. He then seemed to decide that the meeting had run its course.

"Anyway, you think you can drop a heavy drug network in East Harlem? It's your headache. If you find something, let me know. Have you checked with the Manhattan North borough commander? Inspector Donegan?"

"I was going to. I know Harry Donegan. He's a good man."

Deputy Inspector Harry Donegan was easy to get along with. His tone and manner made it clear he felt no insecurity about McCrae's working his territory. Sure, Donegan said, there was probably dealing going on in the Two-five and in East Harlem, but was it more than in other places? He wouldn't know. They busted their share of street pushers and runners, but dealers in heavy weight? He couldn't tell; the Two-five didn't have the manpower for it, or the buy money. That stuff was really up to the feds.

McCrae also asked Donegan about social clubs and bars where dealing might be investigated. Donegan said there were clubs, bars, restaurants, and whorehouses all over the precinct where dealing could go on without his people knowing. There were just too many, and there wasn't much he could do without buy money and wiretaps. It was up to the feds.

"We're OK with Donegan," McCrae told Steve and Bill later. "He thinks he convinced me it was hopeless, and that we won't bother. Now, let's see about Olivares, your 'Louis Afro.' "

McCrae set up a meeting with Captain Hugot of the task force. At the meeting he said they'd favor making a deal with Olivares because he used to operate out of an East Harlem bar called Tina's East.

Artie Ackerman, one of Hugot's men at the meeting, was knowledgeable and mentioned other bars Louis frequented, including one on Pleasant Avenue.

McCrae said he'd very much like to squeeze Olivares for anything he knew about Funzie Sisca, and Ackerman also knew about places Sisca frequented, mentioning Pleasant Avenue among them.

Finally, Ackerman wondered out loud what McCrae planned to do, specifically where he was going to focus his investigation. McCrae said they were still working in a preliminary way and hadn't yet picked a target.

"For what it's worth," Artie said, "my opinion is that you could get into Tina's with a wire and an undercover—it's possible—and you might get into Diane's, up the street from Tina's—that's possible. But if you are thinking of anything on

119

Pleasant Avenue, forget it. Nobody, but nobody, gets in there, nobody even walks on Pleasant Avenue except he's known to them or he lives there."

"You are probably right," McCrae said, turning a bland look toward Bill and Steve.

After the meeting, driving back to their own office, the three hashed it over. Bill said, "Olivares knows half the dealers on Pleasant Avenue. His father used to work for the Ruggerio brothers. He could go in and say he's looking for a new connection."

"You really think so?" McCrae asked.

"Sounds good," Steve said.

Bill started smiling, and when the other two looked at him questioningly, burst out laughing.

"Bullshit," he said. "You have to know I'm joking. Nobody would trust Louis."

"You mean Ackerman's right?"

"Yes. Of course. You heard what he said—nobody gets into Pleasant Avenue except he's known there or he lives there."

"Well, isn't Olivares known?"

"Who cares, if we live there?"

# 13

Pleasant Avenue is a sixteen-hundred-foot strip of asphalt road, trash-strewn sidewalks, small stores, and six-story tenements, bordering the East River and running south from the Triborough Bridge. Its cross streets run from East 120th to East 114th.

It is difficult to find on most city maps, being obscured by immediately adjacent landmarks. At 120th Street, the large, impressive Robert F. Wagner housing complex backs up on Pleasant Avenue, and at the lower end there are the Thomas Jefferson Park, the Benjamin Franklin High School, and Balsamo's Funeral Chapel.

Despite its importance in the drug rackets, Pleasant Avenue and the surrounding East Harlem section is largely unknown to the general public today. The reason is simple. In the outpouring of "Mafia" books, movies, and television tales from the 1930's to the present, the Lower East Side and the Mulberry Street neighborhoods were usually the background settings shown. East Harlem never got publicity, even though it was a much larger settlement of Italians, and was of comparable importance to organized crime. East Harlem spawned plenty of notorious characters including Frank Costello, Trigger Mike Coppola, and Three-Finger Brown Lucchese. Louis Terranova, the once-famous "Artichoke King," came out of East Harlem, but even after Joseph Valachi, another native son, became a household name across America, East Harlem continued to be overlooked by the public.

"Harlem," of course, is a name known around the world, but it is identified with blacks—their music, life-style, exotic pleasure lairs, and their miseries. A minority of New Yorkers are aware that there is also a so-called "Spanish Harlem," where the early Puerto Rican immigrants who gave Mayor La Guardia his political base settled on the ghetto blocks next to black Harlem. But "East Harlem" is a term known to very few people who are not Italian intellectuals, social reformers, or members of the New York Police Department.

Even among the cognoscenti, Pleasant Avenue never became notorious. Somehow cops and crime reporters adopted a practice of referring to criminal groups as "The 105th Street Mob," the "107th Street Gang," and similar labels related to the east-west streets. Thus, Pleasant Avenue never achieved an identity of its own, like, for example, President Street, where Joey Gallo's gang made its base.

Crime aside, East Harlem has a unique history, reaching back to the days of Peter Stuyvesant three and a half centuries ago when the first settlement there was named "Happy Valley." The original Dutch settlers were followed by French, Danish, Norwegian, and Swedish immigrants. By 1900 the area had filled up with Jews, tens of thousands of them, until it was often referred to as a Jewish city. After World War I, they too were displaced, this time by a wave of migration from downtown Manhattan. The Italians took over, moving up from the incredibly congested living conditions that once characterized the Mulberry Street ghetto of Little Italy. And it was this fifty-year-old, tight-knit, well-established community that Del Corso and Erwin proposed to penetrate.

"What you are saying," McCrae declared, "is that their countersurveillance is so good—"

"No," said Bill, "not good. Perfect."

"You're saying that whole street is like a safe house for them."

"That's about it," Steve said. He looked around for a piece of paper and took a ball-point pen from his pocket. He began to draw a diagram.

"Here's 114th Street. It goes one way, into Pleasant Avenue. Here's 115th Street. It goes only one way, out of Pleasant Avenue. Here's 116th Street; it's an exit from the East River Drive. Here are 117th Street, 118th, 119th—they are dead-end, blocked off by the fences of the warehouse, right? And 120th Street is one way, into Pleasant Avenue."

Bill said, "Nobody comes in without being looked at. There's nothing on that street that would bring strangers in—unless they're coming to place a bet or make a deal for some junk. Everyone else you see lives there."

McCrae looked at the diagram and back into their faces. "Well, I guess that's—"

"Right," Steve interposed.

"We move in," said Bill, "and we live there."

"Who does?" McCrae asked.

"Couple of fellas from the unit—Larusso, Cabalo, Fiorentini, Spinelli—we got enough guineas."

"You're crazy," said McCrae. "It would never—"

McCrae gave Sergeant Varella the job.

Pablo Varella was unique. He didn't speak English. For

everyday use he had a language of his own invention, combining Spanish and English words.

He was a small, animated man, a dynamo of energy. His face was tanned and creased, and he wore a Fu Manchu-style mustache. Cops liked working with him, though few knew how he became a sergeant. To prepare for the sergeant's examination, which was in English, he took a dictionary and made for himself a complete translation into Spanish of the regulations and the study materials. He answered all the test questions in Spanish, and then, using a dictionary again, translated his answers back into English. He scored toward the top of the list.

Pablo Varella was a Spaniard from the Basque country. He'd run away from home as a teenager, gotten a job on a freighter, and spent World War II having merchant ships torpedoed out from under him. When he first arrived in the United States he was an illegal immigrant, but somehow he got into the U.S. Army and gained citizenship after somebody bent the rules a little.

For the Pleasant Avenue job, Varella decided that the worst tactic they could adopt would be trying to look unobtrusive. For their neighborhood debut, he and Steve drove up in a bright green gypsy cab and parked in front of the Church of the Holy Rosary. They went into the church and talked to the charwoman they found mopping the floor, asking to speak to the priest. She eventually produced Father Bruno and an old man who seemed to be the caretaker, and the two cops told their story. They were a group of gypsy-cab drivers who needed a centrally located place to sleep where they could get away from the regular cabdrivers and cops and hack inspectors who were constantly bothering gypsy cabbies. They and their buddies would be sharing the rent and would be taking turns using the apartment when they'd worked late and were too tired to go home before their next shift. They had chosen Pleasant Avenue, Varella told the priest, because Steve's family had lived in the neighborhood—on 109th Street and First Avenue—and it was like home to him. It was also a good location, just off the Triborough Bridge. Perhaps Father Bruno could help them find some rooms, speak to a few people, look around with them?

Father Bruno did not know of anything, but he walked around the neighborhood with them for a little while, and his caretaker tagged along. Father Bruno stopped people on the street and asked if they knew of rooms, explaining that these men were driving cabs to serve people who were ignored by the regular taxicab companies, that they served people in Harlem and the Bronx and Queens, and Steve's family used to live in the neighborhood.

Father Bruno spoke with one man who wore a leather cap and sandals, and another who had a limp and walked a black-and-white dog. Neither of them had any help to give, but they looked searchingly at Varella and Steve. Varella guessed that these two were watchers, and Steve whispered he was sure of it; he thought he recognized them. They let Father Bruno do the talking while they stood looking simple and hopeful, and Steve threw in a few Italian phrases.

Soon after this encounter, Father Bruno said he had to go attend to other matters but his caretaker would stay and continue helping them. They stopped and inquired at the fruit store and at the grocery store and in the beauty shop, each time repeating their story.

By then Varella had surveyed the possibilities and knew what they wanted. There was a red-brick three-story building on the northwest corner of 118th Street and Pleasant Avenue. It was slowly disintegrating, with a broken iron fence, peeling paint, and trash in its tiny front yard.

Varella thought it looked good. The church caretaker went to fetch the superintendent from the basement apartment, and when he came out to speak with them, four little faces peered from the doorway behind him. He was a dark-skinned man, and when Varella spoke to him in Spanish, he answered in Puerto Rican. He said the first floor and top floor were occupied but the second floor was empty.

125

Varella and Steve trooped upstairs and made a cursory inspection of the three nondescript rooms. The walls were crumbling, the floors were covered by worn and torn linoleum, the bathroom fixtures were chipped and discolored, and the walls were broken through in a couple of places. Steve made several dispirited circuits through the apartment, peering with distaste through the bathroom doorway, nauseated when he looked into the tiny kitchen.

Varella thought it was perfect.

He pretended to look around, but his attention was actually on one window, in the living room. From it, there was a clear view down Pleasant Avenue, from 118th Street to the end. In the gray light of the overcast day he could see the grocery store on the near corner, several shops, the parking lot, more shops, and a tavern on the far corner. Past the street crossing there were other shops, tenement buildings, and a two-story green-painted structure, more shops, and Balsamo's Funeral Parlor, and the street crossing. Beyond that was the pillared portico of the two-block-long high school.

The super had stood aside all this time, eyes turned ceilingward. Varella asked who else lived in the building; they were taxi drivers who worked hard, and they needed a quiet place where they could be sure to get some sleep. The super said the floor above was occupied by a family, very nice, quiet people, with three children but very well-behaved, he thought, but you know how kids are. Varella smiled and said he had five kids himself, and he asked how many the super had. The super said four that he knew about, and they all laughed. It was time for business. The super said the owner had told him to get two hundred twenty-five a month. Varella said two hundred was plenty, and could they move in right away? The super shrugged. Varella said OK, they'd move in tomorrow morning. He pulled a roll of bills from his pants pocket and counted out two hundred dollars, plus an extra ten for the super.

They got back into the green gypsy cab and drove into the Bronx, to a truck-and-trailer-rental agency on Willis Avenue.

126

Varella rented a U-Haul trailer, and they drove to a thrift-antiques-secondhand-and-junk shop run by the Salvation Army. By the end of the afternoon they had pots and pans, tables, chairs, a sofa. Then they drove to their office on Park Avenue South and loaded on eight cartons containing radio, telephone, tape recorder, and other equipment, and one carton containing two 35-mm. cameras with telephoto lenses.

Next morning, with Varella talking a rapid-fire stream of orders, jokes, and nonsense in Spanish, he, Steve, Cabalo, Tomas, and Fiorentini moved the stuff off the trailer and into the apartment. Using materials they had brought with them, they reinforced the apartment door with a plywood panel half an inch thick, and added two strong locks.

Then they hung curtains on the three windows facing Pleasant Avenue, and on the three facing 118th Street. When the curtains were up, Varella had them cover the whole of each window frame with sheets of dark brown cloth, tacked to the frames. Only the corner window on the 118th Street side was treated differently. The lower sash was raised six inches from the bottom, and the coverings also left this space open.

Chairs were placed four feet back from that window, so that a man sitting there could observe the street without being seen. They were to use binoculars and take photographs with the cameras. With a tape recorder set up on a table nearby, they could record observations into a hand-held mike.

The rooms were hot and humid. Varella promised to acquire two or three electric fans at once.

The day had been gray and drizzly, but as evening came on the sky brightened and a reflected golden light glowed from the rectangle at the bottom of the window. Cabalo and Tomas took the first shift, and Tomas sat down in the chair facing the window opening.

Suddenly, in a voice that was choked with surprise, he said, "For Chrissake!"

Varella sat down beside him in the other chair and looked through the window opening. About 150 feet away, double-parked in the middle of the street, a four-door black Ford was standing with its trunk lid raised. A stocky man in a sport shirt, blue jeans, and white sneakers was talking to a tall slender man in a plaid jacket and gray slacks. The stocky man had a soft white package under his arm and was counting out money from a letter-size envelope. The counting finished, the stocky man dropped his soft white package into the car's trunk, whereupon the tall slender man closed the lid, got into the car, and drove away.

Automatically, Tomas intoned, "Yankee-Pudding-eight-oh-four-five, New York," into the microphone of the tape recorder.

Fiorentini and Cabalo had bent down in time to see the last part of the action. They were all quiet, digesting their astonishment. Tomas shook his head as if to clear it. "Right there on the street!" he said wonderingly.

Cabalo recovered first. "This place may look like a shithouse," he said, "but, man, you can't beat it for action!"

# 14

Tomas and Cabalo, on the first shift, sounded a radio alarm:
"Calling all cars! We are surrounded! There's about a hundred fifty cockroaches creeping up on us. They've got reinforcements in the next room—a thousand, maybe more! This is Roach Base. Do you read us?"

Bill promptly responded from his surveillance car, latching on to Cabalo's inspired code name. "This is Roach One, we read you. Don't panic."

Mike Larusso, from his surveillance car, came on. "This is Roach Two. Help is on the way." And Richie Spinelli from a third surveillance car announced he was Roach Three standing by for all eventualities.

A daily routine was quickly established. The men in the apartment logged their observations of known and suspected drug dealers, and photographed them, as opportunity presented, through the telescopic lenses of their cameras. They noted dealers' cars by color, make, and license number. They radioed the departure of dealers and customers to the surveillance cars waiting outside Pleasant Avenue, and those detectives would then tail the dealers, hoping to observe packages of heroin being sold or transferred.

Steve Del Corso and Jake McNamara worked in the office on Park Avenue South coordinating daily reports from the apartment and the surveillance cars. The photographs and the automobile information were used by Archy and Bobby, who were trying to identify individuals by researching files.

By coordinating the reports, McCrae expected eventually to observe a pattern of activity that would show how the network operated, which dealers had transactions with which customers, and which customers were in turn dealers to customers at the next level. Then a plan for busting the whole network would be drawn up.

They quickly observed that activity centered on the east side of the avenue from 118th Street to 116th, around the tavern on the corner of 117th and the two telephone booths on the sidewalk outside it.

On the corner of 118th Street was a grocery store. A social club was next door, then a barbershop and a ladies' beauty salon. The bar on the corner of 117th was called the Pleasant Tavern.

Across 117th Street the corner store was boarded up. There was an auto-body shop next door, then Barone's Bar with its entrance several steps down and a private club on its first floor above the street. A boarded-up store was next, then the entrance to a tenement, then Balsamo's Funeral Chapel on the corner of 116th Street.

On the surface there was little to distinguish this neighborhood from hundreds of ghetto blocks in New York or other big cities across the country. Trash cans, garbage barrels, and sacks of rubbish were often curbside or against buildings, and people seemed to regard them as a normal feature of the landscape.

There was one distinctive feature, however: the presence of Cadillacs, Lincolns, and other high-priced cars which came and went, starting in the early afternoon, building up a

130

congestion in the roadway and parking lot during the evening and into the night.

As the days went on, they developed lists of men who came regularly, frequently, and intermittently; who spoke with whom; and who drove off afterward in which directions.

The telephone booths on the corner were used for both incoming and outgoing calls, they observed, exclusively by men they identified as dealers. When a phone rang, whoever was nearby answered it and called a dealer out from the tavern or barbershop or from down the street. On one occasion a derelict came by and started whacking the phone to extract money, but one of the regulars quickly came over, admonished him, and sent him on his way.

Sometimes the men in surveillance cars picked up information; other times they would be led on wild-goose chases, tailing a departing dealer or customer all the way across the city to the house of the dealer's girlfriend, where he'd spend the night, or to a restaurant, where he'd have a luxurious dinner with friends. The man on that surveillance run had the choice of hanging around for all hours with probably nothing to show for it, or of breaking off the surveillance without being positive that a transaction was not going to take place.

Nevertheless, by mid-June McCrae decided he'd accumulated enough information for a detailed description of how this network of heroin dealers was operating.

He listed major violators frequenting the area, their seconds and their satellites, beginning with Louis Inglese. "Fat Gigi" Inglese was identified as an important member of the organized-crime family headed by Tramunti. McCrae charted eighteen principal and secondary dealers linked to him.

He listed their links to drug distribution in the Bronx, Queens, Brooklyn, New Jersey, Westchester, and Long Island. He estimated they transacted from twenty to thirty-five kilos of heroin a week, and possibly more.

He calculated that he would require extra men—about twenty-five or thirty to supplement his own unit in gathering the evidence needed to make arrests—wiretaps and bugs to be placed in the tavern, the barbershop next to it, the candy store, and in the cars that came regularly to the avenue. For the final stage, when they made the arrests, he would also need an additional thirty men.

He spread his coordinated information before Inspector Kramer, and Kramer was impressed. The inspector even agreed they should not chance a leak by bringing in the SIU manpower that had been promised them, and which they had been instructed to use. Then Kramer hit on the idea of immediately consulting the district attorney, Frank Hogan, and bringing his people into it, particularly Ron Otis, the special assistant for narcotics cases. The D.A. had his own squad of detectives and he would be concerned with the quality of evidence brought to him on a potentially good case. With support from Hogan and Otis, Kramer and McCrae would be in a stronger position for bypassing the SIU.

Kramer arranged a meeting. The result was disastrous.

The special assistant for narcotics cases said it was all very interesting, but McCrae simply did not have a case, and the D.A. agreed with that opinion.

The meeting was private, but the men in McCrae's unit immediately sensed something was wrong from the lieutenant's bearing and the look on his face. McCrae didn't fill them in, so the next afternoon Steve "happened to be passing" the D.A.'s office and called his friend Pat Vintriano, head of the D.A.'s detective squad.

Since it happened to be lunchtime, he and Steve went out for spaghetti with clam sauce and Pat ran down the meeting with McCrae and Kramer, which he had attended.

What it all came down to, Pat told him, was that Hogan, the D.A., and Otis, the special assistant, were skeptical that anything substantial would come out of McCrae's proposal.

What, they'd asked, did McCrae really have to go on? A long series of observations that certain people regularly came together in a certain location. The American Constitution guarantees freedom of assembly, and there was no way of proving that these men were engaged in drug traffic rather than gambling. On several occasions they'd seen the men handling plastic bags of a soft white substance that looked like heroin? They were a long distance from corroborating the fact that it was heroin they'd seen. These were Otis' outspoken opinions, and the others had to agree. McCrae did not even have probable cause heavy enough to get wiretaps or bugs in New York City, where judges were very wary of criticism from civil-rights groups and New York *Times* editorials.

What it came down to in the end, said Pat Vintriano, was that the D.A.'s office was already committed to supporting other investigations.

"What investigations?" Steve wondered.

"Well, Lieutenant Shandel's, for one," said Pat. "Shandel has a squad working on a situation similar to McCrae's in the Bronx."

"Do they have a wire in, or a bug?" Steve asked.

"Both."

"What comes over them?"

"On the wiretap, nothing they can use. But off the bug—" Pat laughed. "Wow! That Jerry must be one helluva cook. He fixes great meals every time they meet—it's what the talk that comes over the bug is about."

"Unless," Steve said, "it's their code talk for deals."

"That would mean they're wise to the surveillance." He shrugged. "It's Shandel's problem." He called the waiter and ordered zuppa inglese and espresso. Steve ordered tea and lemon. Sintriano picked up the check, and Steve protested they should share it. As each dug into his wallet for money, Sintriano remarked, "I get carried away. We're such big spenders now."

"Who?"

"Us, in the D.A.'s office. Twelve and a half million. You didn't know?"

Steve shook his head. Sintriano said, "The D.A.'s special

assistant for narcotics cases has received a federal grant, twelve-and-a-half million clams. You hadn't heard? I thought that's why McCrae came around, to get a piece, like Shandel did."

Seeing Steve's puzzled look, Sintriano went on. "We're hiring lots of staff, buying special equipment requested by the Police Department, putting out buy money. Narcotics enforcement is big this year, you know."

"This year?"

"Yes, election year. The President. They want to show big results fighting drugs, to help Nixon get re-elected."

"I'm just a dumb cop," Steve said. "Explain it to me."

"Actually there's a double connection. There's this new Rockefeller get-tough law, to make judges hand out stiff sentences on junk dealers. Rocky would like to show results, which means more and better cases—so he goes to the President and sells him the idea of putting big bucks into the New York drug scene which is where the action is.

"Meanwhile, Nixon's got his 'War on Drugs'—he's doing so lousy in the war in Vietnam, he'd like to show success at home with the war on drugs. So Rocky scored, and we are up to our belly buttons in nothing but money."

"Too bad McCrae didn't get a piece," he added as they said their good-byes. "Maybe another time."


McCrae evidently was going to try again. His men might be discouraged, but he believed in what he was doing. He had Kramer's support, and he'd be goddamned if he'd let Shandel get away with the stuff he pulled.

The men, though dispirited, continued to do their jobs. Some switched assignments to break the monotony. Steve asked to stop working in the office checking logs and coordinating reports to take an assignment in the field. Sergeant Varella said he was revising the schedule of men assigned to the apartment and would use Steve there.

Bernie Turner was full of bounce, however. At one of their unit meetings, McCrae remarked that they needed to put more "sell" into the presentation of their proposal, and Bernie came up bubbling with ideas on that. McCrae was naturally partial to a guy with unqualified enthusiasm, and pretty soon Bernie was continually running into the boss's office, becoming more and more private about what he was doing. The busier Bernie became, the more irritated the other men became.

Evidently there was to be another videotape presentation. Bernie was spending all his time either out shooting tapes with his own camera or in the office playing them back. But he had positioned his playback equipment in a corner so that nobody else in the office could see the pictures except by coming around into his corner. He pointedly invited no one and was uncommunicative when anyone asked what he was working on. From time to time he asked McCrae to come out and look at something on his tapes.

Steve had been working at the apartment for a couple of weeks when he got a call from Bill to meet him in the office. When he got there, Bill was working with some papers and asked him to wait a couple of minutes until he was finished. Steve greeted other guys—Jake McNamara was there sorting mug shots, Ralph Tomas and Richie Spinelli were on telephones, Sergeant Varella was speaking Spanish to someone on the telephone.

Suddenly there was a yelp from the corner where Bernie Turner was running videotapes on his TV monitor. He was staring at the television screen, his gaze riveted. The sounds coming from his mouth and throat might have been giggles, might have been sputters of rage. He lifted his gaze and looked around the room angrily at the men who were now watching him inquiringly. He would have preferred to say nothing, but some explanation had to be given.

"Some sonovabitch," he said, "has been tampering with my tapes. Who was it?" He again looked around the room at each of them in turn, seething with frustration.

135

"These tapes are highly confidential," he said, "department property. They might be evidence. Tampering with them might cause all kinds of trouble for someone." He swallowed. "Might be a criminal offense," he said defiantly.

A couple of the men went around to see the television screen but he had stopped the tape and the screen only flickered with light. Others came and crowded around. Mingled voices asked to see the tapes, but Bernie refused, then switched to the "off" button just to be sure. The other men persisted.

"C'mon Bernie, what the hell is it?" Bill said. "Let's see. You can't keep this a secret from the unit." The others agreed loudly and waited for Bernie to move, and finally he submitted.

He rewound the tape, then started it again. It showed street scenes. People were standing or walking, alone or in groups, or talking. Most of the footage was jerky or fuzzy.

Bernie explained, "There's narcotics dealing going on here and I was trying for shots of the action without being noticed."

Most of the scenes had been filmed from inside an automobile and suffered from glare, vibration, sudden blackout, jumpy images, lack of focus.

Suddenly the scenes were clear, in crisp focus, well lighted and steady. They were close-ups of a man and a woman in a bedroom. He was wearing a shirt and tie and no pants. She had on stockings, a brassiere and a garter belt. They stood at a sink and although his buttocks concealed the action she was evidently washing his penis. The camera held on them until they moved towards the bed. Then the scene panned sideways to frame another lighted window, with another close-up of a couple sitting nude on a bed. The camera panned again to close-ups of a man and woman prone and intertwined on a bed but the only illumination came from a lamp on a night table. Next the camera panned, still in close-up, through a window into a bedroom where a man fully clothed sat on the bed while a nude woman kneeled before him, her head bobbing in his lap. The camera panned up to a window on a

136

higher level but the lighting in that room was dim. The next room over was unoccupied. The next after that showed a man on the bed nude and a nude woman standing over him.

Suddenly Bernie switched off the set. Voices went up in good-humored protest, and some of the men stepped up to Bernie and congratulated him.

"Which of you sonsabitches did it?" Bernie asked. But he was laughing now, though still uncomfortable. The men all shrugged, laughed, and got ready to leave. Bernie packed away his tapes and playback equipment in a locked cabinet.

Somebody predicted McCrae would get a promotion for showing those tapes to his superiors, and somebody else said Bernie's technique had greatly improved.

When Steve and Bill were out of the building and were getting into Bill's car, Steve said, "How'd you do it?"

"Wasn't so hard."

"It was the Haynes Hotel, across the street, wasn't it?"

"I just shot from our windows, which are opposite theirs. With our lights out. Theirs are always on."

"When did you learn to shoot movies so good?"

"A neighbor of mine works for CBS. A cameraman. He showed me. It's not so hard. He loaned me the telephoto lens and a camera and showed me how to use them. Some things Bernie doesn't know."

"Bernie keeps the tapes locked up."

"You know how hard it is to pick a Police Department lock. I shot the tapes and edited them in, all the same night."

Steve laughed. "The expression on Bernie's face was—" Steve laughed harder and Bill joined in.

Steve said, "Probably the best thing ever happened for the unit's morale. That Bernie and his magic movie machine were becoming the world's biggest pain in the ass. It sure took him down."

They laughed as the road and landscape sped away behind them, but the lift in morale lasted only just so long. The men were gloomy; they had the feeling that Shandel's squad was close to making a move, that the SIU would score a bust on Capra's Havemeyer Avenue club, and that leads from the "Wednesday Night Club" would probably put Shandel into position to take over the investigation on Pleasant Avenue. They felt as if they had worked more than two months for nothing.

The July Fourth weekend was the final wind-down for them. Everyone in the squad asked for leave. McCrae saw no point in resisting and said they could all have it.

# 15

The men came back drag-ass on Tuesday after the weekend. In the office, the early shift was drinking coffee with that look of cops who couldn't care less. McCrae arrived and walked through to his private office, pretending not to notice—but he did notice two large shipping cartons on the floor just inside the door.

"What are these things?" he asked.

Nobody knew. Richie Regan said they'd been there when he arrived that morning.

McCrae was annoyed—damn their "don't-care" attitude—and his voice had an edge to it: "Why doesn't somebody open them up and see?"

Richie Regan split the sealing tape and started to unload the cartons. In seconds there was curiosity all around him, then amazement. The cartons held expensive pieces of equipment. Richie pulled out a videotape camera about the size of an encyclopedia, a heavy-duty tripod, a tripod platform that was elongated to receive attachments, a foot-long telescopic zoom lens, a huge cylindrical object more than one and a half feet long marked "Owleye," another foot-long object marked "Nitescope," a videotape playback deck, a television monitor, and yards of cables. Altogether, there was about a hundred pounds of equipment. An invoice packed inside one of the cartons itemized the shipment. The Owleye alone was priced at $7,500. The total was $24,892.12.

Documents inside the boxes showed they had been consigned to the Organized Crime Division of the Detective Bureau. By mistake, they had been delivered to the Organized Crime Section of the Intelligence Division. The Intelligence Division clerk must have assumed they were for McCrae because his group was known to have been working with TV and videotapes.

Richie Regan looked at McCrae questioningly.

McCrae said, "Get hold of Sergeant Varella."

Bernie Turner showed them how to hook up and operate the equipment. Later in the early evening, Sergeant Varella and Danny Fiorentini arrived on Pleasant Avenue in their gypsy cab and unloaded three canned-goods cartons, two large shopping bags, and a fat bundle of carpeting. After giving the neighborhood a good look, they carried their supplies up to the apartment.

When Steve arrived at eight o'clock to relieve Ralph Tomas, he found the video camera set up on the tripod, with a telescopic lens, the Owleye, and Nitescope in place. It was aimed out the window from six feet back in the room. Wired to it was a television monitor and a setup of controls for focusing and maneuvering the angle of sight. Reels of tape were on the table with pads for logging the scenes. Ralph showed him how to work the equipment.

It produced startling effects. The combination of telescopic, Owleye, and Nitescope attachments brought scenes and people astonishingly close to the viewer. For the first hour or so Steve always felt like jumping back when he zoomed in on people. Through the special close-up lenses of the camera, details could be seen more vividly than with the naked eye. Even though it was nighttime and there were only a few streetlights illuminating the scene for the camera, Steve could see all the way to the end of the street at the high school and Jefferson Park. He could even see inside the cars parked and double-parked on the other side of Pleasant Avenue from 116th Street to 118th.

At first they ran the machine almost continuously from 6:30 in the morning until about midnight. The videotapes piled up fast and the logging became almost impossible to maintain. Within a few days they were videotaping selectively, learning to judge which scenes, persons, and action were significant.

The selectivity itself brought new insights. Individual bits of action, carried out by one, two, or three people, would form a sequence that was obviously a drug transaction, although the actual passing of money and heroin usually occurred out of sight of the camera.

When Pleasant Avenue had first come up for discussion, McCrae had called it a "safe house" for the drug network. That had seemed a bit extravagant at the time, but no longer. After looking at a few tapes, it became obvious that the dealers, major violators and minor ones alike, felt completely secure.

McCrae made his move now, with confidence and precision. He set about putting together another "Walter Cronkite" show, employing charts, narration, scenes highlighting the drug traffic, long lists of violators who frequented Pleasant Avenue, and criminal biographies that explained each individual's place in the drug network, both in the city and nationally. A few of the biggest, like Herbert Sperling and John Capra, he linked to the international drug traffic in France and South America.

With his videotape presentation in the can—McCrae was beginning to adopt showbiz expressions—he again asked Inspector Kramer to arrange a meeting so that he could pitch for manpower to push the investigation to a conclusion. Kramer suggested that this time they try laying it on Captain Hugot and the joint task force. He would remember the JC case, which he had backed them up on and thereby earned excellent credits.

Hugot was impressed. He thought the idea had lots of merit. But he could not release men to McCrae or in any other way get involved now. He was fighting a takeover by the federal narcotics bureaucrats. According to Hugot, the new Office of Drug Abuse Law Enforcement (ODALE) was out to gobble up everything in sight. Hugot had already lost a couple of his best units to ODALE and was having a tough time holding on to the rest.

When they walked out of Hugot's office, McCrae felt uncomfortable. He had drawn Inspector Kramer into the position of being turned down by a captain. McCrae tried to think of something to say, something less banal than, "Well, you can't win 'em all," but when he turned to face Kramer, the inspector was smiling.

"It's the way to go," he said.

"You really think so?" McCrae wondered what he meant.

"Why not? They have the power, and they have the money. If we can get ODALE to back it, why not go with a winner?"

Mike Andrews, regional director for ODALE in New York, was cordial and friendly, and interested in McCrae's videotape. Andrews' chief investigator, Brig Jenkins, sat in on the meeting, saying nothing until toward the end. Mike Andrews complimented McCrae on his voice and said if he left the police he'd make big money as a TV commentator. They had lots of laughs together, but when Andrews turned to his chief investigator for another opinion, Jenkins simply got up and said, "Not for us. This is a long, tedious undercover job. Our charter from the president is to get cracking fast and show action. This will do nothing for us." And he walked out.

Mike Andrews shrugged. "Well, you can't win 'em all. He's the chief investigator, I'm only the boss."

He called in his deputy director, Al Cherne, and briefly outlined McCrae's proposal. Al's face lit up. He outlined a plan, "off the top of his head," to organize a special force of ODALE agents, FBI agents, and city police. They'd cordon off the area and conduct a roundup of Pleasant Avenue drug dealers, and they'd tip the TV news networks in advance. That would really let the country know that ODALE meant business in the war on drugs. This would put the New York ODALE people right up there where the White House would take notice. If they planned it for mid-October, before the election, the White House would see that they got top priority in cooperation from other agencies.

McCrae was sweating. If such a scheme came to pass, he'd look like a horse's ass. He said he doubted that such arrests could be made to stick. Cherne replied that they would work through the federal courts and prosecutors—the attorney general would see to it they got cooperation—and they'd hold the suspects at least until after the election. Meanwhile, they'd have terrific media coverage.

By now all McCrae wanted was to preserve his case from federal interference. Mike Andrews came to his rescue, closing the meeting with the decision that it wasn't a solid case, and was unlikely to produce the kind of evidence they'd need to go to court. McCrae's try at ODALE led him to think about other federal agencies. He spoke to a friend, Joe Quetarro, a unit chief in the Bureau of Narcotics and Dangerous Drugs.

The effect was electrifying.

News spread quickly by word of mouth among McCrae's men, in the office, on surveillance car duty, in the apartment.

Joe had spoken to his boss, and he had spoken to his chief, and so on up the line. They'd each asked to see McCrae's reel of tape, and there was a stream of federal narcs coming into McCrae's office for closed-door meetings.

It looked like heavy support.

The federal agents of BNDD were in the market for something new and dramatic in their struggle to resist takeover by ODALE. A conference was set up between McCrae and Burt Williams, the feds' regional director, and his chief assistants.

The outcome was a standoff. The feds were definitely interested, but to make a case that would hold up in court, they'd have to have witnesses to bulk drug transactions, and corroboration.

McCrae ordered the sergeants to round up the men for a meeting that evening. After they had all assembled, McCrae arrived, carrying a gallon jug of red wine. Mike Larusso, dropping his voice to an audible whisper, said, "Looks like bad news tonight. See what he's carrying?"

The men broke out their coffee mugs, passed the wine, and settled down to listen. McCrae sensed that was a bad sign—passivity. One or two bastards among them must have heard of the turndowns by Hugot and Andrews, and they didn't understand the situation at BNDD. They were tired, bored. He'd have to let them ventilate their feelings.

"Well, men, there's bad news, and there's good news."

"Keep talking, coach," Mike Larusso said.

"BNDD is with us. They've got the manpower and the money, so their support means we're on the right track."

"We've been on it for a year," Archy Brown Barton said, "and all we've got to show is a bust of some nigger dealers in the Bronx."

"Why don't we find that leak," Bobby Macon said, "and take care of him, but good."

McCrae said, "I know some of you are finding your assignments a little boring, but—"

"Sitting day and night by that damn video camera is very boring, Lieutenant," Ralph Tomas said.

"If you think that's boring, what do you think it's like in the surveillance cars?" Spinelli asked him.

Charlie Cabalo answered, "It's not as bad as being cooped up in that shithouse twelve hours a day. In the cars, you guys get around, and you can stop off for a decent meal. We're stuck with sandwiches and Cokes, and the same walls to look at day after day. We're even glad when a new cockroach makes the scene."

Jake McNamara said, "You could try running cockroach races and filming them. The tapes you send us are absolutely the most boring thing to look at. I'm going cockeyed watching them."

McCrae rapped on the desk with an ashtray.

"Anyone who wants out, say so, and the sergeants will fix it. We happen to have picked a tight little community as our target, a community fiercely loyal to certain drug dealers, dealers who are deeply rooted in that community. But the BNDD feds will go with us.

"We all know what we must have to make our case: legally valid corroboration. That means witnesses who'll stand up to defense attorneys—and stay alive. We'll have to find informants, and get undercovers in to make buys.

"Starting tomorrow, that's what we're looking for. We've worked on this more than a year, we have a big investment in this case, we have to protect it."

He spoke with fervor, looked each one in the eye, then turned away to signal the close of the meeting.

He pretended not to hear someone mutter, "Bullshit."

As they broke up, Bill Erwin spoke to Jake McNamara about switching assignments. Bill was as bored in his surveillance car as Jake was in the office. They both cornered Sergeant Fitzgerald and made the switch.

The next night was Bill's first in the office. He spent some time screening tapes and ID-ing Pleasant Avenue suspects. He phoned Steve at the apartment to let him know he was in the office now. The video monitor was running, and on screen, Ernie Boy Abbamonte was in conversation with a dark-skinned Hispanic male who was accompanied by an attractive lighter-skinned female.

Steve picked up the phone but didn't say hello.

"Who's the broad?" Bill asked without preliminaries, and Steve immediately recognized his voice.

# 16

There was something special about her.

Young women came and went on Pleasant Avenue, as they did wherever men gathered with money to spend. They were varied—British, Scandinavian, and German, as well as Italian, Hispanic, and black—and they played the traditional role of camp follower, whether for backroom partying in the clubs or as companions for a night on the town.

Dolores was tall, pretty, and vivacious, it was clear from the video monitor, but it was also evident that she was one man's woman or possibly his wife. They were together whenever he was on the scene, presumably to deal for a package. This alone made her different: she was the only woman on the avenue who was present where dealing went on.

Steve recalled having seen her when he was a rookie working Harlem, and knowing she was Gabby Condotti's girlfriend. And she'd lived on Pleasant Avenue when her brother was killed, so she must have been well acquainted with its activities; she must also have been an accepted member of the community. Steve thought of McCrae and the pressure they were all under to make the arrests. After his shift at the apartment was over, he met Bill at the office and suggested Dolores Gomez as their undercover informant. She knew everybody, and everybody knew her. If she and her husband were arrested, and talked to, and induced to work for the police ...

Bill listened thoughtfully, and looked at a number of tapes in which they appeared. He didn't quite see it as Steve did, but when Steve said they'd been sitting on Pleasant Avenue since June with nothing to show for it except a few miles of videotape, he didn't say no. But he couldn't help mumbling that someone might just get killed.

McCrae listened to their idea and watched in silence as they ran off sections of videotape in which Dolores Gomez and her man appeared. Then he said, "If we arrest them, there are likely to be two troubles. The guy looks weak and the girl looks strong.

"Let's face it, though it's only a guess," McCrae continued. "The mob would scare the shit out of him, like they did JC, and he'd clam up. And the D.A. wouldn't scare her—she looks too sharp, and she probably knows the courts would go easy on a woman.

"Besides," he continued, "our friendly feds at the Bureau of Narcotics tell me they've got a real live one."

He leaned back expansively. "Craziest damn thing. A guy walks in off the street, into their office at 90 Church, and he says—just like that—'I want to tell everything.' They didn't believe it, but he checks out perfectly.

"They still don't believe it: he wants to give up Pleasant Avenue! He's lived around there for five years, and he knows everybody."

Then he added, "I like your initiative, men. Good thinking. Pass the word to the others, will you, that we got it made, the feds are coming into our case."

# 17

"Fat Jimmy," sometimes called "Jimmy Fats," was a shot in the arm. McCrae's men had been poised somewhere between lethargy and rebellion until Jimmy turned up. They turned enthusiastic overnight, and the feds who expected to work on the case couldn't wait to get started.

"It's an agent's dream," said Jeb Sanders, an agent friend of Joe Quetarro at the Bureau of Narcotics, "a once-in-a-life-time."

He was taking Bill Erwin to meet Fat Jimmy, since Bill had the job of coordinating information on the tapes and logs. As they drove to the hotel where the feds were keeping Fat Jimmy, hidden and guarded, Jeb said, "He's been living on 109th Street near Second Avenue and, listen to this, he's been actually working next door to Diane's Bar on Second Avenue near 105th Street."

"I know the place," Bill told him, "a hangout for the Pleasant Avenue bigshots."

"So you must know who owns it."

"Sure, Steven Delacava."

"Yeah, Beansie. Well, this guy Jimmy says Beansie also owns the air-conditioning agency next to Diane's on one side, and he's a half-owner of the Phy-Cul Club on the other side. Jimmy actually works for Delacava. He knows them all up there." Jeb chortled.

"What made him do it, give them up?" Bill asked. He wasn't skeptical, but he was warier than Sanders, who didn't seem to question their once-in-a-lifetime good luck.

"Scared. He happened to be around where he could see a couple of guys get into the car in which the Manfredi boys were whacked. He says he's sure he's been marked for death, and he came begging for protection, in exchange for information."

"And you believed him."

"Not right away. But Joe Quetarro came in to question him, and he thinks he's for real. Joe knows the East Harlem scene from way back."

Sanders remembered something else and added, "Maybe the funniest part with Fat Jimmy was when Joe started talking. Joe would say, 'You know Fagioli?' and Jimmy says, 'Sure I know Fagioli. You know Fagioli?' And when Joe starts reeling off what he knows, Jimmy's mouth drops open with amazement—he thought none of us knew anything about what goes on up there. Fagioli is Beansie Delacava—*fagiolo* is Italian for 'bean.' Joe says Jimmy's for real, all right."

"What I actually said," Joe Quetarro told Bill later, "was that he seems to know all the dealers and their satellites quite intimately. He describes people and places we know, and he's quite accurate.

"I'm a little hung up, though," Joe continued, "because if he's so deeply involved, how come we never heard of him before, and neither did your people?" He and Bill were meeting to arrange for exchange of information between Mc-Crae's unit and the feds.

Bill said, "Maybe we'll find him on the tapes if we look hard enough. What's he look like?"

Joe laughed. "That's another funny thing, Bill. You know what Inglese looks like? Jimmy's a fat guy and looks a lot like him. Spittin' image."

"Does he know Inglese?"

"Yes. Matter of fact, he says Inglese gives him one of his old suits from time to time. He acts kind of proud of that. Even his name, Fat Jimmy Rinaldi, sounds like Fat Gigi Inglese."

Joe was laughing. "You should have seen his face when I said to him, 'That's a big favor you do for Fat Gigi, to wear his suit.' He says, 'What do you mean?' I said, 'From the back you look alike, so if somebody wants to take a shot at Inglese, they might get you instead.' He says, 'Yeah? Gee! I never thought of that.' Nice guy, though."

Bill asked, "What are you going to do with him? Use him as a witness? Could he bring in undercovers to make buys?"

"It's too soon to tell, but one thing is definite. He corroborates everything we knew before, and lots of the new information that came off your tapes."

Bill said, "McCrae must be happy about that. The D.A. and his special assistant, Otis, can't kiss him off any more and say the work we've done doesn't mean anything."

Joe said, "It's even better than that. Jimmy says he knows where all the traps are. He's been describing places where they stash their heroin, so that should make for a lot of search warrants. We should be able to fill in the chain of evidence on particular transactions—like when Lentini walks around the corner out of your camera range on 117th Street, where's he go? Jimmy says he's got a trap in the butcher shop around that corner."

"So he would be a good witness," Bill said.

"He describes places you wouldn't believe, like Delacava's setup, including his air-conditioner shop. It looks like an ordinary messy store, but in the back there's a hidden compartment, a whole room built behind false walls, where Beansie has a luxurious office for conducting his important deals."

A couple of weeks later, Jeb Sanders told Bill of further

results in the questioning of Fat Jimmy. The feds were putting him up in hotels, moving him frequently, collecting large folders of information. Sanders reported that from the information Jimmy was giving, he must himself have been an important member of the network, with connections in Canada, several southern states, and Cuba and Argentina.

He was a sort of manager of deals, assuring delivery of bulk heroin shipments, supervising operations such as a caravan coming in from Montreal, or a private plane delivery from Florida. He told how he had worked his way up by doing several jobs as a hit man, and he named names, dates, and places where he'd been present at deals made by Louis Cirillo, Louis Mileto, Al Catino.

And then the whole thing fell apart.

Bill found out from Detective Jim Nauwens, one of his joint-task-force contacts. He called Nauwens to get some information for a folder he was assembling, and when he mentioned Fat Jimmy, Nauwens started laughing.

"Don Blanchard spotted right away that he was a phony. Don's in the same unit with Frank and me. They sent us over to the Prince George Hotel to debrief him on smuggling, which he said he was involved in. Don asks him what he knows about heroin coming in from Puerto Rico, and he tells us about coming in with a delivery by helicopter, landing on Key Largo, and a truck pickup there. He described the helicopter perfectly—Don was a helicopter pilot in Korea—but Don also says there isn't a helicopter in this part of the world that could make the trip nonstop from Puerto Rico. You should talk to Joe Quetarro—he's on to him now."

Joe Quetarro wasn't sore about Jimmy. "Poor bastard," he said. "Sure, he worked with Delacava and knew everybody—he used to cook for them.

"He finally told us the whole story. He went up to East Harlem about five years ago and got a job as a short-order cook in Diane's. Then he did the cooking for one of Delacava's

152

parties, and they liked it so well they helped him open a restaurant.

"He says it was a smash hit—for one week. He made a couple of thousand bucks' profit right off. Then everybody started eating there—but after the first week, they ate on the cuff. In the second week he was bust and in debt, so Delacava gave him a job, as go-for, air-conditioning repairman, and chef whenever somebody wanted a special meal.

"That part is absolutely true—he's cooked some dreamboat meals for us at a motel we had him in. It could also be true about him witnessing the Manfredi boys killing and being scared. Also, he's probably just a nut.

"The biggest laugh is when he said he was a hit man—he's the mildest, sweetest guy you'd ever want to know. That's why he knows so much—they never had any fear of him, so they'd talk their deals openly when he was around cooking and serving the pasta and the scallopini. And he's cooked for all of them. But, he doesn't even know what heroin looks like.

"Sure, Blanchard caught on right away, but so did we when he started talking about deals—he didn't have the foggiest notion about how much junk sells for."

Bill asked, "What are you guys gonna do now?"

Joe laughed. "Hell, man, we're back on square one. We need a witness, we need undercover buys, we need to get this show on the road somehow."

Bill put in a call to Steve at the apartment on Pleasant Avenue and asked whatever had become of Dolores. If Steve felt like dusting off some tapes in which she and her husband appeared, he said he thought Lieutenant McCrae might be more interested in listening.

# 18

McCrae was edgy and depressed after the BNDD fiasco. He was barely cordial when Steve and Bill arrived to talk about Dolores, but little by little he began to perk up. Soon he was talking fast, asking questions, making decisions. He told Steve to put together one reel of videotape that would show six or eight scenes of Dolores in action. He told Bill to assemble information from the logs and the files, and then have Steve narrate the information on the soundtrack of the tape. By the time the meeting broke up, they were laughing and joking. "We started as detectives," Steve said, "then you went into show business, and now we're all in it."

"TV's taking over; there's hardly anything on except cop shows; it's only fair if us cops get into TV," Bill said.

McCrae said, "Just make sure what you come up with will play south of Canal Street."

The Bureau of Narcotics office was on Church Street, ODALE was at Federal Plaza, and the special assistant for narcotics cases was in the D.A.'s office on Leonard Street—all south of Canal Street in Manhattan. Steve and Bill got the message. McCrae was going to go around the track again, fighting to get the extra men he needed.

"Gotta hand it to him," Steve said. "He doesn't give up, even after his last show got good reviews and nobody bought tickets."

Bill laughed and said, "But now your Dolores is the star, and she's prettier."


McCrae didn't go around the track again.

This time he pulled strings and set up one big meeting, to which he invited them all at the same time. Three high-ranking feds came from the Bureau of Narcotics, the regional chief of ODALE sat in, the special assistant for narcotics cases attended with two of his assistant D.A.s. Inspector Kramer chaired the meeting, which was held in the D.A.'s conference room. McCrae explained all over again why the case was important, and how additional manpower would enable his unit to bust a major drug-dealing network. Steve ran the videotape reel of Dolores.

Driving home with Bill later, he said, "It was funny. McCrae talked, I ran the tape, and one by one it dawned on them that this is a damned good case. Before the meeting was half over, everybody wanted in."

"No wonder McCrae was so lively when he got back to the office."

"The second half of the meeting was for the bullshit about cooperation—but each one had the idea *he* should run it."

"Who won?"

"Can't tell yet. I bet there'll be lots of infighting before that's settled."

Bill said, "So nothing definite happened."

"Except that we're working for the feds, you and me," Steve said. He described their new employers to Bill.

The deputy assistant regional director of BNDD was a man

named Anthony Pohl. At the meeting he had said he would like to study the tapes in detail, and asked if he could get a set of them duplicated. McCrae said his unit didn't have the money—reels cost thirteen dollars each—or the equipment, or the space to do it in. Mr. Pohl had said that was no problem— his office would buy the reels, and he'd provide the equipment and the space. Could McCrae let him borrow a man who was familiar with the videotaping to make the dupes? Mr. Del Corso, for instance?

Pohl was a big guy, tall, over two hundred pounds, but with a quiet, easygoing voice. The others called him Tony. He didn't say too much, but Steve thought he was smart. Andrews, the guy from ODALE, must have thought so too, Steve said. As soon as Pohl had been promised the tapes, Andrews had said that he would like to study the files, so could McCrae make them available to him? Along with one of his men who was familiar with the files and could analyze them?

"That's you," Steve concluded.

"What about the D.A.'s special assistant, Otis? What did he reach for?"

"He's already got. Twelve and a half million bucks of federal funding. With that he could hire enough investigators to take over our case."


When Bill went over to work at ODALE, he found himself a spectator at a struggle whose intensity astonished him.

Mostly it was beyond his understanding. The only thing that was clear, he told Steve when they met for coffee or lunch, was that Dolores and Pleasant Avenue would have to wait until these characters finished their fight for power. After that was settled, they'd see about fighting drug dealers. After months of being an orphan, their case was now a hot property and everybody wanted a piece.

Otis, the special assistant, was proposing to Andrews that they work together and run the case. They were old friends.

Andrews was evading that alliance. As a federal man appointed by the White House, he didn't want to risk playing second fiddle to a city D.A. Meanwhile, he was propositioning Pohl that *they* work together. Pohl could be in charge after transferring from the BNDD to Andrews' organization, ODALE. He and Pohl were old friends too, and now that he had the White House back of him, he could get anything for Pohl that he wanted.

Pohl was humble. He said thanks, but he couldn't just go and "take" a case—he had to be assigned to it. Andrews said he'd fix that and phoned Pohl's boss, Burt Williams, urging his assignment as a matter of national priorities and the president's commitment to the American people.

Pohl's boss agreed, and next Pohl said he'd like to read all the files so he could make up his own mind.

Meanwhile, Otis came up with another angle. He was already supporting the investigation handled by the SIU squad under Lieutenant Shandel; he'd lent some of his men for the investigation of the Havemeyer Club in the Bronx and of the Wednesday-night apartment in Queens. Shandel's targets included many of the same narcotics dealers who were on Pleasant Avenue. He proposed to McCrae that the two units and investigations be combined, and that he then put more of his own men into it.

This scared the hell out of McCrae. He'd kept the Pleasant Avenue operation under tight security for so long that he'd taken it for granted. The Meat Market had blown after only one day of surveillance. If Pleasant Avenue blew now, after all these months ... McCrae quickly arranged a meeting of Otis, Kramer, and himself, where they quickly made it clear that the SIU was not invited to the party.

By this time Pohl had told Andrews that he was declining his offer, because he disagreed with ODALE's policy of making lots of cases to impress the president with statistics. Andrews was in a fury. There was a nose-to-nose shouting match in which he accused Pohl of a double-cross. Tension between the old friends mounted. The president's own special consultant on drug matters, Special Assistant Attorney General Myles Ambrose, came up from Washington, whether to make peace or to put pressure on Pohl, no one was sure. In any case, Pohl resisted and Ambrose ordered him to appear in Washington for a confrontation with the attorney general himself.

Meanwhile, ODALE and Ambrose were being criticized in Congress for their announced plans for a "concentrated assault on street-level heroin pushers" and "special grand juries to gather new intelligence."

Steve, working in the BNDD office, told Bill that Pohl seemed strangely unagitated. He had calmly told Andrews that if ODALE wanted this Pleasant Avenue case, why didn't they just take it and run it themselves? And leave him out of it. Next they heard that the United States attorney, Whitney North Seymour, Jr., had called a conference at his office in the Federal Courthouse. They met for coffee and asked each other what that meant.

Steve said it looked as if their whole case was going to drown in bullshit while these guys fought over who was to control it.

Bill said he thought maybe not. "Watch Pohl," he said. "That's one smart son of a bitch, and they say he really knows the narcotics rackets."

"That still doesn't explain why the U.S. attorney is getting into the act now," Steve said.

"Figure it this way. Pohl's got the tapes, and he's got the files—that's two legs of the trophy. If he gets the U.S. attorney—who is part of the Nixon administration—on his side, it would be a third leg, and permanent possession."

"Since you started working at ODALE," Steve remarked, "you're getting to be a real political expert."

In the next few days they learned that Bill's guess was on the right track. While others were visiting McCrae and maneuvering for position, Pohl had been sitting up nights studying the files. Now he had come in with a strong idea—to have lawyers in the U.S. attorney's office work directly and closely with the detectives and federal agents assigned to the case. The case was incredibly complicated, he said, and was only going to get more so. When the arrests were finally made, the defense lawyers would kick and scream to get the evidence thrown out of court. And the case would be vulnerable on two counts—charges of invasion of privacy and violation of due process. The police would be accused of using television as a publicity stunt and thereby destroying any possibility of a fair trial.

So, he said, if the U.S. attorney were to assign lawyers to the case now, they could guide the detectives and agents on bringing in "clean" evidence that would be acceptable to the courts. Later those same lawyers could be assigned to try the cases, and they would know that much more about them.

Evidently this idea appealed enormously to Whitney North Seymour. He may have had some political scores to settle with several of his colleagues in the Nixon administration, or perhaps he simply felt strongly that the president's men were attacking the heroin problem the wrong way.

Late in the day of the conference in Seymour's office, Bill and Steve made it their business to look something up in the files in McCrae's office. He came back from the conference but walked right by, pretending he did not know why they were there. But he was too elated to keep up the suspense very long.

"Pohl's going to take charge." McCrae leaned back in his swivel chair, with his feet on the desk, hauled a big cigar from his pocket, and lit it. "Before the meeting was half over, Pohl had it, hands down."

He was the picture of contentment, filling in the details of the meeting between puffs. "It took a little while for the others to realize what was happening. What he'd done is to convert the action from a bunch of drug busts—which Otis would like to prosecute in the state courts—into a multiple conspiracy case. That puts it into the federal court. At the same time, the ODALE guys couldn't touch him because Pohl has done his homework, he really has, and he was able to start outlining a plan of action, a strategy that had them goggle-eyed.

"He wants the target to be a five-way network, taking in narcotics violators from all parts of New York City, Westchester, Connecticut, New Jersey, and Long Island—guys who supply the Northeast all the way to Chicago. Our Pleasant Avenue operation would become just the center hooking it all together."

Steve and Bill left McCrae's office and stopped in at the Belmore Cafeteria for a coffee before parting. "You know what's really funny about this whole thing?" Steve said. "It all hangs on Dolores. Remember when you said on the phone, 'Who's the broad?' "

"When was that? Middle of September?"

"Yes," Steve said. "And now it's December. The feds have been in the apartment and in the surveillance cars for the past two months, and they're thinking big, but what we had in September is still all we've got to go on in December."

The day was December 7.

On December 9 Bill phoned Steve and said, "There she blows."

"If she does, tell her I'm busy now and I'll come later. What else is new?"

"Somebody from the SIU has been asking about Pleasant Avenue."

"Who?"

"A lieutenant. Myron Bransla."

"Do we know him?"

"McCrae's checking him out."

"What's he up to?"

"His squad is working on Dolores Gomez and Pedro Melicio."

"You think something leaked?"

"Can't say yet."

"McCrae think it's gonna blow?"

"He didn't say. Lieutenant Bransla is getting ready to arrest Dolores and Melicio."

"It's gonna blow. *The whole fucking case!*"

161

# 19

"Actually, I was going to arrest them several weeks ago," Lieutenant Bransla said.

"Why didn't you?" asked McCrae.

"Because of that woman, Mrs. Melicio; she mentioned Pleasant Avenue," Bransla said. One of his detectives, Vince Lazarri, was with him, and McCrae had asked Steve and Bill to sit in too.

The two visitors seemed casual and relaxed. McCrae and his two men were agitated but under control.

"We were set to drop them, but we aborted when our undercover got into a hassle with her."

Lieutenant Myron Bransla was a tall man, a Slavic-looking six-footer with blue eyes, fair skin, and reddish-brown hair. He was serious in manner, soft-spoken, not much given to smiling.

In August he had arrested a Puerto Rican male on the Lower East Side, whom they were able to flip. The new informant revealed that his connection was a Puerto Rican from the Bronx named Pedro Melicio. The informer introduced Bransla's Hispanic undercover to Melicio, and a buy was set up. The undercover bought only an eighth of a kilo, the idea being to establish confidence by having the undercover seem cautious, wanting to sample the merchandise before making a large purchase.

"Melicio was OK to deal with," said Bransla, "but his wife starts to butt in. She's needling him for bothering with chickenshit eighth-kilo deals, and she didn't like our man hanging around asking a lot of questions.

" 'C'mon, c'mon,' she says, 'you want to buy or don't you? We ain't got all night.' I don't know what our undercover said to irritate her, but she got pissed off at him. Later she told the informant, 'That one I don't like. Don't bring him around no more.' And we had to put another undercover on them, who started right off with a quarter-kilo buy."

McCrae, Steve, and Bill smiled sympathetically at the discomfiture of their colleagues, as Bransla continued:

"Well, one of the things that riled her up was when our first undercover asked if their merchandise was really good. She said, very sharply, 'Good? It's the fuckin' best there is. It comes straight from the Italians on Pleasant Avenue.' That's when we got the idea of checking into Pleasant Avenue."

Bransla sent a couple of his men to check Intelligence Division files for recent information on narcotics violations and investigations on Pleasant Avenue. They found that application for wiretaps and bugs had been put in by something called the Drug Intelligence Group, of which he'd never heard before.

So they obtained the name of the commanding officer, Lieutenant Robert McCrae, and now Bransla was there to hear whatever McCrae could tell him about Pleasant Avenue.

McCrae tried not to appear evasive. He said they hadn't yet received authority to bug or wiretap, and they'd made some preliminary passes at the area, yes, but before he released anything they had he'd like to check with his superiors—could Bransla wait a couple of days?

164

Bransla said yes, that the information wasn't urgent.

McCrae said that what he'd meant was, could Bransla hold off on making the arrests, in case his unit needed to change any of their plans?

Bransla said he couldn't answer that without knowing what McCrae's people had in mind. After all, his squad had already put a lot of time into this investigation, and they wanted to get it over with. There were some peculiar things about this couple.

Like what, McCrae asked, and Bransla summarized:

Pedro Melicio was born in Puerto Rico and his family was still there, in a small town outside of San Juan. Although his police record described him as a small-time street pusher, he was now dealing in quarter Ks, halfs and whole Ks—which was quite a jump for a guy who looked so unprepossessing.

"He's kind of small, you know," Bransla said, "with short black kinky hair, a mustache, and really dark coloring. His clothes kind of hang, and they're always creased, and he has a limp from a busted kneecap on his left leg.

"It's really very strange," Bransla went on, "him being married to this very good-looking broad. I don't know if they're really married or living together, but it's the same thing. They met at a dance about two and a half years ago and started going together, then she got knocked up and had a child over a year ago."

McCrae tried to change the subject again. He asked Lieutenant Bransla if he could lend them any of his own reports, so McCrae could give his superiors some background on what the SIU was up to. Bransla agreed, and he was conscientious. Two hours later he had one of his men in McCrae's office handing over copies of several of the SIU's surveillance reports. McCrae turned them over to Bill, who came back a couple of hours later with a funny look on his face.

He said, "Bransla may not have tumbled yet, but he has either made our case, or he's about to blow it. Which way do we go?"

"What'd you find out?"

"Listen to this, off the SIU report from Bransla's squad:

"October 7, 1130 hours: At Pedro Melicio residence—undercover negotiates narcotics transaction. Hands over $5,500 in marked bills as half of purchase price.

"1205 hours: Melicio and wife leave residence to meet their connection.

"1220 hours: second undercover tails them in their auto, license # 9547YP—loses them when they take the highway.

"1410 hours: Melicio and wife return to residence. Pedro hands over half-kilo package; undercover hands over $5,500 in marked currency, balance of buy money.

"1425 hours: undercover leaves residence. Second undercover remains on surveillance outside residence.

"What were Dolores and Melicio doing when the undercover lost them, from shortly after 1220 hours until 1410 hours? Here's our log, observations through the apartment window on October 7:

"1235 hours: gray Pontiac license # 9547YP pulls up on east side of Pleasant Avenue between 117th and 118th Streets; male Hispanic, Melicio, and woman, exit auto; speak with Lentini; the three enter tavern.

"1255 hours: white male, Georgie Romano, exits tavern and enters barbershop next door.

"1310 hours: Georgie exits barbershop, opens trunk of gray Pontiac license # 9547YP, drops package in trunk, and slams lid shut; takes key and enters tavern.

"1330 hours: Melicio and wife exit tavern, enter gray Pontiac license # 9547YP, and drive north on Pleasant Avenue."

\* \* \*

166

McCrae said, "All right. It's a complete chain of evidence; we got pieces and they got pieces. If we can put them together, we've got a case."

He phoned Pohl, who said to come over first thing next morning. By midmorning Pohl was calling Bransla to request that the three of them meet to work out a plan of cooperative action; meanwhile, would Bransla please hold back on the arrest? Bransla was out of his office but called back at noon.

He said his squad had already made the arrest.

His office had radioed the message to the men tailing Melicio and his wife. But they did not catch the radio call. They had tailed the suspects to Brooklyn and had made the arrest at midnight.

They had collared them as they were about to enter their automobile.

They brought them to SIU field headquarters, and then found that the man was not Pedro Melicio.

Christmas of 1972 brought a welcome break, but only after Steve had had a last-minute panic.

On Friday the twenty-second he suddenly realized he had not put in for leave over the holidays, and by then the department holiday work schedules were all made up.

"I could kick myself," he told Bill. "Loretta asked me more than three weeks ago if I'd put in for leave. But that day something came up, and then, with all the crap that was flying day after day, I forgot. . . ."

Bill wasn't excited. "I put in," he said quietly. "For both of us."

Steve's anxiety promptly subsided. "I knew you would."

"I know you knew. I signed your name."

"You saved my marriage. Loretta was getting ready to do something. She said this morning, 'Do you realize you haven't spent a single evening at home since Thanksgiving, and very few since Columbus Day?' I said I'd make it up to her during Christmas, and then I suddenly remembered . . ."

Bill said, "Phyllis didn't need to say anything to me—the kids have been on my back about it. Anyway, we both got OKs for two four-day weekends."

"You mean you didn't get us the Wednesday and Thursday in between?"

"I didn't think you'd want to stay away from the office that much." Bill was laughing. "You don't know where Dolores is."

"Neither do you."

"But you're more worried about it."

"Am I?"

"You probably would be if you knew they're using her to make buys."

"Who is?"

"The feds. Bransla. She's been up to the Blue Lounge trying to contact Campopiano, and she's been making phone calls to Pleasant Avenue, looking for him."

"She could get killed!"

# 20

"You are my true good buddy," Steve said. "You take away one worry and hand me another."

"You rather I didn't tell you?"

"Go ahead. Lay it on me."

"They arrested her in Brooklyn. She and a guy named Lindy. Vince Lazzari and a woman detective, Elsie Farrel, made the pinch."

"When was this?"

"About midnight, ten days ago."

"What was she doing out in Brooklyn? Where was Pedro?"

"She said Pedro left her. And she was visiting a girlfriend—"

"Come again? Pedro left her? How'd you find out all of this?"

"I talked with Lazzari. I met Vince a couple of times when I used to work Brooklyn Eight-seven. I saw his name on the report as arresting officer."

"Who's Lindy?" Steve wanted to know.

"Friend of Pedro, she said. He was just driving her as a

favor, she said, not involved, but they are holding him anyway so that he won't spill to the mob on Pleasant Avenue."

"They lock her up, too?"

"No. There's something funny going on."

"What happened?"

"They turned her."

"And sent her out to make buys? When?"

"She was arrested on a Tuesday, and they sent her out on the following Friday."

"Goddamn. Is somebody out of his skull?" Steve brought his voice back under control, conscious that Bill's face had a little smile on it, half-amused.

"You want to know what happened, don't you?"

Steve was hungry to know. He shut up and listened.

Bill said, "They brought the two of them in to SIU field headquarters and separated them. Bransla talked to her, Captain Leonard talked to her, working on her to turn right away, but of course she clammed up. Then the feds came over with a search warrant and they took her up to her apartment in the Bronx and found half a K of good-quality junk, and a gun, and six thousand bucks cash. Then they brought her to the Five and booked her, and brought her back to SIU and talked to her some more."

"And she turned."

"Yep. Lazzari said she's one sharp baby. She said she'd make a deal—for herself, *and* for Pedro, *and* for her brother who's in the can on a murder rap, *and* for another brother, Robert, who she says we are holding on a bum rap for drugs."

"And they turned her loose to make buys that fast?"

"I said there's something going on."

"Where is she now?"

"Vince wouldn't say—or doesn't know."

Steve was thoughtful. "If she goes out to buy before she knows the ropes, she could make a false move. If our guys keep her under wraps, it will look funny that she doesn't show up on the avenue. Either way, those rats would smell a rat."

Bill said, "After all the fucking work that's gone into this case, and nothing to show for it—could be the bosses are pushing for results and she is it."

Steve was silent. Bill said, "Listen, we got Christmas and New Year's, so let's enjoy. We can start worrying again next year."

When they came in for their two days on duty in the middle of the Christmas week, the first thing they learned was that Dolores had disappeared.

# 21

Every other day during the New Year's weekend and the first week of January, Steve called the SIU, speaking with either Vince Lazzari or Elsie Farrel—Dolores was their prisoner—but he learned nothing new.

Meanwhile, he had finished duplicating all the videotapes for Anthony Pohl. Now he was screening and rescreening them, making notes, trying to sort out information that would satisfy the government lawyers, who were themselves trying to figure out what evidence would satisfy the courts, when and if the case went to trial.

It was tedious work, not at all like the job of putting together the second "Walter Cronkite" show. Then it had given him a lift to try to figure out what scenes would convey the message to people viewing his tape. It had been his chance to help get them to agree with what McCrae was trying to tell them.

Now he was trying to sort out the activity of the Pleasant Avenue characters into legal evidence. There was no established procedure, and no one to ask for guidance. Cops didn't do this sort of thing. Prosecutors had never done it before; no one had. He was feeling dispirited.

It was lonely work, too, and he became aware of a tendency to let his attention wander, sometimes out the window and back home to Loretta, his kids, his mother and father, his grandmother, whom he had visited when he was a child, when she had lived in East Harlem. And then his attention would wander from the videotapes to Pleasant Avenue. Its people were men like his grandfather, women like his grandmother, children like their children who were his own mother, uncles and aunts.

At such moments his frustration with the job would evaporate as he imagined being with them on Pleasant Avenue, the ordinary folks and kids who were not dealing heroin, just living there, working, raising families. They were his people and he knew them; he felt close to them. Long-forgotten memories surged through his head; undefined feelings stirred in his gut. A whispering sound came up off the running reel he had on the tape deck that day. On the monitor screen, the street was filled to overflowing with people in a religious procession. Toward the front, men were carrying on their shoulders a life-size statue of the Virgin on a platform. In the crowd that followed, hundreds of lighted tapers were held aloft. Men dressed in suits and neckties; women in their best dresses, even if they were only freshly laundered housedresses; children in neat clothing with their hair carefully combed marched slowly across the screen, evidently moving toward the Church of the Holy Rosary. Many of them walked barefoot. The expressions on their faces were part of a timeless tradition of the towns and villages of Italy.

As the church procession moved out of camera range, all that was left were the streamers stretched across the avenue, fluttering on the light breeze, catching little patches of illumination off the streetlamps.

The whole scene was familiar to Steve. He remembered it

174

from the times they had visited Grandma on feast days, and from the stories his mother used to tell him at bedtime. Memories flowed over him in waves, and his head seemed to become lighter than air, as if he were floating to a hilltop and looking down into himself. He now owned a part of himself he'd forgotten. In the days before the celebration, when he had been on duty at the window aiming the video camera at drug dealers, he had seen people putting up those streamers. But until this moment he had not known why they were doing it. Now he remembered.

He was no longer feeling dispirited, but he wasn't happy either. He had entered the community through the lens of a video camera. It was a telescopic intrusion, affording unilateral intimacy. He still felt lonely, and ignorant of what meaning it all might have.

Roger Coston, who was coordinating the case for the feds, came by and saw that Steve was down. He took him to meet Anthony Pohl, who had set Steve his task in the first place. He let Steve know he was keenly interested in the job Steve was doing, and that he expected it to play an important role in the final outcome of the case.

Steve appreciated this encouragement from Pohl and Coston. But he still didn't know exactly how to give them what they wanted.

That afternoon one of Lieutenant Bransla's sergeants, Sam Spaida, came over with a message. On orders from Pohl, Steve was to show a few reels of tape to some people. Spaida would escort him to their place.

Steve loaded up—a monitor, a converter, a tape deck, cables, a package of reels—and drove across town with Spaida acting as guide. They turned into West 72nd Street and parked in front of the Olcott Hotel.

The two of them hauled the equipment up to the third floor, to room 310, and the sergeant knocked.

Detective Elsie Farrel opened the door.

Spaida said hello and went in.

Elsie said, "Steve, meet Didi."

Steve eased the equipment to the floor and turned to face the other person in the room.

It was Dolores.

She was dressed in green slacks and jacket with a blouse the color he thought of as Puerto Rico pink. It set off the olive tone of her face and hands. She sat upright with hands demurely in her lap. She quietly acknowledged Elsie's introduction, and her voice, as much as he could hear of it, was light and melodious. Her large dark eyes were alert and interested, her full lips, with just a touch of crimson coloring, were composed. For a moment, the only thing that appeared to connect her with the woman he had seen on the video monitor was the long black hair that hung almost to her waist in back and framed her face and shoulders, catching bits of soft light as she moved.

Steve did not speak for a moment.

Then he said, "It's nice to know you, at last—in person."

"What does that mean?" She leaned forward, tense, suspicious.

Elsie said quickly, "Didi, this is Detective Del Corso."

Steve said, "I feel I know you from watching you on television."

Emotions registered easily on her face, and, automatically, the detective deadpan look came over his. But in an instant their expressions changed, hers to curiosity, his to pleasure that she was alive and well and prettier than her pictures.

He started to set up the video equipment, talking as he worked, and she was responding easily, comfortably.

He asked, "Everybody call you Didi?"

"All my friends."

"I thought it was Dolores."

"Yeah, you saw it on my driver's license, that time."

"You remembered." Steve kept on working without looking up. He was aware that his face and neck suddenly felt warm. He covered the moment by a touch of gallantry. "You must have a very good memory."

"In my business, ya gotta remember the fuckin' fuzz or you're dead."

He shut up and kept on working, but she kept the conversation going. "What's that?"

"The converter. It converts what's on the tape into a tiny electric charge, and each little charge turns on a tiny spot of light in the television tube over here. Millions of these spots make up the picture—it's like regular television, except it comes in through these cables and the converter box instead of through the air."

"What'd you need all that shit for? Why not just plug it in and turn it on?"

Steve was uncomfortable. He had heard women swear— prostitutes protesting an arrest, ghetto women declaiming against their husbands in a family fight, a junkie cursing out her connection—but invariably these women had been unkempt, uneducated, unattractive. Funny, he was still shocked at hearing a pretty, well-groomed woman talk dirty.

She was standing near, and he caught a slight trace of some sort of perfume. She was intent on his work, and ... Well, maybe he'd misjudged. Maybe she hadn't intended to put him down. Maybe it was just her way of talking when she was comfortable with someone, with a man, whom she liked. He decided that was how it was.

Meanwhile, Sergeant Sam Spaida had dropped into a chair in a corner of the room and was reading a newspaper while munching an apple. Joe Caesare came in from using the bathroom, said hello to Steve, then sat in another chair and resumed reading a paperback novel.

They were in a two-room hotel suite, a sitting room with a bedroom through a doorway on the left, a bathroom through a doorway on the right, and a bathroom off the bedroom. Spaida, Caesare, and Farrel were on bodyguard duty. Steve asked if anyone else were coming, and Elsie Farrel said two or three others were often there, but she couldn't say when they'd arrive.

He spoke to Didi. "Where were you after Christmas?"

"Puerto Rico." She pronounced it "Pwerrto Rrico." "I had business there." She pronounced it "bizziness," but except for a few words, she spoke with very little trace of accent and used much less "New Yorkese" than many of his cop friends.

She said, with a giggle, "Roger was very mad."

"*Por qué?*" Steve asked.

"Hey, man! You capish 'Spañol!"

"*Poco, poquito.* That's about it." They were smiling at each other, and he glanced over at Elsie Farrel, who'd been silent; he did not want her to feel left out. Elsie was half-smiling, the look on her face saying very plainly that another cop was falling for this little smart-ass drug dealer.

"Let's all go to the movies," Steve said. He was finished setting up, and a reel was on the deck. Didi pulled up an armchair, and Steve switched on the monitor. At once, Pleasant Avenue lit up. A sunny October afternoon. He was twisting knobs to adjust the picture when suddenly there was a little scream from Didi.

All the cops in the room spun around in her direction, and so did Steve. From the look on her face, she was entranced. She hadn't screamed, really. She had said, "It's me!" in a high-pitched voice.

For the next twenty-five minutes they watched in silence, Didi utterly absorbed in the picture tube, Steve watching her, Elsie dividing her attention between the picture tube and the animation on Didi's face. The other two cops watched in silence.

When the reel was finished, Didi erupted with laughs and questions, while Steve said he would tell her some other time how they did it. Could she tell who the people were in the pictures? Did she recognize them? What were they doing?

The telephone interrupted, and Elsie went to answer it. She finished her very quiet conversation and said that Roger—Agent Coston—would be coming over in about an hour.

Didi resumed talking about Pleasant Avenue. Sure, she recognized the scenes. That was a Monday, about three months ago.

178

Steve looked at the box the reel was stored in. She was right on the money: it was marked Monday, October 9. He rewound the reel partway, and started showing it again.

"That's Pedro and me talking to Moe. That's Ernie Boy going over to talk to us. There's Johnny Echoes coming over, too.

"I just got out of the car. There's Johnny and Ernie going around the corner—they had a stash someplace on 117th Street around the corner from the tavern, and that's where they are going. We were trying to buy a kilo that night, and they came back later with . . . That's Pedro going to drive our car into the parking lot. That's Pedro and me going into the tavern. There's Johnny and Ernie Boy going into the tavern. They came in to sit with us. Johnny had the package. That's Johnny coming out of the tavern—he's going to the parking lot. He's opening our car door and he's putting the package—you can't see because he's bent over, but that's what he's doing—he's putting the package on the floor under the seat. There he is going back into the tavern. We had a customer waiting in the Bronx, we were already late there. That's us coming out. Hey, the door was open—son of a bitch, Johnny left it open, didn't snap down the lock . . . I told him . . . that's us driving out on Pleasant Avenue. That's Ernie and Johnny coming out of the tavern—son of a bitch, I keep telling him, 'Lock the fuckin' car, man. . . .' "

Steve started another reel going, but before it had gone very far Roger Coston came in and he shut it off.

Roger was a big handsome Texan, blue eyes, rugged face, shock of yellow hair, husky build, deep slow Texas voice. He said a solemn hello to Elsie and Didi, then to Steve and the other detectives in the room. He said Vince Lazzari would be along in a minute—he was finding a place to park. Then Vince came in.

Meanwhile, Steve became aware of a fast change in Didi. She had shifted her focus of attention from the videotape show to Roger Coston. She wasn't talking much at first, just looking at him. There was a new little sparkle in her eyes. He wore a

179

plaid jacket, which he dropped onto the sofa shortly after he came in, and a blue patterned shirt, snug-fitting "Texas"-style pants, and cowboy boots. His necktie consisted of plaited leather thongs with a worked silver closure at the throat.

"Any calls yet?" he asked Elsie.

Didi answered quickly, taking the play away from Elsie, "Should be any minute now. I told him I wouldn't be in until about now."

As if on cue, the telephone rang and Didi went to it. "Hiya, Johnny, how ya doin', man?"

She had slurred her voice into the street jargon and pumped it up with put-on heartiness. Steve noticed there were two telephones in the room; the one Didi was using was attached to a tape recorder, which had automatically switched on when the telephone rang. Everybody else in the room was deathly silent.

Didi listened and talked and said sure she'd be there, right after the show, and when she hung up she turned to the others.

"He says we should have a meet, in front of the movies on 72nd Street and Third Avenue."

Roger Coston played back the recording, then said, "That's fine, real fine. You go ahead and meet him. Elsie will wire you."

Didi and Elsie Farrel went into the bedroom. When they came out, Coston said, "OK. I'll go on ahead, with Detective Norman. He's waiting downstairs. We'll be around for the meet, don't worry, and don't look around for us, whatever you do. Lazzari's your cabdriver. He's got the cab downstairs."

After ten minutes, Lazzari went down, and ten minutes later Didi followed him.

Steve stayed behind. Spaida and Caesare said they'd go out and get a bite to eat. Elsie said she was going to take a nap; she was bushed after the hours she'd been on duty. He asked about the telephones, and Elsie told him to stay away from the one attached to the tape recorder; that was strictly for Didi's calls. The other was a special line to the Police Department. It

180

was also connected to the communications base for this undercover operation.

Steve sat around awaiting Didi's return. After about twenty minutes he began to fidget, and after half an hour he called the base. He identified himself and asked what was happening.

"We're not sure. When she pulled up in the cab, two of their guys were waiting for her in a black Caddy. She got out and went over to them. They told her to pay off the cab, which she did. Then she went back to their car, and one of them said, 'C'mon, get in, we're going for a ride.'"

"Did she?"

"Yes. And they drove away. She was sitting between them on the front seat. They drove south, on Second Avenue."

"What else happened?"

"Don't know. Our agents ran to get into Lazzari's cab and followed. We haven't had any more reports since."

# 22

Steve settled down for a long wait. It might have been an hour, it might have been two; he dozed off and lost track.

He heard a key in the door and sprang to his feet.

It was Dolores.

She said, "Hi, there," and came in. Vince Lazzari came with her, carrying a white shopping bag.

He put the bag on the table as she took her coat off, then went to the closet to hang it up. She sat down on the sofa where she had been when Steve first saw her earlier that day. A sweet and demure young woman. Straight from the company of killers and dope dealers.

Roger Coston came in with Norman and Wells, two other federal narc agents. They went immediately to the white shopping bag and unloaded from it several magazines, an empty Johnnie Walker scotch bottle, and a half-kilo package of a white powdery substance.

As Coston and Norman watched, Wells put the package into a tan paper envelope, sealed it, and wrote his name and the date. Coston witnessed it with his name and the date.

Wells departed with the package, and everybody relaxed. Elsie had come into the room, and Didi went with her into the bedroom to take off the wire she'd been carrying inside her clothing.

When they came back, Norman opened the attaché case he'd been carrying, with a tape recorder in it, and as they sat around attentively, he started playing it back.

They heard the voices of Didi, Johnny Echoes Campopiano, and Ernie Boy Abbamonte—Johnny telling Didi to go pay off the cab, then telling her to get in his car, they were going for a little ride, then Didi asking where they were going, Johnny saying, "Downtown for a drink," she asking, "Where, 79th Street?" and Johnny saying, "No, a new place I want you to see."

Ernie Boy's voice came on. "I got good news. We got some goods for you. We don't know exactly how it's gonna be, because Georgie is waiting, and he's gonna let you know."

The tape ran silently. During a pause in the recorded conversation, Didi said, "We went to the Beef East, on 38th Street and Second Avenue. Georgie was there when we got there."

The tape recorder resumed—greetings, ordering drinks, Campopiano saying, "I got to talk with Georgie."

Another pause in the recorded conversation. Didi said they had gotten up and gone to the front of the restaurant to talk, and Georgie handed him something little, then Johnny . . . Ernie Boy Abbamonte's voice came back on, saying they had half a key for her, and Georgie would tell her where. Didi's voice came on saying that was fine because there was a dry on the street and she could use anything. Campopiano's voice came on saying that when she was ready, Georgie would tell her where.

Didi said, during another pause in the recording, "He gave me a key and told me it was for a locker in the airline terminal, then I went over to Georgie."

Georgie's voice came on the recording, giving directions on

184

how to walk from the restaurant to the airline-terminal building on East 37th Street between Second and First avenues, and how to find a particular locker there. Then Campopiano's voice came on again, saying he'd telephone that evening asking if she'd have some money for them, that if they had the money they could get more stuff later on. Didi's voice came on saying fine, call her anytime.

The taped conversation seemed to be over, and Norman shut it off. Didi said, "After that I did like they said, walked to the airline building, went where Georgie said, and opened the locker, and there was this shopping bag in it. I took it out and went to where the taxicabs pull in, and I saw Vince Lazzari in his cab waiting, so I got in and came here."

Roger Coston said, "Do you think he will call tonight?"

"Johnny? Sure. He's gonna want his money."

"When?"

"In the next couple of hours."

Roger Coston thought for a moment. "We'll stick around. Anybody hungry?"

Elsie said, "I noticed a pizza place around the corner on Columbus Avenue."

Norman was dispatched to bring back two large round pizzas in flat square boxes, which he somehow balanced in one hand while carrying a bag of canned Cokes and beers in the other.

At just before ten o'clock, the call came in and the tape recorder activated itself. It was Campopiano. He was asking her to meet him at a restaurant called Chances on East 58th Street.

Roger Coston nodded his head yes, she should meet him.

She went into the bedroom with Elsie, to be wired, and when she came back into the living room, Coston counted out $5,500, which she tucked into her pocketbook. Then he made a call over the second phone.

"Vince's relief will be driving the cab. Andy. You met him two days ago."

Didi nodded. Roger and Norman left, and five minutes later she went out. In less than an hour they were all back.

They sat around feeling relaxed, as Didi recounted what had happened. She had joined Campopiano and some stranger at a table. They ordered a drink for her; she told Johnny that she had something for him, and they went upstairs to where the rest rooms were. She handed over the $5,500 and Campopiano sent her back to the table while he extracted his share of the money. Then he came down and took the stranger aside, handed him some money. The stranger left, and then she left the restaurant.

But not before Campopiano invited her to join him and his friends at Bachelors III later that night.

"What for?" Coston asked.

"Just to hang around. They're always doing that."

"How about you?"

"Sure, why not? We've been doing it all the time. Pedro wasn't so much for it, but now they think I left Pedro, so there's no reason for me to refuse."

Roger was dubious, but she said, "Listen, we're supposed to be friends, known each other a long time. It will look funny if I stop hanging out with them for no reason."

Roger said, "OK. Might be good. We might pick up some good material off the wire."

She said, "Uh-uh. I can't go wearing no wire."

"Why not? It will be concealed."

"Well, I gotta wear a dress, I can't go like this. The wire would be noticed."

They were arguing now, and Roger wanted to know why it couldn't be concealed on her body—it was no bigger than a pack of cigarettes.

"So where you gonna conceal it, man? Where they won't notice? Under my tits? Between my legs? It'll get noticed, all right." She stopped, then smiled broadly at the look of distress on Roger's face. "This is social, man, sociable-like," she said. "Lots of fooling around, dancing, and, you know."

186

After a moment she added, "You know, I been doing nothing for a long time, haven't gone out for weeks."

Coston said, "Well, be careful."

Elsie Farrel said, "What about the wire?"

Didi said, "No wire."

"No wire," Coston said.

Elsie went with her into the bedroom and came out with the tiny apparatus. Didi emerged after a while, looking beautiful. Her long black hair was piled up and shaped elegantly; she wore a black sheath dress patterned with bright pink, red, mauve, and orange flowers. She had on high-heeled pink shoes and a matching necklace and bracelets of gold set with green stones.

She came through the doorway, posed, then struck another pose and said, "I look OK?" She took her coat from the closet and started to put it on.

Steve got up and went to help her on with it.

Nobody said a word. Didi smiled at Elsie. "Don't wait up for me," she said, and was gone.

# 23

Del Corso, Coston, and Norman left the hotel together. Out front Steve found a parking ticket on his car and said, "Looks like somebody's trying to tell me I've been here a long time."

Coston was busy with his own thoughts. Norman was scanning the street for a cab.

Steve said, "Don't think it hasn't been fun, Mr. Coston, but. . . ."

Coston took another second to focus.

"I know, Steve, I know," he said softly, his drawling voice full of contentment with this day's progress. "Ya don't want to just sit around while she's out galavantin' and makin' buys. We've got to do somethin' about that. Meet me at the office tomorrow, first thing. We'll talk about it."

Steve had difficulty falling asleep that night, thinking of Didi out partying with hoods she was working to destroy. He knew what they'd do to her the moment they had the smallest suspicion. Coston hadn't wanted her to go out alone, and he'd been right. He should have insisted. On a mental video screen he saw Didi at a bar surrounded by hoods who were dancing, laughing, leering, reaching. . . .

Next morning, driving down to Coston's office, he felt curiously refreshed. The feds had moved north of Canal Street, to new quarters on the top floors of the Ford Motors Building, West 57th Street, with a view of the Hudson River, the Jersey shore, and the brightest January sky since New Year's.

It seemed to Steve that Coston had been reading his mind. Actually, he must have had the same concerns. "She's a natural," Coston said. "Takes to this job like a real pro. I've had Pohl listen to the tapes off her body-wires. He thinks she works like a top undercover."

Steve said, "You think she realizes?"

"Indeed she does, Steve. We have been over it with her. She knows we're goin' all-out to put her friends on ice for a long time, and it's what she's to help us do."

"Sounds good," Steve said, using an expression of Bill's. Depending on inflection, it could mean he was dubious or satisfied.

Coston said, "So, we're not worryin' about her. She's willin' to make all the buys we need."

"Well, do I lay off screening videotapes with her?"

"No way, Steve. We need her to make buys, and we need her to go over the videotapes with you. . . ." He paused. "This is absolutely confidential; we haven't even discussed it with her yet. We need her as a witness. We expect she'll identify every dealer on Pleasant Avenue and tie them into specific transactions—it's what those miles of tape are all about, isn't it?"

"OK. So when do we screen tapes?"

"That's the question, Steve. Seymour, the U.S. attorney, has put two teams of lawyers on the case. Phil Wallace heads up one team, and he's hot on us getting lots of buys. Dick Webber is in charge of the other, and he needs a thorough analysis of all the Pleasant Avenue tapes from the beginning."

"And her friends need her for partying. She's going to be one busy little girl."

190

"Don't worry. It'll work out. You've got the video machines up at the hotel. You go around every day and screen tapes. When there's a chance for a buy, well, she'll just go to it, and when she gets back, you can continue screening. OK? See how it works?"

"Why not?" He got up. "Might as well get started."

"I'll go with you. She says they might have something for her today."

At the hotel, Steve set up the equipment and began screening tapes with Didi and making notes. Almost immediately a phone call came in from Ernie Boy Abbamonte.

They arranged a meet, on East 72nd Street in front of the movies. Federal Agent Alice Martinson, who was filling in on Elsie Farrel's day off, wired Didi while Coston counted out $7,000. An undercover detective drove her in a taxicab, and two narc agents tailed her in their car.

She returned and said it was a standup.

Steve started to screen tapes again. There was another phone call and conversation with Johnny Campopiano. He explained that Ernie Boy couldn't make it that day but they'd have something for her, definitely; he'd let her know.

Steve started again, and there was another interruption, Johnny calling to say she should meet him at the 58th Street place. Alice again wired her, Coston again counted out the $7,000, and she left with the same entourage.

She came back empty-handed. Johnny had met her at the bar of Chance's Restaurant; they'd gone up to the rest rooms and she'd given him the $7,000. He had promised to get her a whole kilo this time, and she could pay the balance of the money later.

Coston had a fresh idea. Could she work it so that the delivery would take place out on the street?

He would have agents on hand with a concealed mobile video camera as well as radio pickup of the voices—could she fix it so the camera crew would have time to get into position?

No problem, she said. And she did it.

191

She talked Johnny into making a meet in the open, on Second Avenue and 72nd Street. Steve was given the resulting videotape and made a duplicate, for study, while the original was sealed and marked for use in evidence at the future trial.

There were laughs when he screened the tape for Coston and the others. A rainstorm had come up, and, on camera, there was Georgie, standing about awkwardly under a dripping umbrella, hugging an attaché case to his bosom for protection against the wet.

The attaché case contained $80,000 to $100,000 worth of heroin. Evidently he had other deliveries to make.

Didi arrived by car, driven by an undercover cop she pretended was her boyfriend. They stopped the car, Georgie got in the back, opened his case, and took out Didi's kilo, handed it over, then got out of the car and scurried through the rain.

As he did so, Didi's recorded voice, clear as a bell, was heard on the tape. "Hey, man, did you see that? He had a whole fuckin' case full of shit!"

The detectives and agents viewing the tape agreed it would be sensational if this tape were offered in evidence in court at a public trial. The lawyers later thought it might pose a problem for the court's dignity.

In the days that followed, Didi's buys became routine. Concern for her safety evaporated and the atmosphere in room 310 at the Olcott Hotel was relaxed. Steve doggedly went about screening tapes whenever he could get and hold Didi's attention.

He would have liked to talk with Bill about his feelings of frustration—they had always helped each other let off steam that way—but Bill was tied up on a new and demanding assignment: he was working with a young British woman who'd become a junkie in New York and might be turned into an informant. She had the improbable name of Primrose Rodman but she had been Afro Louis' girlfriend, and the lawyers thought she was likely to be a valuable witness.

Roger Coston had moved on to some other part of the case, and Lieutenant Myron Bransla was in full charge of the work with Didi.

February 4 was a lazy Sunday. When Steve arrived at the hotel, Bransla, Lazzari, and a federal man, Jeb Sanders, were huddled with Didi in one part of the room, planning the next buy. Sam Spaida, Joe Caesare, and Sergeant Larry Barcos were sprawled on chairs at the other side of the room, listening to Elsie Farrel.

Elsie was all charged up. When she let Steve in she brought him into the conversation right away. "I was just telling the fellas about my new car. I got me a Caddy!"

The men all knew her as an efficient no-nonsense detective who had a good sense of humor, so they enjoyed seeing her go on this way. The new car evidently had a special meaning for her.

"I just took possession last night and drove it to work for the first time this morning," she said. "It's not new, of course, but it's *like* new, in beautiful condition, all shiny."

There were big smiles all around, maybe too big. She wanted them to understand:

"You have to know—ever since I was a kid, I dreamed of owning a Cadillac. We lived in Brooklyn then, next door to a garage where rich people used to keep their cars, and us kids on the block used to watch them go in and out, and they all looked so happy. In my fantasy, having a Caddy meant having a beautiful life. . . ."

She hesitated, and laughed, glanced anxiously at their expressions, and said to Steve, "They think I'm nuts."

"Not at all, Elsie. We're just thinking its previous owner was that little old lady . . ."

Proudly Elsie said, "It's only got 18,423 miles on it, and not a scratch, and—"

The phone was ringing, Didi's phone. Conversations stopped as she went to answer it.

She said her hello, starting to slur into her way of talking with Ernie Boy, Johnny, and the others, but her manner quickly changed as she listened.

She seemed puzzled, said, "What?" and "Hm," then, abruptly, "Wrong number," and she hung up.

As conversations resumed she said, "Somebody asking for a Joan or Joanne or something." Moments later the other phone rang, the one with a direct connection to the Police Department.

Elsie Farrel answered it. She listened a moment, then abruptly said, "No. Wrong number," and hung up.

Conversations resumed, but Larry Barcos was heard to mumble, to no one in particular: "It's funny, kinda. Two wrong numbers like that—back to back."

He didn't say it loud, but somehow the words carried.

Seconds later, Bransla was on his feet in the middle of the room, looking troubled.

"What do you mean?"

"Oh, I don't know. Just . . . seems funny."

Bransla went to the tape recorder attached to Didi's phone and replayed her last call. He asked Elsie to listen closely, and played it again. She said it was the same voice she had heard.

Bransla thought about it a moment longer. Then he told Sam Spaida to check with the department's communications unit to see if anyone had been taking an interest in their phones, which were unlisted confidential installations.

The others resumed their conversations but Bransla remained silent and thoughtful as Spaida made his calls. After a while, Spaida reported that the department knew of no questionable contacts regarding these phones.

Bransla reacted with unexpected asperity. "The hell with telephoning. Get yourself down to headquarters and run it down yourself—don't let those dummies bullshit you!"

"Yes, *sir,*" said Spaida. But the look on his face and the way he put on his coat announced loud and clear that he thought the lieutenant was off his chump.

After he left, Bransla ordered Lazzari and Caesare to cover

194

the windows, and Sergeant Barcos and Jeb Sanders to cover the doors.

He got on the phone, and next thing they heard, he was asking for a detail of men with shotguns and flak suits—about eight to start with. He might want more later, he said.

Didi was puzzled and wandered off to the bedroom. Steve and Elsie felt awkward hanging around. They felt even sillier when the first of the men with shotguns and flak suits arrived.

Sam Spaida phoned from headquarters. He had personally checked every place he could think of. There were no outside contacts of any kind relative to their confidential unlisted phones.

Bransla's men were wondering how the lieutenant was going to extricate himself from an embarrassing loss of face when this story got around the department. He was taking ridiculous measures over nothing. Bransla must have sensed their attitude, but he wasn't backstepping yet. He told Spaida to get down to the telephone company, fast, and check it out there.

The faces of the cops with him were deadpan. Time went by slowly.

Spaida was on the phone again, from the special unit of the telephone company that handled confidential police services. Thirteen men and a woman watched the lieutenant's face as he took the call in silence.

He slammed down the receiver.

"Security has been broken," he said. "Someone's been asking about our location here—and someone at the phone company gave it to them. The supervisors say they don't know how it happened, but it's on the record. The caller gave a cop's name and badge number, probably phony."

He started answering their questions before they could ask them. "Didi's cover is blown. We got to get her out of here before the torpedoes arrive—if they're not here already."

He was talking fast. "Steve, call your people at the Pleasant Avenue apartment. Find out how things look up there. By now, they probably know if the operation blew. I think the

195

whole operation is gone. They should be getting themselves and their gear the hell out of there on the double. Tell them to ask for as many backup guys as they think they'll need, on my authority."

He added, "Call as soon as this phone is free," and he put in a call to headquarters again, asking for ten marksmen to be posted on rooftops, and three cars with men for a convoy.

As Steve took the phone, Bransla was redeploying his men: Lazzari to take two men and cover the lobby, Caesare to take three and cover the back entrance of the hotel, Barcos to post a couple of men at the elevator and himself with another man at this end of their corridor. "And for Chrissake, everybody move quietly and keep your hardware out of sight, but seal up this place.

"And somebody get on the telephone-recording equipment, pack it, and get it out." He called to Steve, who was talking on the phone: "Get your video gear packed to pull out as fast as you can.

"And Elsie! Where's Elsie? Elsie, where are you parked?"

"On 72nd Street, near Amsterdam."

"We'll be taking Didi out of here in your car. How long do you figure it will take you to bring it around to the back door? Fifteen minutes? OK, back door in fifteen."

As she put her coat on, he called Barcos in from the corridor. "Time Elsie, and thirteen minutes after she leaves, you and the three men posted in the corridor take Didi down in the elevator.

"In the lobby, you turn right and head down that hall, all the way, to the back door of this place. Three of our guys have it secured. Elsie will be waiting outside.

"Meanwhile, I'm calling the Two-oh Precinct to send every squad car and uniformed man they can lay hands on to the front of this building on 72nd Street. That will be a diversion while we take Didi out the back.

"OK. Everybody move it."

Steve had finished his phone call. He told Bransla that

Ralph Tomas, on duty at the Pleasant Avenue apartment, had said that something funny had been going on since early afternoon. He said there was hardly any action on the street, and now, when it was usually jammed with cars double- and triple-parked, the street was practically dead. None of the familiars had showed up. In fact, he had already been wondering if it blew.

Lazzari called from the lobby. The desk clerk, the porter, and the elevator starter had all noticed four men around the lobby a short while back, men who did not seem like their regular run of hotel guests. They had assumed them to be customers of the hotel bar or the restaurant. Lazzari didn't have very good descriptions yet; there was a lot more questioning to be done, to find out where they went.

"OK," Bransla said. "But first, keep security in the lobby tight for at least fifteen more minutes. Elsie's OK?"

"She came through at least ten minutes ago."



As Elsie reached her car, the squad cars were rolling up around the front of the hotel, their roof lights flashing and spearing the darkness. As she got into her car, she rapidly figured her driving plan—northbound on Amsterdam Avenue to 74th Street, which was one-way eastbound, around on Central Park West southbound and into 73rd Street westbound.

Her destination was somewhere on that block, but she didn't know exactly where—she'd never been on 73rd Street before. Both curbs were tightly packed with parked cars, and there was no sign marking the back door of the Olcott Hotel. There were many dark places in which a gunman could hide. She could only estimate when she'd gone far enough along the block, and she slowed to a crawl.

Suddenly a splash of light appeared against blackness, figures bursting out and toward her. Four men and three shotguns were silhouetted—and a woman. They yanked her doors open and piled in.

A car came up from behind them, and the driver signaled Elsie to follow him. Two cars stayed back of her. They were in motion as a convoy.

The lead car took them through dark and quiet streets, maneuvering and turning as they all watched to discover if they were being followed or observed.

The lead car finally took them into the garage of the Hilton Hotel on Sixth Avenue. Elevators took Elsie, Didi, and eight of the men up to a high floor. Elsie and Didi were guided to a room they would share for the night, while the men arranged themselves in adjoining rooms and the corridor.

With the door to their room locked, Elsie flopped on the bed, closed her eyes, threw her arms wide, and took long deep breaths. When she opened her eyes, she saw Didi darting about in a state of excitement, opening closet doors, examining the bathroom, looking out the windows at the city and its lights.

"Isn't this something?" She was giggling with delight. "Hey, this is fun!" Her eyes were shining; she sat on a bed and tested its bounce.

Elsie raised up on one elbow.

"Hey, woman," Didi said, "what's the matter? You look terrible."

She was solicitous, and surprised, too. Elsie had always seemed so tough. "What's the matter?" she repeated.

Elsie was becoming annoyed. "What do you mean, what's the matter—don't you realize what's been going on?"

"Oh, sure," Didi said, "there might have been shooting, people killed. But I wasn't scared. Were you scared?"

"You're damn right I was scared. It didn't mean a thing to you, but some son of a bitch might have started shooting and putting bullet holes in my new Caddy."

# 24

Saturday, February 17, was a clear, cold day, with brilliant blue sky, cotton-white clouds, and hardly any traffic on the road. A stream of warm air from the car heater cut across the iciness coming off the glass windows so that Steve was not uncomfortable as he drove along, but he was not particularly happy either.

He was reflecting on a dumb thing he had done. He had failed to suggest to Roger Coston that they should use a motel in the upper Bronx or Westchester. That way, the driving would have been a cinch. He just hadn't thought of it in time, and they'd gone ahead and set Didi up in a motel way the hell out in Queens, near Kennedy Airport, which meant he had to drive nearly two hours from his home in Rockland County across the Bronx and then clear across Queens. And then two hours back. Damn. He just hadn't been thinking.

Room 236 at the Skyrider Motel was on the second floor and at the far corner. Steve knocked, and after a brief pause while Elsie looked through the peephole, he was let in. A scene of total chaos surrounded him. Eight cops and federal agents were sitting, standing, and slouching in the two adjoining rooms; shotguns were laid across the beds in each room; paper cups from coffee and Cokes and sandwich wrappings were on every flat surface; cigarette butts were everywhere in ashtrays and dishes; and in the middle of this a two-year-old little girl was the center of attention as she ran, jumped, crawled, and climbed everywhere on furniture and people—Didi's kid, Tania.

Didi came over and greeted him affectionately, and the child ran to him immediately. Didi started to scold her; Steve bent down to talk with her, and she ran away. The press of people in the two rooms seemed heavy, like a dull party that had run its course. Detective Elsie Farrel was there, and Agent Joe Caesare, whom the feds had assigned to help Steve with the tapes. Steve was so new at it himself, though, he didn't know what to tell a helper to do. The other cops and feds were known to Steve only by sight or not at all.

He set up his equipment in the second of the two connecting rooms and ran the first videotape for Didi. Then he ran another, but the atmosphere was distracting and Didi was wondering what this was all about. Steve really wasn't sure how to explain it to her.

The next day, Sunday, was also wasted, in Steve's opinion. He went to church early and arrived at the motel while everybody was slipping into a restless Sunday mood waiting for football games to start on television. Didi's child had thoroughly gotten on everyone's nerves, and Didi was half-apologetic, half-resentful. Steve set up the equipment and actually did try to get her attention onto the tapes, but it was difficult. He gave up early, packed his gear, and went home.

On Monday he went to the office on 57th Street for a sitdown with Roger Coston, Anthony Pohl, and Captain Leonard of the SIU.

He found that Coston had already reached the same conclusion: they had to move Didi out of the motel. In fact, having eight armed cops in two rooms with a woman and baby was really not very safe for any of them—in case of trouble they could end up hurting each other. The motel had been an emergency measure, affording maximum protection for Didi after the Olcott Hotel incident, but renting motel rooms on a daily basis was not likely to sit well with the government's budget officers once the immediate crisis was over. They would have to find Didi an apartment of her own.

That last point squelched Steve's other idea, to get Didi set up in a motel in the Bronx or Westchester, and when he talked with Bill about it afterward, he suddenly found himself laughing.

"Here's a meeting of high-powered government bosses and what are they discussing? Like a bunch of housewives over the back fence, they're discussing Didi's apartment in Queens and, Chrissakes, it's like someone was getting married."

Bill said, "Well, they got to take care of her."

"Protecting her life is the easy part. They got to find an apartment which is nice enough to live in for a while but where the rent is low, the plumbing works, and the shopping is convenient; and they got to get furniture, and dishes, and pillows, and sheets and towels and spoons, and pots and a million little things, and, well—it's what we leave to our wives and the mother-in-law. I'd like to have a tape recording of that discussion. It would be a very funny bit to play later on."

"What about the kid? Must be nice having one around."

"They're getting Didi's mother to come and live there and take care of the kid while I'm working with Didi. Run the house, that sort of thing."

"How's her cooking?" Bill asked. "Let me know if I should come over."

"You like Spanish?"

201

"I don't know. Never tried it."

"Me neither," said Steve.

A week later, Steve reported the meals were fine. It had taken him a few days to get used to it, but now he was trying to get Loretta to fix chicken the way Mrs. Gomez did.

Dolores and her mother had a three-bedroom apartment, with living room and dining area, kitchen and bath, in a twelve-story apartment house off Queens Boulevard. Three agents were on guard at all times, rotating in shifts. Dick Webber, one of the assistant United States attorneys assigned to the case, sat in with them every day while Steve reviewed the videotapes with Didi.

By the start of the second week they had a routine going, and were becoming a tight little family group. The agents and Steve and Webber were all calling Mrs. Gomez "Mom," and Didi's child, Tania, was getting used to having all these men around, as well as Detective Elsie Farrel, alternating with agent Alice Martinson—"Aunt Elsie" and "Aunt Alice." Mrs. Gomez usually had a pot of chicken and rice on the stove or a black-bean soup simmering, and everyone got along fine—except, said Steve, when a couple of the guys forgot to chip in for the grocery bills, and Didi said that was why she liked the cops and hated the agents, because the feds were the ones who were so cheap.

They were even feeling secure enough to go on small excursions outside the apartment—little walks, and then some restaurants, and little shopping expeditions on Queens Boulevard. Didi was transported with delight by the shops, the like of which she had never seen. To her they were fabulous, beautiful, palaces of luxury where customers were treated like queens by the princesses who waited on them. It took Steve a while to visualize this ordinary middle-class shopping neighborhood through the eyes of a young woman born and raised in the ghettos of Harlem and the South Bronx.

For Didi, it was evident, a new world was also unfolding in the postures men and women took toward each other. She had been raised to be tough and smart, to receive rough treatment as well as dish it out. The men of Pleasant Avenue had treated her with more regard than they treated other women; they had accepted her as one of them, almost, but their behavior was harsh and vulgar compared to the treatment she was receiving now. The men around her, the agents as well as Steve and Dick Webber, were courteous and considerate, and even when they laughed and joked together it was with a tone of personal respect. It was amazing to her that in a restaurant, and sometimes even when they ate at the apartment, one or another of them would pull out her chair at the table, or hold her coat when they were preparing to go out. And Steve was charmed at her surprise and delight, and how easily she took to it.

For Washington's birthday, Steve stopped on his way to Queens and bought a large ice-cream cake decorated with a cherry tree, a hatchet, and an American flag. As they gathered around to cut and serve it, Mom said there had been a telephone call for Steve just before he arrived.

Who was it? he asked.

Mom didn't know. One of the agents had taken the call. Steve asked around. Oh, yes, Osborn had taken the call and had said Steve hadn't arrived yet but was due any minute. No, the caller didn't give his name but said he was going to call back.

Steve's heart stopped. He immediately went to the phone and called Coston at the 57th Street office.

He had not given the phone number at the apartment to anyone. No, not even to his wife, no, not even to Bill. Not to anyone.

For a moment there was panic in the apartment. Phone calls

were made. In minutes unmarked police cars started to arrive on the street and detectives were deployed in the halls and on the roof and around the back of the apartment house.

Within forty-five minutes everybody had their coats on, Didi and her mother had thrown a few clothes and toilet articles into small satchels, and Tania had her teddy bear. They left everything else as it was and moved out in a convoy of cars, along back streets to the highway, then eastward out of Queens, scooting along the expressway into Long Island, while the slices of ice-cream cake slowly melted on plates in the kitchen.

# 25

Pleasant Avenue in East Harlem came alive, as always, at precisely 6:30 in the morning. The earliest of the shopkeepers appeared, the man with the pasta belly marched through, and Daniel Iello took up his post in front of the barbershop. The working people started coming out of their homes, the housewives started coming out for shopping, and those among them who were Dan Iello's patrons stopped to greet him and declare their daily number preferences. At eight o'clock, as usual, Angelino arrived to open the luncheonette, "The Head" arrived to open the club over Barone's Bar, "The Mona Lisa" walked across 118th Street while "The Blond" and her three kids noisily crossed 117th Street. But by the time the two sons of Angelino arrived to take up their positions for accommodating the sports bettors, there was the beginning of a change in the street routine.

The gypsy cabdrivers who had the upstairs apartment in the corner building on 118th Street did not make their appearance. One of them used to come in every morning, about eight, and a short time later one used to leave, but they didn't anymore.

Everything else seemed about the same during the morning, the kids running off to school, and the young man coming to open the tavern for the day's business. But there was one other slight change about now, when the superintendent of 320 Pleasant Avenue did not go to open the barbershop next to the tavern. Women and men of the neighborhood moved about as always, the gamblers gathered at their usual time to discuss trends in the day's wagering, and the morning wound down past lunchtime into afternoon, when the gamblers departed.

Then changes were noticeable. Johnny Echoes Campopiano did not appear, even though it was past one-thirty. Georgie did not appear, nor Castellazzo nor other regulars; nor did Moe Lentini, who lived on the avenue across from the tavern, make his appearance, nor, as the afternoon went on, did the congestion of automobiles build up, nor did the parking lot fill up, nor did the stream of irregular visitors come by.

At the Federal Narcotics Bureau office on West 57th Street, phone calls and teletypes had gone out to narcotics agents in Florida, Arizona, southern California, and one or two other states, requesting them to be on the lookout for John Campopiano, Oreste Abbamonte, Thomas Lentini, and a list of others.

At 432 Park Avenue South, the offices of the Drug Intelligence Group were empty. The group had been disbanded, its members reassigned to other units or lent out to work with the feds, and Lieutenant McCrae had been sent into a new headquarters job, recommended for promotion to captain.

In Hartsdale, upstate, the Erwin household was enjoying the unaccustomed treat of having Bill working relatively regular hours, going and coming at about the same time as other daddies on their street. Phyllis was amused to see Bill trying to catch up with neglected winter chores around the house at the same time his neighbors were getting their front and back yards ready for spring, which was just around the corner. She sensed that he didn't expect his regular hours would go on forever, and she was right. For now Bill was still debriefing Primrose Rodman, the British junkie, and he was working on a team with a BNDD agent and a state-police investigator. Debriefing sessions were held daily, in a comfortable Church Street office, with federal marshals escorting Primrose to and from her hotel hideout. But from the leads coming out of those sessions, there was going to be a lot to do very soon, and Bill knew he'd be in on it.

In Nyack, across the Hudson River, the Del Corso household was under the severest strain it had ever known. Loretta felt completely isolated from her husband, and the children seemed to have accommodated to an uneasy schedule of Daddy's not being there, yet not being invisible either. Most mornings Steve was on the road with the earliest of the commuters, driving down the Palisades Highway, over the George Washington Bridge, down the West Side Highway, turning off at the 125th Street exit, passing down Riverside Drive, making a brief stop to pick up a passenger, Dick Webber, at 95th Street, then across town on 125th Street, over the Triborough Bridge, out the Grand Central Parkway, then swinging the interchange onto the Long Island Expressway.

He would be traveling upwards of sixty miles an hour without knowing his destination.

At some point as he tooled along, his car radio would sound off with instructions to leave the expressway at a certain numbered exit and to look for an automobile with a certain license plate. From this moment on he and his passenger would make constant observations in the rearview mirrors on both sides of the car, and Steve would execute a variety of maneuvers: changing speed, changing lanes, occasionally leaving the highway and getting back on it.

At the exit designated by radio, Steve would turn out, notice the car with the designated license plate, drive past it, slow down so it could pass him, and then follow that car.

It would lead him to a motel and then depart. A different motel each day.

Joe Caesare would come out into the parking area and bring

him and Dick Webber to the motel room that was their destination for the day.

Meanwhile, two federal agents would have brought Didi to the same motel in their car, followed by two more agents in a second car. No mention was ever made of where she was living, although from passing remarks and references, Steve could have figured it out if he had tried. Didi sometimes complained of how early she'd had to get up, or how long they'd been on the road, or she mentioned sights she'd seen for the first time in her life that surprised or delighted her—hints that might have added up to her hiding out at a one-story converted farmhouse out toward Montauk, if he had wanted to figure it out.

Each day Steve would transport the video monitor and equipment in his car, set it up in the motel room, and spend six or seven hours with Didi and Dick Webber reviewing the tapes. They had begun with the earliest and were running consecutively through all the hundred and six accumulated during the previous summer, autumn, and winter.

For Steve it was tedious. For Webber it was frustrating. For Didi it became more and more fun.

Steve had been through the tapes several times. There was absolutely nothing new about those characters for him to see.

Webber felt he had material that would convict some dealers, but not the very big ones. Considering that he was an assistant U.S. attorney working on a new technique for prosecuting a case, it didn't look as if he would be accomplishing anything spectacular. There had to be something more in those tapes that could be gotten out of Didi.

Didi enjoyed being the center of the men's attention. In her world, respect was paid to mobsters who were arrogant, made lots of money, and had connections. In the past few months she'd lived a different life. She had met people who had education and power, too, though they didn't make huge amounts of money. They were lawyers, and agents, and cops with special jobs; and they were Jewish, Irish, Italian, Spanish, Greek, and black. In her world, the important people were

Italians; the others were less important or they were nothings. In this world, all kinds of people had importance—and she was the center of their attention. She loved it. Buying junk, for instance, used to be an everyday, ordinary activity for her, but they had carried on as if it was marvelous the way she did it. Before, when she was on her own, she had had to carry a gun in case wise guys tried to cheat her out of a package or heist her for cash. Now she always had at least three bodyguards, like a real bigshot mob boss. She loved it.

And all she had to do all day was watch TV and see herself and her friends. And that was real fun. People she hadn't seen for a long time came on, and she saw things she'd only heard about: the fight between Johnny and Spike—that was terrific— and Moe with his crazy antics, and those broads the guys used to screw around with.

It bothered her that Webber was impatient and disappointed, and Steve she knew was disappointed, but that was because Webber was. She wanted to please them, but what the hell did they want from her?

Webber particularly. He was getting to be a pain in the ass. He explained what he wanted to know, and she told him, but he acted like she wasn't getting it right even when she tried, real hard, to understand him.

Steve tried to please him too. "Look," he would say, "she's identified Armand Cassonia; we've never known what he looks like, and she's picked him out." Another time Steve said, "Look, she's identified Nercessian, 'The Arab,' and we didn't know what he looked like. Now we know."

"Yes," Webber would say, "that's very good. Your guys can start surveillances on them. But it doesn't help the case any."

Steve protested, "They're believed to be very big in junk, very big operators. We now know what they look like, and we know they are tied into Pleasant Avenue. And we've never been able to pin Capra before, or Guarino, and she's made positive identifications of them doing business on Pleasant Avenue."

Webber again spoke with impatience. "So what? She corroborates what we see on film, but for a judge and jury, does it prove beyond doubt they were transacting junk deals? And Zanfardino—when do we see him handing over a package or receiving a payment?"

Steve said, "They never handle it. They got guys to do it for them. Henry Ford makes cars, but you won't see him on the production line."

"So I end up convicting who? Runners. Some dealers. Maybe Abbamonte, who's been taken before. Christ, those guys are strictly expendable, and Pleasant Avenue would be back in operation the next day."

Webber seemed almost bitter. Steve thought of him getting up at dawn to make the long trip, putting in six or eight hours, and then the long trip home. Federal lawyers weren't used to that—but then, neither were detectives. He himself was doing it, so he, too, had to be some kind of nut.

"Let's run this tape again," Webber said.

"Let's play some basketball," Steve said.

"Let's eat," Didi said.

Joe Caesare made a habit of carrying a basketball in his car, and the men used to take a break by throwing it around on whatever play space the motel had, or in the parking lot if that was the only space available.

Didi said, "OK. You guys go play a little ball, I'll take a nap, then we eat, then we run the tape again. OK?"

The agents who escorted Didi back and forth always had the job of scouting the motel restaurant to see how good the food was, or to discover where in the area they could get good sandwiches to bring in. This day they ate sandwiches. As they relaxed in their room unwrapping food, opening plastic containers, and popping cans of drinks, Steve remarked to Webber, "I noticed when we were throwing the ball around your mind was on something else. Was it?"

"I guess so. I know she's trying. It must be my fault. I'm not getting through to her what we need. This is a new procedure, and to tell the truth, I guess I'm not clear myself exactly how to define it."

"Maybe you try too hard questioning her."

"What else can I do? If we don't pin guys at Zanfardino's level, we've put in a huge effort for—you know, the mountain labors and brings forth a mouse."

When they ran the tape again and came to a scene where Armand Cassonia made his appearance, Steve stopped it and asked Didi how she knew it was him when nobody else he knew had any idea what the guy looked like. They were astonished at Didi's reply: "I was out to his house."

"Where?"

"In New Jersey."

"When?"

"When I was going with Gabby. He took me. A bunch of us went to a party. What a place. Everything white, the furniture, the rugs, the curtains and walls."

She smiled at the recollection, and when Steve resumed running the tape, she continued to smile as she commented on the scenes and the people. Then she started laughing.

"It's Johnny," she said, "and Spike."

Johnny Echoes Campopiano came rushing across the screen, picked up a garbage can from the sidewalk, and turned to assault his adversary, Leo "Spike" Guarino, who came at him brandishing a golf club. People came rushing out of stores and houses until it looked like a mob scene.

Guarino was in a rage, Campopiano in a frenzy as they had at each other, while the crowd whooped it up.

"I used to hear about this fight," Didi said.

"What was it about?"

"Money, or a customer, I don't know. I wasn't around, but it must have been great fun, the way they told about it."

She laughed some more, then she said the garbage can had reminded her of the time Campopiano left a package for her in a garbage can.

"Why'd he do that?"

211

"Must have been because Georgie wasn't around. Georgie used to deliver the packages. He'd put them in your car, in the parking lot, or he'd drive the car somewhere, put it in the trunk, and drive back."

"To make sure no cops saw them?"

Didi looked at them both, puzzled. "No," she said, "so that nobody'd see where the stash was. So that nobody'd try to raid them."

As the next tape ran, Didi's mood continued to be bright and gay, her commentary animated. Indeed, the activities on screen did not at all seem serious. She saw Moe Lentini walk down the street in the sunshine carrying two umbrellas unfurled, and was reminded of all the crazy things Moe used to do. Abbamonte borrowed a child's paddle-ball set and played with it, reminding Didi that he was a cheap son of a bitch, never bought when they were out partying.

Then she talked about the partying: how nice Johnny Echoes was, always buying, and how they used to tease Ernie Boy for being cheap and they would all joke when it made him sore.

Then a scene came on that Didi thought could be used in court. Ernie Boy Abbamonte was on the sidewalk handing over a bag of soft white stuff to a man named Angelo, receiving from him a fistful of bills which he proceeded to count while still standing on the sidewalk. Then Ernie Boy turned to an elderly, short, stocky man with gray hair, and handed him some of the money.

Didi explained that the elderly man was Funzie Sisca's father, who lived on the avenue and was always walking his little white Scottie dog on a leash. Steve mentioned he was one of the watchers. Didi said his son, Funzie, was Ernie Boy's brother-in-law. And as long as they were talking about people's relatives, Ernie Boy's mother owned the store next to the barbershop where Jerry hung out, where people went in to see him.

Webber was about to ask something, but Didi spoke out

212

sharply: There was Joe Mack, she hadn't seen him for a long time. He was a real boob, she was through with him and his partner, that louse Nonni. She was making a delivery to them once and the bastard pulls a gun on her! What for? To make sure the deal would go down OK, he said. Thought he was a tough one. What did she do? She pulled her gun on him, said she'd blow his head off if he didn't cut out that shit. He did.

Speaking of guns reminded her of times these Pleasant Avenue guys turned nasty, like when one of them gunned down a stranger because he thought he heard him make a remark to his sister; another time, two of them heard a man in a bar say something about "wops" and chased him in their car. They ran him down, then pumped bullets into him. Didi said she heard that when the police came the killers calmly handed over several thousand dollars and walked away. That was how she'd heard it.

Webber waited for her to finish this story, then went back to something that had occurred to him, about Jerry Zanfardino hanging out in the barbershop where people could come to see him.

"How long do you know Jerry?" he asked.

"Since I was a kid. I used to live on the avenue. He was around lots of the time."

"You knew him to talk to?"

"Well, just hello, when I was a kid. But then when I used to go with Gabby, Gabby knew him to talk to, and I'd be with him."

"But when you grew up? When you were dealing yourself?"

"Well, only to say hello. Jerry's the boss."

"How did you know?"

"Everybody knew."

"How about Inglese, Gigi?"

"He's Jerry's boss."

"How do you know?"

"Everybody knew."

"Did you ever buy from Jerry or Inglese?"

213

"Of course not."

Webber was talking with animation. "Georgie would actually deliver, or one of the other runners, right?"

"Right."

"When Ernie Boy or Johnny told him to?"

"Right."

"Steve, let's put on that reel where Pedro and Didi are double-parked and talking with Moe Lentini, and where Abbamonte comes over."

Webber was humming. When Steve had that segment on, he asked Didi to tell what was happening.

"That's Pedro and me, talking with Moe. Ernie comes over. We wanted to buy a key. He goes to tell Johnny, then he goes with us into the tavern."

"What about Johnny? Why doesn't he go with you into the tavern?"

"He has to speak with Jerry."

"Jerry?"

"Jerry in the barbershop. There, see, he's coming out of the barbershop, and he goes into the tavern. He came to sit with us inside. We had drinks. Johnny said the deal was OK."

"Why'd he have to speak with Jerry?"

"Well, that day we only had half the money in front, and he had to ask Jerry if it was OK."

"But you were buying from Johnny, and Ernie, so why did he ask Jerry—did Jerry give you credit?"

"They always said they had to ask Jerry, even when we had all the money up front."

"Why?"

"Like I said, Jerry's the boss. Everybody knew that."

"Did Jerry always say OK?"

"Lots of times not. Depends on what they got and who's asking, and how much of the bread was up front. They knew I was good for it even when I only had part."

Webber told Steve he wanted to run over every scene that Didi appeared in. As they spoke, the tape was still running.

"Wait a minute!" Didi said. "I never saw her before. It's Moe's girlfriend. So that's what she looks like!"

Steve said, "Quite attractive."

Didi said, "She looks like a whore."

"You don't like him, do you?"

"He's a louse. And he cheats on her. Later on, this same day, they brought in other girls, took 'em into the club over Barone's Bar, for a real sloppy party. Bunch of whores."

Steve was about to turn it off, and go on to the scenes Webber had requested, but Didi said, "Let it run. I heard about these broads but never saw them before."

Didi was enjoying herself again, feeling superior, feeling appreciated by her new associates, the cops, who needed her.


Driving home that night, Steve commented on this new side of Didi, her pride in being needed by them.

Dick Webber agreed. "But don't kid yourself," he said, "she needs us, too. She is reliving parts of her life that must have been hard to take, even if she is a tough baby, and she's reliving her experiences from a vantage point that must be very satisfying to her."

Steve said, "You seem in a good mood now this day is over, a lot different from when it started."

"Steve," said Webber. "I think she's got it."

He began to sing, "The rain in Spain stays mainly in the plai-ain. . . ."

# 26

The finish began suddenly and dramatically, with a shoot-up, raids in the night, and mass arrests. To protect against leaks, false diversionary plans were drawn up and these false plans were subjected to full security. False assignments were made to detectives and supervisors. For newspaper reporters with contacts in the Police Department, a fake inside story was devised, and an informant was hinted at—Jimmy Fats. Months after his exposure as a fake, Jimmy's colorful, knowledgeable, and eccentric "exploits" were duly reported in the press, in magazine articles, and in books written about the Police Department.

As for the real case, its windup was a surprise, even to the cops, agents, prosecutors, and officials who had spent a year preparing for it. The final stage began inadvertently and proceeded irreversibly, almost as if it had a will of its own.

It began at the end of March, with a predawn shoot-up on Second Avenue and 38th Street.

By then the investigation was running smoothly even though

its staff came from various federal and state agencies, and from city police. The secret was its unified line of authority. Anthony Pohl, one of several deputy assistant regional directors of the Federal Bureau of Narcotics and Dangerous Drugs, had requested, some say demanded, complete authority to run it. When first asked would he like to "take the case," he'd replied that as a federal employee he didn't "take" cases, they were "given" to him. Some officials had let it be known they would have liked to be given parts of this complicated case, but Pohl had suggested that whoever was given the case should be responsible for the whole of it. The number of candidates for that assignment suddenly diminished to one.

When the case was placed in his hands, he promptly announced formation of a special group, Tactical Unit Two, and requested the loan of more than 120 police officers, detectives, federal agents, state police, Customs Bureau agents, Internal Revenue agents, and lawyers from the offices of the district attorneys and the special assistant for narcotics cases— and he got them. In New York City, in 1973, the coordination alone was a major accomplishment.

Anthony Pohl had been born of French-Alsatian parents on Manhattan's West Side forty-six years before. He had been educated at French schools and universities, in Strasbourg, Bordeaux, and Lyons. He served with the U.S. Army as a CID investigator, then remained in the European theater of operations when the war against the Nazis ended, and he joined the opening phases of the war against drugs. He worked with the flamboyant narcotics battler Charles Siragusa, who afterward took him to Washington, where Pohl held jobs with the various agencies that succeeded one another in what many regarded as a hopeless battle to restrict narcotics use among Americans.

On March 30, when Pohl had been "generalissimo" over the Pleasant Avenue case for about four months and was meticulously developing precise plans for concluding it, word came of a shoot-up on Second Avenue.

Previously Pohl had had information that Campopiano,

Abbamonte, and others of the Pleasant Avenue crowd had gone to Florida when Didi's activities had leaked. Orders had been cut to request their arrest and extradition.

Suddenly they were accidentally discovered at five o'clock in the morning, partying on their old stamping ground at the Beef East Restaurant in New York, happy as loons, firing guns in the air like television cowboys—Campopiano, Abbamonte, Frank Stasi, Georgie Romano, Alphonse Sisca, John Della Valle, Salvatore Sally Moon Tomasetti, Pasquale Prisco, and Ray Ray Rescildo.

Since no one was hurt when the One-seven Precinct cops came around, except a patrolman who was bitten on the pinkie, the incident was regarded as comic—bigshot mobsters arrested for drunk-and-disorderly conduct.

Pohl read about it in the *Daily News* under the headline SHOTS IN THE DARK BRING BLUES IN THE NIGHT.

His first move was to tease a few subordinates for trying to arrest people in Florida who were having a party in New York. His second move, instantly following, was to start revising his timetable for the windup of the case.

Outwardly, the only thing that seemed to happen was that there was some delay in arraigning the men who'd put on the cowboy act. Somehow, judges were not available that weekend. The nine had been arrested in the early hours of Friday morning, but it was a beautiful spring weekend coming up, so they were told that judges had left work early on Friday, that none were around on Saturday or Sunday, and somehow the paperwork got screwed up at the beginning of the following week. The cops at the One-seven did their best to make them comfortable in the detention cells of the East 51st Street station house, which, fortunately, was in a new, modern building. By then Pohl's timetable was revised.

Steve got word Monday morning while driving with Dick Webber to the usual Long Island rendezvous with Didi. The radio message was different this time. As he went zooming down the Long Island Expressway, he was told to turn around and head back to the city. He and Dick were to report to their offices.

Didi and her convoy, also en route to the motel rendezvous at that moment, were redirected to a small county airport near Riverhead, where a NYPD helicopter was waiting. She and two federal agents were flown to the helicopter pad in lower Manhattan, transferred to a two-car convoy, and taken to the U.S. Courthouse in Foley Square.

A couple of blocks north, in the State Supreme Court Building, a grand jury of the State of New York was in session and the special assistant for narcotics cases was presenting drug charges against nine recent patrons of the Beef East Restaurant. Indictments were voted, Campopiano, Abbamonte, and Georgie Romano were rearrested, and now there were plenty of judges around for the arraignment. Bail was set in amounts up to half a million dollars.

"That will keep them out of circulation for a while," Bill said when Steve caught up with him at the office on West 57th Street.

"What else is new?" Steve asked.

"Nobody says anything, but I suspect we are rolling down the homestretch."

"I'm glad we're not making a lifetime career out of this case."

"They've got me and about twenty-five guys working up folders on those characters. We're only doing one or two each, and the daily message is hurry up."

"What are the folders for?"

"For the lawyers, they say, in the U.S. attorney's office."

"So maybe a couple attorneys there are going to have lifetime careers prosecuting our gang from Pleasant Avenue."

"Who knows? I'm sick of it. This paperwork, I've had my bellyful of, for a long time. When I finish my two folders, I am asking for a transfer."

"What about the leak?" Steve asked. "You want to leave before we find him?"

"The answer will have to come off the telephone tracings, and Lieutenant Bransla is on that," Bill said. "What've they got you doing?"

"I don't know yet. I've turned in the videotapes and the video equipment that I've been dragging around every day for a month. I feel a hundred pounds lighter, just knowing I'll never see any of that stuff again."

A great calm settled over the nineteenth floor of the office building at 57th Street and Tenth Avenue, but the beginnings of a frenzy were felt on the eighteenth floor. Federal agents and city detectives were being pulled in and told to stand by. Steve was told to report there, and Bill was sent along as soon as he finished his folders. An intelligence report, it was rumored, had come in from Bangkok that a large shipment of Southeast Asian heroin was about to be landed in New York and that its destination was Chinatown in lower Manhattan. Agents and detectives were being briefed in small groups for raids, arrests, and seizures. Security rules were so tight the various units had difficulty coordinating with each other. As a result there seemed to be an extraordinary amount of discussion, and lots of feeling that the operation was bumbling. The bosses seemed to feel uncertain, too, since after several announcements and cancellations they kept delaying the signal for launching the Chinatown raids.

Friday morning, some groups were sent into position in lower Manhattan station houses to await further orders. In the afternoon there was another delay, so further surveillances could be conducted in Chinatown. Two helicopters were sent up on surveillance. Meanwhile, more agents and detectives were asked to come in and stand by at the feds' regional headquarters on West 57th Street.

By then the intelligence report from Bangkok was widely known; everybody was talking about the long, secret telegram that had come in from the American ambassador. By evening more than two hundred agents and detectives were crowded in the large eighteenth-floor conference room. At eleven P.M. Tony Pohl entered the room, accompanied by First Deputy Police Commissioner Arthur McNeil and Captain Dan Leonard.

Pohl announced immediately that they should forget the Chinatown raid completely; it was a fake-out. In actuality, the federal grand jury had been in almost around-the-clock session and had handed up indictments of eighty-six drug dealers. Second, they were about to take part in a massive roundup of these dealers that would be carried out simultaneously in all five boroughs of New York City, in New Jersey, in Connecticut and counties outside New York, and in other places as far away as Washington and Detroit. Some dealers were already in custody.

Third, he announced, they were being divided into teams of four or more, and each team would be given a folder of information on the drug dealer it was to bring in. They would be given one hour in which to study their folders, and then they were to get going. Some would go out a second time, and perhaps a third.

They were to bring their prisoners to the 57th Street building and take them up by freight elevator to space that had been prepared to hold them securely.

Shotguns, sledgehammers, rifles, bulletproof jackets, and other special varieties of equipment would be issued in accordance with the estimated needs of each team. A contingent of men would be held in reserve to dash in and assist wherever help became necessary. Each team was to keep in constant radio communication with headquarters as it progressed.

Pohl himself would control the operation from a special command center on the nineteenth floor, with several men standing by as aides. He'd be monitoring the raids through the night, and would report progress to them by radio from time to time.

He said at least 250 men and women were participating in

222

this night's work, in New York and other places. He then introduced Arthur McNeil.

McNeil's voice was charged with emotion. "This is an historic night," he said. "It will be a landmark in the future of American law enforcement. Many of you have worked in narcotics a long time but you could not have even dreamed such a thing could happen as is about to happen tonight. Now you know we have eighty-six indictments, but you are going to be shocked at the names of those to be arrested tonight—people who were confident they could not be arrested, and who were thought to be impervious to arrest by many in law enforcement itself. But no longer.

"Many," he continued, "are killers, and will not hesitate to hurt you to get away. One has a machine gun and will not hesitate to use it. Many have world-wide connections where they would find welcome and sanctuary if they could escape. They shall not escape.

"When tonight's work is done, you will tell your colleagues and your wives and your children about it, and in years to come you will be proud to say 'I was there.' Good luck and God bless you." He sat down, and heavy silence filled the room.

As Captain Dan Leonard started making assignments and announcing the names of each team's target, there were, as McNeil predicted, gasps of surprise from cops and agents who had not been at the center of the investigation. Folders were handed around. The "Chinatown raid" fakeout was a great joke but they didn't have time to enjoy it.

Each folder contained background on one dealer, and indicated where resistance might be expected. The teams that were briefed to expect resistance were instructed to draw special weapons and request extra manpower from the reserve contingent. Shortly after midnight, all the teams began moving out and continued to do so through the night, to surround bars, private clubs, apartments, private houses in the suburbs.

In the nineteenth-floor command center, large paper charts

covered an entire wall. That wall contained the only existing map showing what this night's work was about.

The drug dealers who conducted business from Pleasant Avenue were all named in a display of boxes that showed their relative importance and their connections. But that was only the centerpiece of the entire display.

There were five such groupings, networks of dealers headed by John Capra, Herbert Sperling, Gennaro Zanfardino, Louis Inglese and Joseph Cappuccilli of New Jersey.

The eighty-six indicted dealers were ranged in configurations around these five, and dotted lines marked interconnections between the networks.

Pohl entered the room with McNeil and the others, slammed the door locked, turned on the closed-circuit television, opened the radio channels, and switched on a large coffeemaker.

Over the radio channels he would be able to hear the teams as they moved on their missions, and make sure prompt support was rushed in if unexpected problems arose.

On the closed-circuit television he could monitor the prisoners as they were brought into the building, to be held until the roundup was completed. By holding them temporarily in a huge office building on the western edge of the city, he would reduce the chance of anybody tipping others on the list.

By 2:30 A.M. the first of the prisoners were being brought in. At about that time Bill was leading a team of two agents and two detectives down East 118th Street to a building several doors from Pleasant Avenue. They rang a bell, knocked on a door, announced they were police officers with warrants for Frank Bassi and Antoinette Bassi. The arrest was made quietly and the prisoners were swiftly transported to the West 57th Street office building.

Some teams did not have it that easy. A large force assembled at the 32nd Precinct and then rushed the Purple Manor Bar on 125th Street. The place was crowded with patrons, and the police found several handguns on the floor, but the man they were looking for was not there. Their folder had a list of other places he frequented, and they went off to check them out one by one.

In an Upper West Side apartment, the residents would not answer the police knock so they sledgehammered the door open. Inside they found a woman and child and an open window leading to a fire escape. The man had escaped. They too had a list of places he frequented and went along to check them out. Lawsuits would be settled later.

Steve's team headed for Bachelors III on Lexington Avenue, one of the favorite bars of the Pleasant Avenue dealers. His team's assignment was Gennaro Zanfardino, and Friday night was Zanfardino's night on the town. As the team drove into the neighborhood at about 12:30 in the morning, they noticed other unmarked cars of agents and detectives, some standing at the curb and some cruising. "Looks like a convention," one of the agents in Steve's car remarked.

The bar had been staked out earlier when reports were phoned in that Delacava and Lentini were also spending the evening there. With the three teams converging on this one bar, all of them became cautious of tripping over one another. Even more serious was the possibility if they went in and made arrests, somebody in the bar might get to a phone and send out an alarm to others around town.

Team members consulted with each other and decided to wait until their quarries left the bar and could be picked up alone. A detective on surveillance inside the bar reported to headquarters that he had seen Zanfardino pass an envelope to the young woman who appeared to be spending the evening with him.

About 2:30 A.M. Zanfardino and the young woman left the bar, after one of the waiters came outside to get them a taxi. They were in the cab and on their way before Steve's team could intercept them, but they went only as far as 38th Street, and entered the Beef East Restaurant.

About two hours later they came out and got into a taxi, again obtained for them by a waiter, then headed for the

Tudor Hotel on East 42nd Street. Here Steve's team closed in and arrested Zanfardino.

Steve watched while Zanfardino was handcuffed and placed in the second car used by their team. Zanfardino's young woman friend slipped back into their taxi, but one of the agents ordered the driver to stay put. He asked the young woman to allow him a look into her pocketbook. She became frightened, showing signs of hysteria. Clutching her pocketbook in her arms, she fiercely refused to yield it and screamed he should not touch her. He seemed surprised and shaken by her outburst, and may have been overcome by fatigue—some of the men had been on duty now for more than thirty hours. He started to walk away. Steve walked over to the young woman, leaned in, and snatched the purse from her hands. He motioned her out of the taxicab and into his car. Two agents got in as well, and they followed the first car taking Zanfardino to the 57th Street headquarters.

While agents hustled Zanfardino inside, Steve called Elsie Farrel to take charge of the young woman. The envelope Zanfardino had given her was still in her purse and it held a sheaf of large bills—$5,000 worth, it later turned out. They took her inside and notified the command center they had an extra person in custody.

By then it was past five A.M., and the first dozen prisoners had already been brought in. Reports were coming over the radio of others on the way, but many would not be in hand until later in the day. John Capra, for instance, was at home in New Rochelle, in a closet, hiding from the police who came to get him.

He explained later that his daughters had had some friends visiting and he had stalled until they left the house because he did not want them to see him being arrested.

* * *

In all, sixty-five men and women were arrested that night and over the weekend. Sixteen more of those indicted were already in jail on previous charges, and another five became fugitives, picked up afterwards. The investigation had been so well coordinated, that trials were scheduled to start before the end of June.

Bill told Phyllis they'd soon be living a normal life now that the investigation was finished. He and Steve put in for assignment to the Bronx burglary squad, where they'd have normal working days and could travel home in about an hour.

But first, Bill had just one more thing to do. He had to work up a complete summary of the police surveillance records for the prosecutors, with copies going to the defense attorneys, who were entitled to see all evidence collected by the prosecution. There was a lot of it. Pleasant Avenue had been under surveillance for six months, with four to ten men collecting information all day long every day.

Bill had let everybody who cared to listen know how much he hated paperwork, but he was thought to be the detective most familiar with the records, so that was it.

"It's a fucking mountain of paperwork to plow through," he said to Steve.

"But you have only to plow through it, not carry it on your back. Look at me. I used to be a detective, now I'm a goddamn truck horse."

By trial rules, the defendants were also entitled to see all 113 videotapes before the trial. The court had ordered that they be shown at once so as not to delay the trial. Steve was the detective most familiar with them, so he was the logical person to catch the assignment. Since some of the defendants were in jail, and others out on bail, the court ordered that the screenings be held in the jailhouse.

On May 31 Steve started all over again, carrying a carton of videotapes, a television monitor, a playback deck, and a bundle of cables to and from daily showings.

Bill reminded him of the day he had said with pleasure that he felt a hundred pounds lighter because he'd never see any of that stuff again.

That day had been April 1.

# 27

Steve checked his gun at the control booth inside the door at the West Street jail, hefted the TV monitor, the playback deck, the bundle of cables, and the box of videotapes, and passed through one iron gate, then a second, into the interior hallway.

Behind him the tiny booths where lawyers interviewed clients were empty. To his right, the prison psychiatrist's office was empty. At the end of the hall, in the alcove he'd been told to use, five men waited on chairs.

He knew them: Campopiano, Abbamonte, Zanfardino, Lentini, and Georgie Romano.

Several impressions struck him at once. The alcove was very small, no more than six by ten. There were no prison guards in sight. As soon as he entered the alcove, he'd be out of the line of sight of anyone who might have business in the interview booths or the psychiatrist's office. The TV equipment, cables, and carton he was carrying severely restricted his freedom of movement. His gun was back at the entrance control booth. The men waiting for him in the alcove knew the evidence against them was heavy. Instinctively, he was measuring his responses in case any one of them made a move.

As he stepped into the alcove, he said "Good morning" quietly. They knew why he was there, so there was no need for him to say anything more. There was a desk standing by the far wall, but there was not enough room for him to position the desk between them and him. He eased the equipment he carried onto the desk and they watched him hook up the equipment. He tried not to turn his back to them, but he didn't want to provoke them, either, by seeming to be on his guard.

Then, as he reached for the first reel, the oppressiveness of the atmosphere seemed to lift.

He knew them, but they didn't know him. Carrying the equipment, weighed down by all that baggage, he must look like a flunky of the court or the prosecutor's office. He didn't have to tell them he was to be a key witness. They'd find that out soon enough. For now he would let them think he was only the slob who dragged in the equipment and put the reels of videotape on the machine. Meanwhile he'd be figuring some way of reducing the almost total vulnerability that had given him a turn when he first walked in.

He started the first reel of tape and watched their faces as they watched the video screen. He saw no hostility in their eyes, and he decided that what danger there might be would come from another direction. These men were used to having flunkies do their dirty work. The West Street jail surely held lots of inmates who would be only too willing for such an assignment, to gain the favor of bigshot mobsters, for promises of assistance in getting out, or for a place on the pad, or both. He had no doubt that the murder of a cop could be managed if they wanted. West Street was that sort of a place.

The Federal House of Detention on West Street was notorious, probably best known in the early 1970's for the escapes that seemed to occur regularly. It was a plain three-story concrete-block box of a building, faced by windows with rusted bars and by air-conditioning vents. After escapes, the press would quote unnamed officials as supposing that the fugitives had tied bedsheets together and slid down through the air-conditioner ducts. Knowledgeable prisoners were said to be able to quote prices for a key to the back door. The price varied according to the importance or resources of the individual to be accommodated.

Evidently Campopiano, Abbamonte, Romano, and Lentini had heard about the tapes and were curious about them. They watched in silence as the first reel began, and then suddenly the silence was broken.

Campopiano recognized himself on the screen and let out a whoop. From then on the jokes came thick and fast. They made fun of each other, nagged at each other's peculiarities of behavior, strove to top each other's laughing insults, meanwhile letting go with friendly punches, pokes, and slaps.

Evidently they knew the tapes were going to be used to destroy any alibis or denials they might offer in court, so each rubbed the other's nose in his compromising behavior. "Hey, Moe, you got your laundry in that bag?" one would ask at the sight of Lentini walking across the screen with a bag of soft white material dangling at his side.

"Must be first of the month—Ernie Boy's paying his rent," another would say at the sight of Abbamonte standing at the curb with a thick packet of bills in his hand, counting them and handing some to Campopiano. At the sight of Romano walking from the parking lot to the tavern, one would say, "Looks like Georgie's going for a pizza."

By the time Steve was running the last videotape of the day, they were including him in their horseplay, and by the next morning when he came in with a fresh supply of tapes they were using him as the foil for their jokes. In the scene where Moe Lentini appeared carrying two open umbrellas though the day was clear, Campopiano asked Steve if he thought Moe could get off by pleading insanity. "He is crazy, you know, crazy," and they all laughed. As Campopiano counted a fistful

231

of bills on the sidewalk with Abbamonte watching, Lentini shouted at Steve, "They should ask you to watch he makes an honest count."

Steve was relieved the tension had eased, and joined in their laughter. By then Campopiano had asked his name and was starting to call him "Steve."

As the day's session drew to a close Campopiano asked Steve what his job was. When he said "Detective," there was an abrupt change in the atmosphere. He felt four pairs of eyes boring in on him.

He packed his gear. He hefted it in both hands and under his arms, walked out of the alcove and down the hall to the exit. He knew he would find out what they were thinking soon enough.

He passed through the two guarded gates and stopped at the entrance booth to claim his gun. As he bent to pick up the television monitor he had rested on the ground, Moe Lentini was beside him, having come through the gates after he had. Steve could not conceal his surprise. Moe laughed softly in his crazy way.

"Let me help with that stuff," he said. He stood there while Steve considered. "I'm out on bail, you know. I just came to see the show."

Steve indicated the television monitor. "I'm parked around the corner," he said.

Lentini carried it, walking beside him, and as they came up to Steve's car, Lentini said, "That yours?" in a tone that made the car seem shabbier than it had been before.

Steve said "Yes" as he opened the trunk. "It's no Toronado Special."

With exaggerated care Lentini placed the television in the trunk and looked at Steve with new interest. He knew from that remark that Steve had done surveillance on Pleasant Avenue. Lentini said, "No, it's not, but maybe that's your fault."

Steve said, "Thanks for the help," closed the trunk lid, and as he drove off, wondered if this was a beginning.

They started to reach for him next morning.

As he was changing tapes, Lentini asked, "Is that film flammable?"

Steve said he thought it probably was, but that the police had copies. A little later, Campopiano asked where the tapes were kept. Steve said in a locker at the office.

Next day Abbamonte was the inquisitive member of the audience. He asked how the tapes were stored, and who had the key to the locker. Steve said he had the only key, and Campopiano asked to see it. Steve took it out of his pants pocket and held it in his palm. Campopiano deliberately reached over and took it.

He studied it as if it were a rare jewel, rubbing it in his fingers, and said, "I'll bet that key is worth a lot of money, a lot of money."

"I don't really know." Steve laughed. "Maybe I'll hold an auction."

Abbamonte said, to no one in particular, "He wouldn't have to hold an auction. He could name his own price."

Campopiano handed the key back with elaborate reluctance as he said, "That's the key to my whole life, that key."

On his way home that evening, Steve stopped off to talk with Dick Webber at the U.S. attorney's office.

"I think they are going to make an offer," he said. Webber listened to him repeat the snatches of conversation and told him to be careful not to say anything that might afterward be called entrapment. Webber said they better go talk with his boss, Phil Wallace, head of the group of U.S. attorneys specializing in narcotics cases. They arranged to have a couple of the attorneys give Steve a cram course in the law of entrapment so he could steer clear of it.

In the days that followed, Campopiano asked about police salaries; Abbamonte expressed concern about whether Steve had a lot of bills piled up.

Lentini, out on bail, had stopped attending the daily viewing of tapes after the first few days. Zanfardino, too, was out on bail and had attended showings during the first two days only. Now both came in for a day's showings.

Steve had the feeling they had come to look him over. Now the pressure was getting to him. He'd been going continuously seven days a week, getting up early, getting home late at night. He told Webber he needed a couple of days off, and suggested that Bill take his place showing the tapes.

When Steve came back to work after his days off, Bill was waiting for him in the office where the videotapes and screening gear were kept.

"Why didn't you tell me?" Bill asked.

"What's to tell?" Steve said. But he knew what Bill meant.

"They're going to reach for you."

"You think so?"

"It's as plain as the ..." Bill stared searchingly at his partner. Steve wondered why he was reacting so seriously.

"How do you know?" Steve asked.

"From the way they acted when they heard I was your partner. When I started running the tapes, they were quiet and bored. After a while Johnny Echoes asks who I am, what I do, have I been working this case, how long I know you."

"You told them?"

"Why not? Anyway, they all perked up. When I said we had both worked in narcotics—and I said I had worked in SIU, so they assumed that you had, too, I guess—they started asking questions about you. What kind of a guy are you, can you be trusted, did you ever get in any trouble."

"What'd you say?" Steve was still not clear on why Bill was so serious.

"Oh, that you were OK, natch. I gave you a very good reference." He was smiling. "That you can be trusted. You know the score. And you keep out of trouble." His eyes were fixed on Steve's face.

Steve looked solemn. "Could be a lot of bread there." Then

he laughed and said, "You don't think"—he paused dramatically—"that I'd leave you out?"

Bill laughed, then turned serious again. "Don't be a jerk. I know you, and what you think you're into. Playing that game could be dangerous."

"Don't you think we can handle it?"

"We?"

"You wouldn't want to miss out on it, would you, partner? It's not all that dangerous."

Bill said evenly, "I'm not talking about danger from the mob. I'm talking about guys in the department who hate straight arrows, and who'll put the word around that you took."

"Fuck them. I've already talked with Webber and Wallace, and we'll keep clean. But actually, it could be dangerous. Nothing like a double cross to make the wiseguys violent."

The next time Steve arrived with his tapes at the West Street jailhouse, Campopiano called out, "Hey, Steve, I'd like to mail you a Jew bomb." Steve asked what he meant, and he explained with a laugh, "It explodes. In a letter, it explodes."

Steve asked, with mock fright, "You want to do away with me?"

"Not for you," Campopiano said. "You could put it in with the films to explode. You could."

There was laughter all around, but on June 17 the joking and horseplay subsided. When he came in that morning there was an ominous atmosphere in the alcove. Soon after the first tape was started, Georgie Romano left the alcove and stood a short distance down the hall. Campopiano went to stand at the entrance to the alcove. Abbamonte looked squarely into Steve's face and said: "If you wanted to help us in this case—get rid of

235

the original tapes, and the copies—you could name your own price."

Steve said nothing, stared back at him for a long moment, then winked, half-smiled, and turned away and made a pretense of adjusting the machines.

That evening he stopped off at Assistant U.S. Attorney Phil Wallace's office. "Before, I thought it was coming. Now, it's here," he told Phil, and he described the incident. Talk to Pohl, Phil told him.

In his office on West 57th Street, Anthony Pohl listened impassively to Steve's account and told him what he wanted done. He searched Steve's face as he talked, looking for signs of fear or of undue excitement that might make his judgment unreliable.

"You know what you're getting into?" Pohl said.

"I think so."

Every day, Steve was to be outfitted with a body radio transmitter, called a Kel. It was the size of a pack of cigarettes and was strapped to his leg inside the thigh, wrapped in Ace bandages. A wire ran up to his chest where a microphone was attached with surgical tape.

A backup team of undercover federal agents, marshals, and city detectives was organized for his protection. He was no longer to go into West Street alone, and he was to report each day's developments to Pohl personally.

He stopped off in Bill's office and let him know. "I told Pohl I wanted you with me. If you don't mind wearing a wire, that is. It takes the hair off your chest. You think you can make up some explanation for Phyllis?"

Next day, June 18, was uneventful, but Bill was tense. Now that they knew the bribery attempt was serious, Bill was experiencing the anxieties Steve had had on his first day—checking his gun at the entrance, walking past the iron gates, going down a hall to a secluded alcove to be with four men who faced long prison sentences and had an unknown number of allies whom they could summon inside the building.

236

His anxiety centered on the easy familiarity that had grown up between the dealers and Steve. They had a habit of slapping, poking, and punching people they were friendly with, and an unexpected touch could reveal that Steve or Bill was wired.

On June 19 Campopiano asked Steve if he owned any property upstate. The answer was no. "You help us beat this case," said Campopiano, "and you could have a nice piece of property upstate, for you and your kids, or anything else you may want."

Steve said, "What could you do for me from in here?"

"All you have to do is say the word and everything could be arranged right from in here," Campopiano said.

On June 20 the atmosphere seemed very relaxed until Georgie was sent out of the alcove and up the hall again. Campopiano stood in the alcove entrance and Abbamonte said, "Come on, Steve, you know you can help us beat this case if you put your mind to it. What's it worth to you?"

Steve said, "What do you want me to do?"

"Get rid of all the tapes. What's it worth to you?"

"What's it worth to *you?*"

"Twenty-five thousand dollars."

Steve said, "Well, I'd need help to do it."

"Fifty thousand dollars."

"I don't know. I think it's worth more than that. Anyway, I don't feel like talking in here. It's not safe."

Abbamonte said, "Let me make a few phone calls tonight. I'll see how much we can get together."

"Maybe we'll talk tomorrow—on the way from court."

On June 21 the defendants were ordered to appear in court and Steve arranged for himself and Bill to transport Abbamonte and Campopiano back to West Street when they were through. As soon as they were in the car and on their way, Abbamonte said, "We could put together two hundred thousand dollars if you can get rid of the tapes, the originals and the copies, and all other evidence."

Steve did not doubt he was telling the truth. Evidently Ernie Boy had found a way to make his "few phone calls" from the prison, and in privacy.

Abbamonte asked, "Do you think we could beat the case?" He was including the two detectives in his "we."

Steve had difficulty believing all this was real—that he was actually being offered a huge sum of money for becoming a colleague of these people. He felt he was playacting when he answered, "Yes, I think so, you could. Don't you think so, Bill?"

He was driving with Abbamonte beside him in the front seat. Bill was in the back with Campopiano, and he now said, "Yes, if someone got rid of the tapes and other evidence. Your only other problem then would be the witness."

Abbamonte said, "You could hit her for that price, too."

The unreality struck Steve even harder: he was being asked to kill Didi. He started to say calmly, "You want us—"

Bill cut in over his voice and said, "You want us to hit her, the deal's off. We don't hit for nobody."

Steve, surprised, glanced at Bill in the rearview mirror and thought he caught a signal. He didn't understand, but he said, "Right!" and gave Abbamonte a dirty look. "We want no part of that."

"OK, OK, we take care of the hit on her."

When the prisoners had been checked back in, Steve asked, "What was that all about? I was going to say we'd do the hit. It's only talk, you know that."

"Don't you think they'd know it too? They were just testing, to see how far you'd go. You go too far or too fast, it looks phony. They must be still wondering if they can trust us. They think we gotta be figuring can *we* trust *them*."


That afternoon, Zanfardino and Lentini appeared at a tape screening for the first time in nearly two weeks. As soon as a tape was in place and turned on, Zanfardino and Lentini went with Campopiano and Abbamonte into a corner of the alcove, and Abbamonte said in a loud whisper, "We made an agreement with them. It's going to cost two hundred thousand dollars."

Zanfardino held up two fingers and soundlessly mouthed the words "Two hundred thousand?"

Abbamonte said, "Yes, it has to be."

Bill and Steve were sweating. Zanfardino's actions—not speaking certain words aloud, and holding up fingers—meant that he was wary of eavesdropping devices. He was a wily old man, they thought, smarter than his cronies; he might even tell them to check the detectives out for wires.

But he did not. Instead he asked in a whisper, "What about the girl?"

Abbamonte said, "They want no part of her."

Zanfardino, looking at Steve, said, "OK." Then, looking at Campopiano and Abbamonte, he said, "But she's got to go."

Abbamonte walked away and the other two continued to talk in whispers until Campopiano went over to Steve and Bill and said quietly, "OK, everything will be set up for the money."

Next day the videotapes ran continuously, but nobody paid attention. While Georgie Romano did guard duty, the others discussed terms and choice of a go-between. Steve and Bill had never done business with them before, so there was no mutually trusted middleman to call in. They argued over terms. Campopiano wanted to pay $50,000 down. Steve demanded a full half of the money up front. Abbamonte wanted them to name a crooked cop who'd vouch for them, and Bill said they had to be crazy. "You think we'd bring a crooked cop into this? How do we know you're not trying to set us up to get yourselves off the hook?"

All the detectives' years of experience playacting roles came into use. Steve acted irritable and constantly flew off the handle. Bill acted the reasonable member of the pair. Steve would scream at them, call them bastards and chiselers and crooks, then Bill would jump in to calm everybody down and reason with Steve. Both of them hoped to forestall suspicion by taking the offensive and frequently accusing the dealers of trying to set them up.

June 23. Time was running out. Once the tapes had all been screened, there would be no reason for them to meet, no way to talk freely. One unresolved question was the go-between, and they wouldn't name a crooked cop. Bill had an idea.

"Joe Sparrow," he said to Steve.

"Who?"

"You remember Joe Sparrow. Didn't you used to work with him?" They were talking in a corner while a tape ran on the machine.

Steve had it. "Joe Sparrow, Joe Chicken—Joe Sporaccio was his real name. Yes, when I was a kid, we both worked in a fur factory."

"What about him for a go-between? If they know him."

"Hey," Steve called over to Campopiano, "you know Joe Sparrow?"

"Yeah. You know Joe Sparrow?" When Steve nodded, Campopiano said to Abbamonte, "He knows Joe Sparrow, he knows."

"Who?"

"Guy who has the pet shop on Third Avenue, the pet shop."

"That's good," said Abbamonte, and he joined Campopiano in a corner for a whispered conversation.

Several hours later they seemed to have communicated with someone on the outside. Abbamonte said to the detectives, "Go there tomorrow."

"It's Sunday," Steve said.

"Yeah. Sunday. Two o'clock. The money will be there."

"How much?"

"The whole fifty thousand dollars."

Steve reared back and screamed, "Bastards! The deal's off."

Abbamonte shushed him. "All right, all right, the whole hundred."

Zanfardino and Lentini came by a little later. Campopiano told them about the arrangement for the go-between, Joe Sparrow.

"Who?"

"The guy from the pet shop on Third Avenue."

"Oh, him! OK."

Bill and Steve drove to Joe's Pet Shop on Sunday at two o'clock. It was closed.

# 28

"You think they don't trust us?"

"Maybe they're trying to set us up?"

"You think Sporaccio queered it?"

"I don't know. He used to like me."

"When's the last time?"

"Couple of years ago, when he was dropped on a small charge of drug pushing. Before that I hadn't seen him since the fur factory. I was just out of high school when I worked there. Even then he was dabbling a little with junk."

"How'd he act when he saw you as a cop?"

"Very friendly. Glad to have a friend on the force. Absolutely no hard feelings."

"What do we do now?"

"We continue showing the tapes."

"It's Sunday."

"So what? We are under court orders to show all tapes as soon as possible so as not to delay the trial. Sunday's just another day, and we're here."

"Should we go in wired? If they're suspicious, they may try to pat us down."

"Let's call whoever is in charge of the backup squad today and alert him. We could have him listen for a code signal in case of trouble and send the guys in for us."

"In case of trouble we could be finished off before they get there."

"Let's go show tapes."

They went to West Street, told the duty officer to notify the defendants that they would be showing videotape evidence in the alcove, and plugged in the equipment. Steve put a reel on, saying nothing, his face expressionless. They were both sweating. Bill took a casual stance facing the dealers, with a measured distance so he could pick up the television monitor as a weapon if a move was made.

Romano left the alcove and stationed himself down the hall.

Abbamonte said, "Hi ya, fellas."

Steve said, "Fuck off."

Campopiano, looking distressed, said, "Something's wrong."

"Son of a bitch," Steve said. "The place was closed."

"We had a little problem, we had. The money will be there tomorrow."

"Screw. Forget it. We want no part of you. There's no deal."

Campopiano seemed genuinely distressed. "Ernie Boy's father came to see him. Then he had to go see Joe Sparrow. Joey said he knows you."

"So he knows me. That's what I told you."

Abbamonte said, "It's there, it's there." He seemed almost pleading, on the verge of hysteria. "You could get it all, tonight, eight, nine o'clock!"

The detectives walked away from him without replying.


They stopped at a Tenth Avenue diner for coffee on the way home.

"Bullshit," Bill said.

"You think they're suspicious?"

"I think they are jerking us around because they're reaching for someone else. They got a friend in the department who'll work cheaper than us."

"What could anyone do for them? The feds control the tapes, and we're the only cops with access."

"How would they know that for sure? Matter of fact, how would we know it for sure?"

Steve thought for a moment. "Let 'em try. They'll come back, unless they're suspicious."

First thing next morning they were talking with Tony Pohl. Thinking about it overnight, each of them had come to the conclusion they should go on with it. Steve said he thought the dealers were not suspicious, that the pet-shop owner had probably said that he did know Steve, and they had probably taken that to mean that Steve was a crooked cop. Pohl said he would order the backup team to deploy into positions around the pet shop. They could continue to work on it, but carefully, carefully.

They left the feds' 57th Street office and decided they'd check out the scene at Joe's shop, just have a look. It was a beautiful June morning, and under a clear blue sky even Third Avenue and 110th Street looked freshly laundered. They felt like this was going to be a good day.

They got there at ten o'clock and Joe was just opening the shop. Steve was wearing his Kel radio transmitter strapped to his leg. They pulled up curbside and called Joey over to them.

Steve asked, "Anybody leave something for us?"

Sporaccio was a tall, skinny, nervous man of about forty; he couldn't seem to stop talking and chattering, and he stuttered. He constantly made birdlike movements, which was why people always called him Joe Sparrow or Joe Chicken. He'd grown up in the East Harlem neighborhood and had been arrested several times on narcotics charges. His pet shop was small and probably doubled as a numbers drop; it looked unkempt and cheap, but had a fairly extensive stock of merchandise, including exotic birds, fish, and animals.

Joey was acting nervous now, but they couldn't tell if it was his normal behavior or if he had some special anxiety. He said he'd been told that someone had some birdseed for Steve, but that was all he knew. Someone had asked if he knew Steve, but he'd figured maybe someone was just throwing Steve's name around, so he hadn't bothered to show up on Sunday. He said he would try to contact the people with the birdseed, and Steve could phone him around two o'clock. When Steve phoned at two, he said he hadn't heard yet; Steve should call him at six.

At six he said yes, Steve could come to his shop at ten after seven. When Steve and Bill drove up, he came out of his shop quickly and talked nervously.

"Gigi wants to see you."

"Gigi?"

"You know Gigi?"

"Yeah, what's with Gigi?"

"You should meet him at the hotel coffee shop on 86th Street and Madison. You know Gigi?"

"Sure, Fat Gigi Inglese," Steve said, and he exploded with a put-on show of anger to cover his puzzlement at this development. "What is it with those bastards! We're supposed to meet with you, Joey, nobody else! What the hell goes on?"

He kept his voice down, but his manner made Sporaccio tremble. At the same time, Joey was terrified of crossing Inglese.

He was chattering, "I don't know, don't know what goes on. He wants to meet you—you gotta do it—Gigi's the main one kicking in!"

Bill said, "When are you supposed to see Gigi again?"

"He's supposed to come by my store at eight-thirty."

"You tell him to wait, we'll be back at eight-forty."

"We're not going to make a meet on 86th Street while our

246

backup guys are set up at 110th Street," Steve said. They were driving around to kill time until 8:40.

Bill said, "I hope they were set up and working just now."

"We could call in and find out. If they're not set up yet, they've still got an hour before the meet."

"That's not so good, if they weren't there when we were talking with Joey," Bill said.

"Why?"

"He just put Inglese's neck in a noose. Let's find out if we can keep it there."

Steve called their communications base and was connected with Pohl, at his home. Steve apologized for intruding, but he had thought Pohl would like to know that they had a tape tying Louis Inglese into the conspiracy—if the backup team at the pet shop had picked up the signal from the Kel radio transmitter he was wearing. He repeated Joey's remark about Gigi being the main one kicking in, and Pohl assured him the backup team had been in place since late afternoon.

Steve repeated this to Bill, who then said, "Now only one thing to worry about—was your Kel working?"


At 8:38 they pulled up across the street from the pet shop. It seemed to be closed and padlocked.

Bill called the communications base and was told the backup team had reported that Sporaccio was inside the shop, as were Gigi and Moe Lentini. They might be armed.

"I don't like this," Bill said. "I think we got a problem."

He and Steve walked over to the shop and saw that the padlock was not actually snapped shut. They went in. Joey Sparrow was waiting, motioning them to the back.

In the back room they found Gigi and Moe Lentini, Gigi seated on a straight-back chair with his fat buttocks spilling off on both sides, Moe on a box. Gigi was smoking his usual big fat cigar. Beside him was a small round table. Lentini got up, smiling and affable, and, Steve thought, looking like Mack the Knife. "Let's everybody shake hands," Moe suggested.

Gigi hadn't yet said anything but now between puffs on his cigar he growled, "So, first you lock us up, and now you're our friends."

Steve measured him, then put some anger in his voice and said, "Why'd you call us? What have you got to say?"

The fat man seemed unperturbed. "It's OK. We're friends. We don't want anybody to feel bad. You can search us, and we'll search you."

He stood up. Steve patted him down while Bill did the same for Lentini. Each had a gun tucked into the waistband of his pants.

Then it was their turn, and Gigi sat while Lentini patted down first Steve then Bill—each of whom offered a silent prayer to whichever patron saint had inspired Steve to remove his Kel radio transmitter and leave it back in the car after Bill said, "I think we got a problem."

They got down to business, and almost immediately it became a replay of previous arguments. Gigi said $100,000 was a lot of money to put together in one chunk; $50,000 struck him as enough. Steve argued heatedly that they had already agreed on $200,000, with half up front. Bill went into his act as peacemaker. When Gigi spoke sharply, Bill noticed that Lentini soothed him down in a conciliatory way. Son of a bitch, he thought, the pair of them are pulling the same stunt as we are.

Lentini finally said, "Gee, if that's what they said, Gigi, if they made a deal, we should do it, we should give it to them."

As if by magic the fat man's argumentativeness evaporated. "You're going to get rid of all the evidence in the case, right?" he said. "We have a guaranteed walk?"

Steve said, "I can guarantee the evidence, but I can't guarantee about the girl."

"I thought you were going to hit her for the money, too."

"No good, Gigi, no deal. It's no deal if that's what you want me to do."

248

It looked as if they were going to start wrangling again, but Bill cut in, "We can get her address, like we said. That's the most we can do."

"I want her hit," Gigi said.

"I know," Lentini said quickly, "she's the only evidence against me, and she's got to go. You get me the address, and I'll make sure she's hit."

Gigi took the cigar from between his lips and held it up like a symbol of authority as he addressed Lentini. "All right, get the money and give it to them."

He turned ponderously now to Steve. "And what can you do for me in my case?"

Bill cut right in again, "We'll look into that for you."

Gigi stared at Bill, then instructed Lentini and Steve: Lentini would bring the money there at one o'clock in the morning, and Steve would come for it himself. Steve said OK, but he would bring Bill with him.

After a little more talk they agreed, and Lentini left the shop with Gigi. A minute later the two detectives left and went to their car.

At just before one A.M. they once again drove up Third Avenue to Joe's Pet Shop. They had begun this final phase of the plot confidently, but now they were a little apprehensive.

By radio the backup team deployed around the shop had reported that Lentini was already inside and that three gunmen were posted in doorways close by.

More disturbing was the report that when Lentini came along he had not been holding a package or bag or satchel or anything a person might use to carry $100,000 in cash.

The pet shop was in total darkness, with a gate drawn across the front. All the neighboring shops were dark and the street was deserted. Steve and Bill did not know how many of their own people were watching them from positions on rooftops, doorways, and second-floor windows. They saw a delivery truck parked across the street and assumed that it held a photo and video surveillance crew.

Joe Sparrow appeared from the shadows of the church that was next to his shop, a storefront church, with a painted sign saying "La Casa de Dios." Joe motioned them to go on in.

They parked in the one spot still vacant on the block. They walked to the pet shop and saw that the padlock was not in place, and there was a small space between the edge of the gate and the side of the doorway.

They pushed through and into the shop, into the total darkness.

Instantly there was a shriek, followed by wilder shrieks, and barks, and howls, then birdcalls and parrot cries as the store came alive with the cacophonous alarm of the creatures caged there.

At the first sound Bill had whipped out his gun, and he knew from the motion beside him that Steve had done the same, both of them frozen in a squatting position.

From the darkness in the rear of the store a voice emerged, high-pitched and nasal like the ghost on the Late Show. "Cummm . . . innnnn . . . Steeeeeeve, annnnnd Billllll."

Suddenly a face appeared in the blackness, lit with sharp shadows, lips moving, eye gleaming—the face of a monkey in the beam of a flashlight. Then the beam swung in an arc and rested on the grinning face of Moe Lentini.

He beckoned them into the back room, turned on an overhead light, and stood there, grinning, in a cherry-red sport shirt hanging out loose over white Bermuda shorts and white socks and shoes.

There was no money in sight.

They sensed he was trying to provoke an outburst of rage, so they held still. Then, with a sudden move, he dropped his hands and lifted the front of his sport shirt up past his chin.

Stuck into the waistband of his shorts were six packages of bills, hundreds and fifties. And a revolver. "One hundred thou," he said.

He went into his crazy laugh as he started pulling out the

packets of bills and throwing them on the little round table. "I see you are smiling now," he said, and then he realized they were not smiling at all.

Steve, in fact, was staring in disbelief. To him it all looked like very little money—this could not possibly be one hundred thousand dollars.

But he had never seen one hundred thousand dollars—how could he know what it looked like? Somehow he had assumed that it would be larger and bulky. This pile of bills would not have filled an average cigar box.

Steve stood there staring at the bills, the object of all those days of finagling and maneuvering. He'd never before held that quantity of money in his hands. He'd never even seen that quantity of cash in the open before. He was worried that now he'd be revealed as an impostor because of his awkwardness in the presence of the money.

To hide his panic he did the only thing he could think of—he reached forward, picked up the nearest packet of bills, and began to count it.

Lentini, taken by surprise, said, "Don't worry about it."

Steve couldn't think of anything to say in return, so he pretended to ignore Lentini, half-expecting him to make a move.

Moe was protesting, sounding exasperated. "It's all there. What ya think? It's there, all of it."

Steve continued to count, rapidly regaining his self-assurance.

Lentini said again, "It's all there, what's the matter, you don't trust us?"

Steve looked up, stopped counting, and said, "If it's short—if it's one dollar short—you get it all back."

"Whaddaya mean a dollar short?" He was sputtering, looking comical, this time unintentionally. "How could that be?"

Steve laughed inwardly. Moe's exasperation was justified. The money was in packets of hundred- and fifty-dollar bills secured by rubberbands. "All right," he said, looking up from the counting. "It's a deal. All set." He packed the money into the paper bag they'd brought along and started to walk out.

"What about the broad?"

Steve's insides jumped. In all the anxiety of figuring how to handle the bribe, he and Bill had somehow neglected to work out what they would say about Didi's address. He could not make up something now, on the spur of the moment, when all he could think of was traversing thirty feet of darkness and escaping out the front door of the shop.

"Sure," he said.

"The broad's address—what about it?"

"No problem."

Lentini was close behind them as they moved to the door, asking over and over again, "What about it? What about it?"

"It's OK, you'll get it." They continued walking. "It's OK, Moe," Steve said, "you'll hear from me. Couple of days."

"It's for me," Moe said.

"Sure, anything you say."

"That's for me—I'm gonna whack that broad."

"Right. I'll be in touch."

"Call me here, this number, right?"

"Right."

Steve shuddered a little. A memory flashed across his mind, of Didi looking at a videotape and recalling the time Lentini had hanged a cat from the ceiling of one of the clubs.

They reached the door of the shop and Steve said, "I'll call you, here, this number. Couple of days."

Out on the street, Steve and Bill were aware that many pairs of eyes were focused on them—the backup men with guns at the ready, a police photographer, two or three agents tending a video camera in the parked delivery truck, and three bad guys in doorways.

Steve felt an enormous exhilaration. The charade was finished. They must have gotten pictures of Gigi and Lentini going into the store, of himself and Bill going in, all of them coming out after the meet. He couldn't resist the impulse to show off for the cameras—he gave the package of money a little extra wiggle as he and Bill strode to their car and got in.

They drove slowly until they reached the next cross street, then scooted for the East River Drive. They turned off at the 61st Street exit and at the end of the ramp picked up Kiley, a Federal agent. Bill reported the pickup over the car microphone, saying that Kiley had taken custody of the money, that he was counting it, that he was handing over a receipt after signing it.

They drove to the BNDD office on West 57th Street, went directly to Tony Pohl's office, and were astonished to discover he was worried. He greeted them with warm handshakes and said they'd done good work. But his compliments seemed perfunctory, and the detectives wondered what on earth could be bothering him in this moment of success.

As far as Bill understood the legal process, everything was in the bag: their own firsthand evidence of top narcotics dealers attempting to bribe two police officers, a complete taped record corroborating that evidence, plus the money itself, plus photographic and videotape records of the meeting, plus corroborating evidence in observations by members of the backup teams. . . .

Bill asked Pohl point-blank what the problem was. Pohl responded frankly. Too many people knew—the backup teams that had provided security were now a source of potential vulnerability. A hundred-thousand-dollar payoff was too exciting and novel to be absolutely secure. Somebody was bound to talk, and somewhere they would be overheard.

Pohl enumerated the risks that would be run if the dealers caught a hint that Steve and Bill were working undercover. They might jump bail, or they might send in hit men—they'd already shown readiness to kill one witness. He did not mention the danger to Steve and Bill, but they knew he was thinking of it when he asked, "Do you want to go ahead with it—that business of Didi?"

They were silent for a moment, glanced at each other, and Steve said, "Yes." Pohl looked at Bill, and Bill nodded.

Pohl said, "This means we hold off on getting their bail canceled, and every minute they're out on the street is a risk the setup will leak. If it does, they'll come gunning. You sure you don't want to pack it in? It's no disgrace. You've got families."

It was June 27 in the early-morning hours when they finished talking with Pohl. They'd been under pressure since about six the previous morning, and they were ready to sleep as soon as they could calm down. They phoned for rooms at a motel near the office and were about to leave when a call came in for them.

It was from the Police Department headquarters, a message from First Deputy Commissioner Arthur McNeil. He wanted to congratulate them in person; they were to please wait for him at Pohl's office.

They sat drinking coffee out of a vending machine until he arrived. He was a white-haired, dignified, and authoritative gentleman of great prestige. He had come alone, without the aides who usually followed him about on departmental business.

He shook the hands of each of them in turn, and he made an eloquent speech of thanks with the glisten of tears in his eyes. Drained as they were of energy and emotion, they were never quite sure what he actually said, and they never could quite remember how they finally did get to bed that morning.

In Nyack, Loretta was on the telephone arranging a long family weekend at a resort upstate. Steve had told her that yesterday would be the finish of the special job he was on. He

254

would take some time off before going back on a normal schedule.

In Hartsdale, Phyllis had obtained several automobile-club folders because the kids had been talking up the idea of a trip to the Grand Canyon. Bill had said that yesterday was to be his last on the special assignment and he'd be taking some time off, then go back on a normal schedule.

From the motel on West 57th Street, Bill and Steve were telephoning home to say they'd be working that day and probably three or four days more before they could break away.

When they got to the West Street jail in the afternoon, Campopiano and Abbamonte were awaiting them impatiently.

As they set up the videotape screening equipment, they crowded close and asked in whispers: "Did you get it?"

Steve nodded yes.

"These cassettes we're running today are the last, all that's left of the evidence," he said.

They walked around the alcove for a bit, smiling, laughing, saying "Good" and "Hey, that's great," and clapping each other on the arms and shoulders.

Then Abbamonte said, "So how about the broad? What about getting us her address?"

"How much is it worth?" Bill asked.

"Five big ones."

"No dice."

"Ten."

"Forget it."

Abbamonte began to protest and sputter. He started to call them greedy bastards, and Steve started to uncork his now-familiar act of uncontrollable anger, with Bill playing the calm counterpoint. Abbamonte, upset, said, "Last time it cost us seventy-five hundred dollars."

Steve stopped at once. "What's that mean?"

"We paid seventy-five hundred dollars. For nothing." He

255

saw the looks of astonishment on their faces, paused a moment, then laughed.

"What are you talking about—last time?"

"You don't know we knew. You guys had her up on 72nd Street, in that hotel near Central Park West. It cost us seventy-five hundred dollars for the information."

Campopiano said, "Look, he thinks we're bullshitting. It was room 310, wasn't it? Turn right from the elevator, go down the hall to the end, turn right, then last door on the right."

They were both laughing at the look on Steve's face. Bill said, "So what? How come nothing happened?"

Abbamonte said, "We were going to hit her right there, but you guys had too many cops around, so we couldn't."

Bill said, "If you paid seventy-five hundred up front, that means the whole thing is worth a lot more than five or ten big ones. We're talking to Moe about this."

"When?"

"Couple of days."


Two days later they were sitting with Moe Lentini in the Steak and Brew Restaurant at 68th Street and Broadway.

He started to ask how they were doing on the evidence, how they were destroying the tapes, but Steve impatiently said they were taking care of it and Bill asked what he wanted to talk about now.

About the address, the broad's address. He had the contract to take care of her.

"What's it worth?"

"What do you want?"

"Twenty-five big ones."

"You're crazy. I might get you ten."

"Twenty."

"Now, listen. I got a better deal for you. For forty big ones, could you get hold of those tapes they made on Sperling at the letter box on Seventh Avenue?"

When they didn't reply immediately, he added, "And fifteen for Didi's address." A pause. "And another twenty for Boo-Boo's address."

The two detectives sat back to digest this. The dealers had apparently found out that Frank "Boo-Boo" Stasi had just agreed to turn state's evidence.

Steve said, "What is this? You're handing us a laundry list."

"You got it. What can you do for Funzie Sisca? He's Abbamonte's brother-in-law. You get him off, it's worth fifty, sixty big ones."

Steve said, "OK. But let's do one thing at a time. Start with Didi. What will you do with her? The guy giving us the address wants to know."

"That's for me personally. I'll cut her, ear to ear, real slow. I'll make her blow me, and put a shot in her head just as I come. I'll—"

Bill said, "You know they've got two marshals with her all the time, sometimes three."

"No matter. They'll have to go, too. They friends of yours?"

Steve shrugged, and hoped he was not about to get sick. Lentini added, "You have to get us her picture for guys we're bringing in to do the snatch."

"You didn't say anything about this before, about getting a picture. You know what she looks like. We thought she was for you personally. Here's what we do. We meet you here day after tomorrow, say ten-thirty. You have the fifteen, we give you the picture, we give you the address."

# 29

"That's great," Pohl exploded sardonically. "They kill our witnesses, and they kill our guys."

Bill said, "They had the layout of the apartment perfectly. Wherever that leak is, it will kill us yet."

Pohl said, "We've got to make special arrangements for your meet day after tomorrow. Meanwhile, go tell Lieutenant Bransla what Lentini said about the apartment on 72nd Street. He's been handling the leak investigation, and he's been making progress."

"I traced those phone calls," Bransla said. "We were completely secure, except for one cockamamy thing that happened New Year's Day.

"Both phones were unlisted and registered to the Police Department. One of the phones was for Didi. She used it to call Johnny Echoes at the phone booth outside the tavern on Pleasant Avenue. But then he stopped using that phone— evidently they'd been tipped off there was a wire in—and he made her give him a number where he could reach her instead.

Except for that, her cover was perfect. She told them she'd broken off with Pedro and that she was living with a new boyfriend—that was our undercover; she introduced him around as Chico.

"Someone called the telephone company's special operator to ask for the location of the telephone number they had—that's how we know a cop is involved. The special operator only gives that kind of information to a verified police officer.

"The special operator did like she was supposed to—she took down the request and asked for a Police Department number where she could call back and verify the identity of the caller before giving the information.

"That's how we traced the inquiry to the Seven-five Precinct in Brooklyn.

"We got the exact time of the request, and we checked the precinct records to find everybody who was on duty at that time, and who was on their switchboard. We checked out everybody in the precinct, including the switchboard operator, and they all checked out clean. Then we went back and checked out the phone-company special operator who was on duty at the time of the call. There we caught something—that operator was clean, but she wasn't the one on duty that day. She had a New Year's Day hangover or something. They had a substitute on for the day.

"The substitute was clean, too, but not so experienced, and she didn't realize that those two phones had to have special security handling. She followed the regulations, took a call-back number, and gave the information to the person who picked up at the Seven-five. And she also, for some dumb reason, mentioned there were two unlisted phones installed at the location.

"Of course, the person who requested the information gave a name and shield number that was a fake—we expected that. So we brought in the cop who was on the switchboard at the time for questioning. It didn't take long to break him down: he was doing a favor for a friend—a retired detective, Pete Vandowson, who had actually worked the Seven-five at one time, and is now working as a private investigator.

"Vandowson's personnel file showed he worked at one time in the SIU, in Lieutenant Shandel's unit—and you know about the troubles with them—so we can guess Vandowson had friends and contacts there.

"We brought him in for questioning, and he swore he had nothing going with anybody there, that he hadn't been in touch with any of his former buddies at SIU for years.

"Checking out the SIU guys is going to be a long job—there's more than forty who've worked for Shandel, and hundreds as we go further into the SIU; Vandowson's contact could be anywhere."

Bransla stopped talking, and Bill said, "That's it, then?"

"Until someone picks up a new lead."

Bill and Steve left Bransla's office in gloomy silence. They took the elevator down to the underground garage, each heading for his own car, to start the journey home and to sleep off the exhaustion of the past several days. Then Steve became aware that Bill had fallen into step beside him instead of going his own way.

Bill said, "Campopiano asked Didi for a phone number because he knew that the Pleasant Avenue phone booth was tapped. But our applications for authorization were turned down. Weren't they?"

"I thought so. Somebody must have reapplied and obtained an approval, maybe when the feds came on the case."

"Why don't we go see." Bill got into Steve's car, and they drove down to the Intelligence Division.

In the files was an application, approved November 10, 1972, for a thirty-day tap on the sidewalk phone booth. There was also a renewal, approved December 9, for thirty more days.

Bill stared, and wordlessly pointed. The original application was signed by Lieutenant McCrae. The renewal request was signed by Paul Butler, detective, NYPD.

"How the fuck did the SIU get into this?"

Bill flipped through some other applications in the file. The SIU had several authorizations for wires into the Havemeyer Club in the Bronx, and in the Queens address where the "Wednesday Night Club" met.

Steve walked over to the officer in charge of the file room, had a short conversation, and came back to Bill.

"On December 9 the SIU knew we had a wire into the phone booth on Pleasant Avenue—and I bet if you check the videotapes you won't see anybody using that phone after December 10."

"And when I talked with Pat Sintriano, he said nothing useful came over those wires and bugs in Havemeyer and the Wednesday Night Club apartment except a lot of talk about spaghetti marinara and veal scallopini."

"It could not possibly be that certain friends are informed when certain wires and bugs are authorized?"

"And what would be more natural than to ask a friend if there's anything funny about a phone whose number you have been given for arranging deals."

"And if the friend found out that that phone was registered to the Police Department ..."

"He'd be unlikely to check out the location of that phone himself—it would be better to work through a former friend with a contact way out in Brooklyn."

Bransla moved at once and had Vandowson in by five o'clock for further questions. The former detective was well prepared. He claimed he had obtained the number for a private client. No, he had no idea what the client wanted it for. No, he did not know who the client was; they'd met by chance in a bar, got to talking, and when the man learned he was a private eye, had asked casually if such information could be obtained. They'd settled on a fee—one hundred dollars—and

262

arranged to meet again at the bar. However, the man had not shown up at the bar to receive the information and pay the fee, so, said Vandowson, he hadn't given the address to anyone, and he knew nothing more about the subject. Period.

Bransla was not to be put off that easily. He spoke to the D.A., and Vandowson was promptly scheduled for a visit to the grand jury the following morning.

"Good try," said Steve, "but he'll probably just take the fifth, and there's nothing you can do about it."

"Let's see," Bransla said, and he got on the phone to someone in the D.A.'s office named Woods.

Next morning, Vandowson was waiting his turn before the grand jury, and Bransla was also there, talking with Bill and Steve, when Paul Butler, a detective from one of the SIU teams, walked in carrying an official envelope of papers.

Bransla walked over and huddled with him in a corner. Woods joined them. Steve saw Vandowson looking at them and becoming more and more nervous. Bransla continued talking with Butler and Woods until Vandowson was called into the grand-jury chamber, and then he abruptly ended the conversation. Butler left, and Bransla was called.

At the end of the morning, Bransla came out and said Vandowson had accepted an offer of immunity, and had admitted he obtained the information at the request of Detective Butler.

"Vandowson saw us talking to Butler and assumed Butler was going to shaft him, so he thought he better get his in first. How did Butler happen to be there? Woods called Lieutenant Shandel and said there was a problem at the grand jury involving wiretap procedures, and he heard the SIU had a man who was very knowledgeable, and could he send him down with some actual examples or cases to explain the procedure.

"After Vandowson's testimony, Butler will be out of narcotics work by tomorrow morning."

# 30

At 10:30 the following morning Steve and Bill were seated at the Steak and Brew Restaurant when Moe Lentini arrived. Moe sat down and without a word took a small radio from his pocket, switched on a rock 'n' roll music statian, and turned up the volume.

Then he smiled and said, "Hiya, fellas." He slipped a hand under his sport shirt and let them see the tip of a bulky envelope, which he then held out under the table. But he held on to it firmly until he felt Steve press an envelope into his other hand. Simultaneously each let go, and below the level of the tabletop each peeked into his envelope.

Steve's held packages of hundred-dollar banknotes. Moe's was flat with only a photograph inside.

"What about the address?" he asked.

"What about the rest of the bread? There's no fifteen big ones here."

"We always go half up front."

"Not on this one you don't."

"When we got her, you get."

"We get now, or you can take this back," and Steve shoved the envelope at him under the table, hoping it would stab him in the crotch.

Moe's blue eyes narrowed, then blazed with that angry look that Didi called "scary," and he started to swear. He controlled himself, and said, "Half in front, half after."

"You already owe us a hundred grand from the first job, and you want a couple more jobs after this one. We're not running a credit business. All now, or forget it." Steve paused. "Good-bye, Moe."

Moe reached up under his shirt, gripped an envelope, and held it under the table as before, until he felt Steve's second envelope in his hand, and each let go again as before. Lentini quickly looked at the small sheet of paper inside.

"How will we know if she's home?"

"She doesn't go anywhere, and you'll be able to see her—the house is one story with lots of windows and a picture window. The kitchen, dining room, and so on are in the center, with bedrooms and bathrooms on each side. She has her bedroom on the left, the men have theirs on the right. Thing to do is wait until you see the marshal go into his room or go outside for a breath of fresh air."

Moe was visibly turning on, probably imagining the action. He started to describe again what he was going to do when he got his hands on her, but Steve kept interrupting with more details about the house.

Moe said, "Let's eat. I'm gonna buy you fellas the biggest, juiciest steaks in this place."

Steve felt close to being sick. Bill said no, they'd just had a big breakfast and couldn't possibly, and they had to go.

Steve said, "About those other things, we'll check and get back to you. Call you at the same place?"

"That's OK."

Outside, Bill started to laugh. "You should have seen yourself. You looked green around the gills for a while."

266

"For a couple of minutes I thought I was going to puke. I had to keep sipping the icewater."

"I couldn't wait to get away from that mother. I almost wish he'd tried something, so I could have pulled my piece and let him have it."

"Did you ever?"

"No. Never fired my gun at a human being, and I always thought I'd never want to, but that guy ..." Bill made a retching sound in his throat.

"Funny. I've known you a long time, but I never knew if you'd ever had to shoot, and I never thought to ask."

"And I never asked you."

"I never have either, and hope I never have to, but with him, there'd be no choice."


An hour later, Thomas "Moe" Lentini was picked up by three federal agents as he left the restaurant.

One of the three backup men called in that they had the cuffs on, and a radio signal went out from their communications base.

In the Country Club section of the Bronx, a team of agents arrested Louis "Fat Gigi" Inglese in his swimming pool. Inevitably, from that moment on, he was known by a new nickname, "The Whale."

Out on Long Island, off Northern Parkway, a team of agents came for Gennaro "Jerry" "Cheraz" Zanfardino. He was mowing the lawn in front of his home.

At Joe's Pet Shop in East Harlem, a team of agents arrested Joseph Sporaccio, also known as "Joey Sparrow" or "Joe Chicken."

All of them went quietly. When Lentini was searched, a marked photograph of Didi was taken from his pocket.

# 31

Didi disappeared on July 27.

It was the tenth day of the trial of the Pleasant Avenue group, in the Federal Courthouse on Foley Square. Two other groups of dealers arrested in the April round-up were on trial at the same time on other floors. Four more trials, of still other groups, were in preparation in other parts of the building.

Didi had been waiting in Dick Webber's office. She, Steve, Bill, and six other cops and agents had already testified in the early days of the trial, but had been asked to stand by in case they were recalled as witnesses.

She had been sitting quietly in a wooden armchair, her two bodyguards, U.S. marshals, nearby. From time to time Steve and Bill would go over and speak with her. They enjoyed being the object of glances and remarks by the other men when they did so. She was looking particularly attractive, now that the strain of being questioned and cross-examined by three defense lawyers was receding.

Around noon, Bill and Steve were called up to the witness

waiting room next to the courtroom, and they hung around while the lawyers on both sides argued over whether they should return to the witness stand. The judge finally ruled it was unnecessary and they returned to Webber's office.

When they got back, Didi was gone.

Big Mike Larusso was sitting in her chair. His 200-pound frame was slouched down, his legs stretched in front of him, his hands resting with fingers interlaced across his belly, the usual big black cigar protruding from the corner of his mouth, his eyes half-closed, an eloquent picture of "detective at rest."

"Where's Miss Gomez?" Steve asked him.

"Dunno."

"She was sitting here." Steve knew that was sort of a dumb remark, but at the moment it was all he could think of to say.

"My feet been killing me, with all this stand-by waiting around. When I looked in a few minutes ago this chair was empty so I grabbed it."

But Mike wanted it clearly understood he was a gentleman, so he added:

"Until she comes back."

"You think she went to the ladies room?"

"I dunno. Hey, Norman! You see Miss Gomez, where she went?"

Before Dan Norman could answer, Webber's secretary came in with a sheet of paper and said, "Mr. Larusso, you're wanted as rebuttal witness." And, raising her voice so the entire group of men could hear, she added, "And Mr. Norman, Mr. Spinelli, Mr. Tomas—you are all wanted. Mr. Webber says please proceed to the witness waiting room upstairs."

As the others got moving, Steve asked her, "Do you happen to know where Miss Gomez is?"

"Mr. Webber sent word she was excused. I guess she left."

"You mean she's through?"

"Yes. The marshals aren't here either. She must have gone with them."

Steve persisted, "How long ago, do you figure?"

270

"Oh, five, ten minutes ago."

Steve said, "Thanks," and turned to Bill. "She may still be in the building," and he started out of the office. Bill was sorry that there had been no time for good-byes, but he could see that Steve was more bothered than he was. He went along after Steve.

As they reached the public halls and made for the elevators, they found themselves moving in and through a large crowd of people, standing about in groups, getting on and off elevators, talking animatedly in a variety of accents. As they threaded their way slowly through the crowd, they began to notice a familiar face here and there. By then they had realized the cause of the congestion: the three simultaneous trials, each with multiple drug-dealer defendants, had drawn an avalanche of spectators from Pleasant Avenue.

The trial of the Pleasant Avenue group, at which Steve, Bill, and Didi had testified, had a dozen defendants; the Seventh Avenue group had more than two dozen men and a couple of women defendants, with Vince Pacelli, Jr., and Herbert Sperling heading the list; the West Bronx group of defendants was smaller, but it included Al Catino, a link to the overseas network.

In addition to the defendants themselves, the halls swarmed with friends, neighbors, and relatives of the accused, mingling with a stream of lawyers, witnesses, and curiosity seekers. The trials were interconnected, so spectators would move from one courtroom to another as each trial's drama or excitement waxed and waned. Word of where to find the action at any given moment seemed to spread mysteriously from floor to floor, as if by some grapevine.

Steve began to feel like the Invisible Man. Here he was, seeing in the flesh people he had come to know intimately through the eye of the video camera, and none of them took any notice of him. There was old "John the Carpenter," shuffling about with his hunched-up posture and imperturbable smile, greeting everyone. Armand Tognino, the "barber"

271

who gave no haircuts, passed by, and they thought they saw John Cassese down at the other end of the hall. It probably was him, since he'd taken time off from his duties as superintendent of 320 Pleasant Avenue to be a character witness for Jerry Zanfardino.

Soon it was beginning to feel like old home week to Steve and Bill as they passed the proprietor of the fruit stand laughing and joking with the luncheonette owner, while Johnny Makris, who operated the Pleasant Tavern, kept to himself in another part of the corridor, and the manager of Barone's Bar stood apart with a couple of his patrons.

Wives and sweethearts were there, too. Steve noticed Condoti's daughter, who'd been married to a schoolteacher but had recently become Moe Lentini's girlfriend, and Bill called Steve's attention to Mrs. Zanfardino waiting for an elevator. She'd been called as a witness that morning, and court-corridor gossip had it that she had attended every session of Zanfardino's trial except one—the day Dick Webber put Zanfardino's girlfriend, Camille, on the witness stand.

The general mood of the crowd was a subdued excitement laced with barely repressed high spirits. They regarded the trials as spectacles, and few of the spectators were concerned that anyone was really in trouble. Certainly the big men, they assumed, would get off lightly or entirely, as they usually did.

Emerging from the press of people inside, Steve and Bill got outside and found that Didi was nowhere in sight. They returned to Webber's office, Steve feeling more depressed than he could account for, Bill empathizing but a little amused, too, at Steve's taking it so hard.

In Webber's office, the cops who'd gone up to serve as rebuttal witnesses had returned and were on their way home. As Larusso, Norman, and Spinelli filed out, Spinelli said, "Oh, Steve, Didi said to tell you and Bill good-bye."

"She say anything else?" Steve asked quickly.

Spinelli shrugged. "Guess she couldn't. The marshals were hustling her along."

Steve didn't answer, and Spinelli added, "The marshals were acting antsy to get going, ya know, on account of Friday-afternoon traffic."

"You see 'em leave?"

Spinelli nodded, then added, "I also happened to see her leaving the building. I was looking out the window."

"Oh?"

"There's a back door to the courtyard that you can see from this window. She came out, the two guys with her. There was a couple of cars waiting. She got in one with the two guys and they took off. The other car went right behind, must have had a couple more marshals in it." Then he added, "Guess she's gonna need lots of protection—she did quite a job on the witness stand."

Bill said, "Her testimony really hurt them."

Steve said, "She murdered the bastards. She made the case." There was pride in his voice.

Bill looked at him, and from him to Spinelli, half-smiling. Spinelli reflected his look.

In the time Steve had sat with Didi, screening videotapes day after day, the two of them had gotten close. Steve had assumed, without ever being told, that when the case was over she would be spirited away, into the government's witness-protection system. But he had not expected the parting to be so sudden, so abrupt, without even a handshake, a hug, or a kiss.

And they were not even allowed to inquire. The only person allowed to know where she had been taken or what arrangements had been made for her was some anonymous bureaucrat burrowing in his office somewhere in Washington. That was how the so-called Witness Relocation Program operated. Under a federal law passed in 1970, the program was intended mainly to help members of the criminal subsociety to shake off their old lives and make a fresh start somewhere as law-abiding citizens after they had testified in a public trial. Government called this being a "cooperative witness." Some people had

other names for it, the least offensive of which was "rat."
Defense lawyer Gallina chose to pronounce Didi a "liar" and
"degenerate" in open court, before an audience of her friends
and former neighbors.

Knowing all this, Steve had to admit that the feds were
right to have moved so quickly. Promptness counted in such
matters, considering how much secret information the bad
guys seemed to be able to pry out of official places. The feds
had moved her out of the line of fire the moment her presence
was no longer needed in the courtroom, even before the trial
was over.

It was a little after five o'clock when the last of the defense
attorneys finished the last cross-examination of Webber's last
rebuttal witness. "No more questions," said the defense lawyer.
Webber echoed, "No more questions, your Honor," and the
judge announced the jury could go home until Monday
morning. On Monday, he told them, the lawyers would sum
up and the jury would retire to deliberate their verdict.

The courthouse halls were deserted now as Steve and his
partner left the building. As they paused on the steps outside,
Steve became aware that neither of them had spoken for—how
long? Five minutes? Ten? Steve looked at Bill with a half-
smile, realizing he'd been deep in solitary thought, but Bill
remarked casually, as if answering a question: "Philadelphia."

"What?" Steve focused on him, puzzled for an instant, then
let out a short burst of laughter. "You bastard," he said,
"you've been reading my mind."

"It wasn't hard. I've been watching you. It's written all over
your face."

"It is?"

"Sure. You've been following her, figuring out the marshals'
itinerary, and where she is now."

"OK, wise guy, so what is it and where is she?"

Bill was enjoying himself. His partner had come back to
earth. "You figured they drove west after leaving the courthouse; driving east would have meant a destination on Long

274

Island or in New England, but there's too many bad guys living on Long Island, and what would a nice Puerto Rican girl do in New England, you figured. Right?

"So, going west would mean heading for the Holland Tunnel to New Jersey. You tracked them through Jersey City and onto the Garden State Parkway, which means that by now they must be in Philadelphia."

"No," Steve said, "my guess is they stop outside Philadelphia, and they spend tonight at a motel there."

"Sounds good. What's after that?"

"They'll sleep there one night, then go into the city. They'll take her to a beauty parlor and get her fixed up different, ya know, some kind of new style of hair and makeup. And they'll buy her a pair of big sunglasses."

"Think they'll make her cut her hair?"

"Yeah, a whole new hairdo."

"What about clothes?"

"Right. They'll take her shopping, probably."

"She used to wear those close-fitting dresses. How about blue jeans and a sweater or workshirt?"

"What're you trying to do, turn her into a hippie? I see her in nice slacks, a blouse, a nice scarf."

"Oh, right, the suburban-housewife look!"

Steve pondered that seriously. "Maybe you're right. I don't know if she'd go for that."

"Well, no matter what they do, they'll have to burn the clothes she's been wearing."

"She won't like that. She had on a beautiful suede suit. Must have cost plenty."

"And it was a present, from Johnny Echoes and Ernie Boy, from the days when she was their pal. She was proud of that suit."

"Maybe so, but I suspect she wore it in court as a way of goosing them. She has a sense of humor, you know."

"Ok. Burn the suit. Then what?"

"It's as far as I got," Steve said. "They pull out of Philly and

275

head west, or south maybe. Maybe Washington. They may have to check in with whoever is running that Witness Relocation Program. Get some new ID, like a fake birth certificate, driver's license, Social Security card, and a whole set of fake background records would have to be made up: school records, employment records, rent receipts, car-insurance documents, credit-bureau records, all that crap. And there's her mother and her kid to do something about, and her brothers and their records. Looks like they're due in Washington tomorrow afternoon."

They were crossing Foley Square, negotiating the late-afternoon stream of traffic. Bill said, "I'm parked in a 'No Parking' spot and probably have a ticket already. Let's forget it and go have some coffee. You could use it."

They looked around, then headed for Angelo's, a favorite cop-and-lawyer hangout near the courthouse. At a table in the corner they saw Frank Jackson and Jimmy Nauwens sitting over beers. Jackson and Nauwens were helping the government prepare its case against the New Rochelle contingent of the dealers arrested in the April roundup. The New Rochelle group was headed by Johnny Hooks Capra and Spike Guarino, and the joint task force wanted them bad. During the struggle with ODALE the task force had had to relinquish Capra's club on Havemeyer Avenue to the SIU. The SIU investigation had been a flop, but Jackson, Nauwens, and the task-force people had made their own comeback with indictments and arrests and—they hoped—solid material for convictions.

Steve said, "I hear you finally got Ramos to cooperate."

"Yup," Nauwens said in a tone that made it clear there would be no discussion of their case outside the courthouse before the trial.

Frank cut in, "And how's yours going?"

"Testimony's finished and goes to the jury on Monday," Bill said.

"We hear Webber put on quite a show," Jackson said.

"Multimedia," Nauwens added.

"Yup," Steve said, "it had everything. TV, audio tapes, photo blowups, charts, graphs, maps."

"And with all that junk," Bill said, "my partner here thinks the best part was a live witness."

"Oh, hell," Jackson said. "With all that TV and tape coverage, you guys handed Webber a sure thing. This case is going to change the face of criminal investigation in this country. You guys have started a new era in law enforcement."

"Yeah?" Bill said. "No shit?"

"We were just talking about it when you came in," Nauwens said. "Don't you understand what the hell's happened? Your unit hit on some kind of new system for taking apart criminal conspiracies, by precisely recording all the pieces and showing how they fit together."

"We know that," Steve said. "It makes the bad guys' invisible activity visible."

"Yeah, but there's something different here. It's not just the videotapes and the wiretaps, which are old stuff. It's the idea. A new way of working, a—"

As he groped for words to express his thoughts, his partner, Jackson, threw in, "It's like dominoes. You stand them up in a row, then tip over the one in front, and all the others go down.

"What's interesting," he continued, "is that it doesn't matter how the row of dominoes twists and turns. Once you tip over the first one, the rest fall the same way, following the twists and turns."

Nauwens said, "Hey, that's good! And the trouble was when each cop or fed was out to grab just his handful of pieces to stay in the game and win some points."

"Now," Jackson continued, "we all worked together and traced the whole row of pieces. Sending Pleasant Avenue down sent them all down."

Nauwens said, "You guys, your unit, figured out a new system. You should get credit for that."

Steve and Bill looked at each other. Bill said with a smile,

"Credit?" Steve said, "We'll be lucky if someone doesn't start a rumor we stashed half the bribe money."

And Bill said, "You're off your chump. Everybody knows there were lots of guys into this. Dozens, hundreds of guys had a hand in making it come out. Our unit can't expect to get all the credit, or even extra credit."

"Well"—Nauwens retreated a little—"somebody must have come up with an idea to kick it all off."

"We wouldn't know about that. Bill and me, we have the worm's-eye view."

"From where us worms view things, it was our lieutenant—he was the son of a bitch who kept on peddling the case until someone listened."

"Maybe it was his boss, Inspector Kramer—at least he gave him support."

"Maybe it was Kramer's boss, Terborg, who is a nut on coordinating intelligence."

"Maybe it was the first dep—he had to buy the package and sell it to the commissioner."

"What about the commissioner? He had to go along with it, and maybe . . ."

They were all laughing and topping each other: "What about the mayor? And that college kid he brought to City Hall to be his police expert?"

"Hey! Can you imagine how it would be if that City Hall kid had gotten his sticky little fingers into this?"

"Wait a minute! I just thought of something! You remember the night of the big roundup? You remember they let four or five newspaper guys in at the briefing that was supposed to be so secret. Who the hell decided to go for big media coverage on a night like that? With the slightest leak, our guys could've got killed."

They were too hyped up to be sobered by that thought. They were still bubbling, letting go of all the tension of the trials.

278

"As long as we're up to the mayor, we might as well go the whole distance: what about the president?"

"Don't laugh," Steve said. "The president had a lot to do with it. Say anything you like against him, it happens to be the president who ordered up the big money for drug enforcement, and that's how Hogan's special assistant got his hands on one and a quarter million dollars, and out of that came a hundred thousand or so for purchase of the video equipment that we funneled into Pleasant Avenue to shoot the tapes to show Jerry Zanfardino unlocking the door of the barbershop that gave no haircuts and which he said he didn't go into."

"Then you and Bill are safe," Jackson said. "If the jury comes down on Zanfardino, he'll have to blame the president."

"Not forgetting the governor," Nauwens added. "He put that new drug law on the books with life sentences, and he had to show results. So he got the president to pony up the big bucks for enforcement."

"How do you know that's the way it was?" Bill demanded.

"Friends. They tell me things."

Steve said, "I'm the one who told you. I heard it in the U.S. attorney's office."

"Bullshit, you did. I got it myself. From my friend the U.S. attorney."

"Curran?"

"Yessir," Bill said. "He personally is going to try the case against Tramunti. We've been briefing him on Primrose, the English junkie."

Steve said, "We'll also have to brief him on Frank Stasi, who is going to testify."

"Sounds good," Bill said. "The U.S. attorney himself trying a case, with the governor and the president and all the brass getting in on the act. And not too long ago—Steve and me remember it—there was our Lieutenant McCrae walking around like Little Orphan Annie with his reel of videotape in

279

hand, begging everybody, 'Please, please, won't you take our case?' "

"I remember him being discouraged at one point," Jackson said.

"Steve saved him when he came up with that Didi tape," Bill said. "That put the show on the road."

"OK." Jim Nauwens sighed. "This is getting to be a bore. Let's say the key people were the president of the United States and detective Stephen Del Corso."

"Wrong again," Steve said. "The key person was Didi Gomez. She was there, and she told us what those tapes meant. I was just lucky to latch on to Didi."

Jackson raised his nearly empty beer glass. "Here's to Didi Gomez. Long may she wave." The four of them clinked coffeecups and beer glasses. "Where is she now?"

"They've taken her into the Witness Relocation Program," Bill said.

"What?" Nauwens exclaimed. "Are you sure?" His joking mood suddenly evaporated.

"What's the matter?"

"They're in trouble." Jim Nauwens was serious now.

"Give."

"There's a big stink building up down in Washington. The word's going around that the bureaucrats running that program don't know what they're doing."

"Who says? When?"

"Jerry Zelmanowitz. About two weeks ago."

"The guy who gave up Gyp Del Carlo?"

"The same. He was beefing like hell that after they fixed him up with a new identity the whole thing blew. He flew to Washington and got some senators stirred up."

"Who blew it?" Steve's face and voice were controlled, but Bill knew there was something going on inside. "Did Del Carlo's mob catch on?"

"I couldn't say. I only heard about this from an FBI friend who was in town last week. Those guys are always happy when other parts of the Justice Department make a booboo. He said Jack Anderson had done several columns on it."

"About Zelmanowitz?"

"Yes, and a couple other cases where bad guys who went into Witness Relocation had a rough time, or so they said. And one guy in the program who got whacked."

"And no one knows who blew it!" Steve said. "Christ, that's lousy."

"Anderson quoted somebody as saying that relocated informants make their own troubles by going back to their old habits, drifting into hangouts like they're used to, and getting spotted by guys from the mob who are passing through."

Jackson said, "I seem to remember that Zelmanowitz was a real jazzy character—brilliant they said, but also a show-off. He could've called attention to himself."

"There must be a couple of hundred informants under protection," Bill pointed out, to ease Steve's feelings. "If there's only a few who get in trouble, that's one or two percent; that's not too bad. Maybe they're improving as they go. And they can't help it if informants go back to their old ways."

"Some just won't learn, Jackson said. "Well, *hasta la vista.* We gotta hit the road."

"Me too," Bill said. "I want to get home before the kids start saying, 'Mommy, there's that strange man coming in again.' Come on, partner."

They shook hands all around and parted outside Angelo's. Steve and Bill walked toward their cars, silent for a moment.

"She'll be OK," Bill said.

"Oh, sure. Goddammit, Bill, what the hell you talking about? That little spic broad who they'll forget she exists up there in all them high and mighty offices"—he swept his arm around across the courthouse and the government buildings lining Foley Square—"she made this case, for us, for the government, for the American people. . . ." His voice and face were full of heat and tension. "Can't they at least guarantee her life and her safety and a decent future?"

"And goddammit," Bill shouted right back at him, "who says they won't?" Then quietly he added, "You heard Jackson: the ones who get in trouble are the ones who go back to their old ways and expose themselves to discovery."

"That's just it," Steve said, lowering his voice too. "She's a young girl, and what's her way of life—going on the town. She's used to hanging around in bars, going around with the crowd. She's outgoing, she loves a good time, being with people, bouncing the night spots. No matter where they locate her, she's gonna find out where the action is. I was with her every day for months. We were always talking, and half the time she was telling me about her life. You think all of a sudden now she's gonna be content to sit at home and knit? Watch TV? No way. Maybe they'll help her get a regular job, but can you see her just going home at five and keeping house? Forget it."

"How do you know so damn much? Maybe she'll change. Maybe she'll take guitar lessons, or go back for her high-school diploma, or study to be a nurse or a social worker—"

"No way!" Steve's voice drowned out the rest of the list. "I know her. I practically lived with her for weeks and weeks . . ."

He stopped short, suddenly realizing that Bill was just joking. "Son of a bitch." He laughed. "Isn't it funny? You have a fantasy of making her over like Phyllis, and I have a fantasy of making her over like Loretta. But I know her—like a sister, of course—she's a powerhouse and she's not going to change."

They reached the side street off Foley Square where cops often parked their cars. There were signs that said "No Parking," but by long-established custom cops regarded those signs as applying to civilians; their function was to keep spaces open for when a cop was in a hurry to get to court, and every month or so there would be a sweep of the street and whoever happened to be there would get ticketed. The theory was that everyone would get it about once a year. Anyone who got caught more often would be entitled to pass the ticket on to someone else's car, to be taken care of or passed along further.

Bill had a ticket this day, and he decided it wasn't his turn. He picked it off his windshield, saw a black Cadillac parked next to his car, and began to slip it under the Caddy's windshield wiper.

"Well, hello there."

The rich and liquid contralto voice spoke from behind him; a moment later his ticket-placing arm had been gripped firmly. "Can I help you, sir?"

They turned, and it was Elsie Farrel. "Hello, Detective Farrel, baby. I was just passing on the Mayor's Delight. To someone who can afford it."

"You're in the right church but wrong pew, Brother Detective. Gassing her up keeps me below the poverty line."

"This your crate? Listen, you play your cards right with me, I don't tip Internal Affairs."

"Relax, boys, owning a Caddy is easier than you think. You just save up your cigarette money for a few years, and you got. I've wanted one since I was a little kid. It's what makes being a cop worthwhile—putting my salary into the monthly payments."

"Is this what you were driving when you arrested Didi?" Steve asked. "It's a surefire way to tail a suspect and not get made."

"I didn't get it until months after that. We tailed Didi in Vince Lazzari's car. So, how is she? Last I heard of her, she had agreed to testify."

"She did, and it's over. It goes to the jury Monday."

She's a nice person. How'd she do on the witness stand? I expect she was a good witness."

"The best."

"She's still got her bodyguards, I trust."

"When last seen, yes. We assume they'll be putting her in the Witness Relocation Program." Elsie nodded, and Bill said, "We were just talking about that. How do you think she'll make out?"

Elsie replied at once, with raised eyebrows, "OK, I'd say."

Steve asked, "OK? Really, you really think, OK?"

Elsie shrugged. "Sure, why not? She's smart, she gets along with people, she's lively. She should do fine."

"We were just wondering," Bill said.

Elsie said, "She's got a chance to make a new life. They'll help her get a decent job, live a normal life with her baby. Probably her mother will join her. She's warm and friendly, and attractive to men—I guess you've noticed—no reason for her to be lonely."

Steve said, "But she's used to the big money. Sooner or later, won't she be tempted to drift back into the racket?"

"Maybe. But I don't think so."

"The way she's used to living—bars, clubs, night spots—she starts that again, they'll find her and whack her."

"I don't think she will."

"How can . . . ? Listen, Elsie, she's one real sexy dame. She turns men on just looking, and she gets turned on herself whenever there's a man in the same room."

"You're talking like a goddamn male chauvinist."

"Male chauvinist?"

Steve's eyes widened. Bill laughed as the other two warmed to the argument.

"Yes, chauvinist. She is a warm, sweet person, and concerned for her family and friends, and if the government helps her, she'll make a home for her baby and her mother. Don't you hand out that sexy-dame shit to me!"

Bill just had to get into it. "You mean us honkies are always thinking every Puerto Rican girl is a sexpot, but it ain't so?"

Elsie refused to take the baiting, but she softened and said, "She really is ready for a normal life, and she has held jobs that she could pick up with, like medical receptionist and dental assistant. With half a chance . . ."

"I hope so," Steve said, "but let's face it. Her life-style was exciting, and it showed in the way she would talk about it, day after day that I spent with her."

Elsie smiled, a knowing look on her dark brown face. "Talk, Steve, just talk. She liked you a lot, and she wanted to please you. She has a natural talent for pleasing men. She told you things you wanted to hear, and besides, it helped you understand things in the investigation. She helped you get insights into the dealer network on Pleasant Avenue like nobody ever got before."

Bill said, "Wait a minute, Elsie. It's one thing to switch from junk dealer's girl to cop-lover—a man's a man—but it's something else to change from bouncing bars and clubs to quiet homemaker."

"What makes you so sure about that?"

"What makes *you* so sure?"

"I lived with her, man! Since the night she was arrested. I was assigned to her almost constantly, slept in the same room. We used to talk. Woman talk.

"You've seen her peppy and full of fun, and you think she's hard. I've been with her in the night when she cried.

"You know what she cried for? Her brother, who was a junkie and got shot by the cops? Sure. Her brother Robert, that we arrested on a technicality? Sure. Pedro, that bastard who skipped to Puerto Rico and left her to face the music? Sure.

"But what she really cried about was all those kids who ate the shit that she was dealing, she and the buddies she went partying with. And what she really, really cried for was herself—the frustration, and the helplessness of being unable to understand where the hell she was in all of this, and why."

"So why'd she do it, if it made her feel so bad?"

"She never would say, but I think Pedro made her do it."

Steve said, "He was just a Bronx street pusher when they met, but she had the contacts on Pleasant Avenue."

"Right. And he sweet-talked her into using them. Then she was hooked, because as soon as she started making money, relatives started coming around for a loan, or a handout, or an emergency—she was a softy for her family, and she knew it.

285

She used to laugh at the way she was accumulating cousins and uncles and aunts."

Bill said, "Yes, she did have a sense of humor. And she needed it. To live that way."

Steve said, "Dealing junk by day, crying for junkies in the night—you may be right, Elsie, but how come she never told me any of this?"

Elsie got into her Cadillac, closing the door tenderly, started the motor, and said, "I'm a woman, you're a man. How could a man possibly understand?"

The car pulled out silkily, turned smoothly at the corner, and was gone.

Steve said, "And she calls *me* chauvinist?"